European

BOOKS IN KAREN BROWN'S COUNTRY INN SERIES

AUSTRIAN COUNTRY INNS & CASTLES

ENGLISH, WELSH & SCOTTISH COUNTRY INNS

EUROPEAN COUNTRY INNS

FRENCH COUNTRY INNS & CHATEAUX

GERMAN COUNTRY INNS & CASTLES

IRISH COUNTRY INNS & CASTLES

ITALIAN COUNTRY INNS & VILLAS

PORTUGUESE COUNTRY INNS & POUSADAS

SCANDINAVIAN COUNTRY INNS & MANORS

SPANISH COUNTRY INNS & PARADORS

SWISS COUNTRY INNS & CHALETS

In preparation:

California: Country Inns & Itineraries
France: Best Bed and Breakfasts

European Country Inns

Written by

KAREN BROWN CLARE BROWN JUNE BROWN

CYNTHIA and RALPH KITE KIRSTEN PRICE

Illustrated by

BARBARA TAPP

HARRAP COLUMBUS
London

First published in Great Britain in 1989 by
Harrap Columbus
A division of Columbus Books Limited
19-23 Ludgate Hill
London, EC4M 7PD

Cover design and painting, and illustrations
by Barbara Tapp

Maps by Keith Cassell and Karen Herbert

British Library Cataloguing in Publication Data

Brown, Karen
European country inns
1. Hotels, taverns, etc. — Europe
Guide-Books 2. Europe — Description and
travel — Guide-books
I. Title II. Series

647.'94401

ISBN 0-741-0089-6

Printed and bound by
The Bath Press, Avon

Dedicated with thanks to

Bill

son, brother, cousin, friend
and computer whiz

Contents

MAP SECTION

INDEX

Introduction

If your only concern is to find the least expensive bed in town, this book is not for you. Our book is dedicated to the discriminating traveller who not only wants to find an inexpensive to moderately priced room for the night, but who also seeks a place to stay with comfort, old-fashioned ambiance and a gracious welcome. We believe that where one spends each night is half the fun of travel. Therefore, each of our recommendations has been carefully chosen – not for *cheapness* but rather for value combined with charm.

During our travels, we are constantly amazed to find that many of our favourites are not the elaborate, expensive hotels, but rather the small, homely ones which exude warmth and charm. From enchanting farmhouses to cosy mountain chalets, our hearts are won by the simplest inns and our lives enriched by the friendships established with their owners – many of the places we love the most, cost the least. Good taste and a flair for style are talents – not always a direct reflection of the price. We have seen hotels which charge exorbitant amounts for rooms with gaudy, tasteless decor. Conversely, we have frequently stayed in budget-priced little inns where the furnishings were simple – yet a basket of flowers lovingly placed on the dresser and pillows arranged with perfection on the turned-down bed made a very appealing picture.

We have roamed the cities and backroads of Europe, ferreting out the very best 'affordable' places to stay – some of those we found are inexpensive, others are moderately priced. By studying the rates, you can decide what your budget will bear. Perhaps the basic pension with the 'bathroom across the landing' will suit your fancy or maybe a small inn offering more amenities will appeal. But only hotels which offer a special ambiance have been included – places to stay with style and romance that do not cost a fortune.

ABOUT THIS GUIDE – HOW IT IS ORGANIZED

In the hotel description section, countries are listed alphabetically and each is featured separately with two exceptions: 'Scandinavia' groups together Denmark, Finland, Norway and Sweden and 'The Benelux Countries' groups together Belgium, Holland and Luxembourg. Immediately after the hotel descriptions, a series of maps shows the location of each hotel within the country.

This guide features the hotels of Europe that in our estimation offer the best value for money. We do not imply that these are the *cheapest* hotels possibly available, but rather a combination of charming places to stay with rates ranging from inexpensive to moderate. Our goal is that your holiday be *very special* and that you will return home with memories of enchanted nights spent in dramatic castles, snug chalets, sunny farmhouses, romantic villas and cosy cottages.

HOTELS – BASIS FOR SELECTION

Each hotel featured in our guide has been personally inspected and chosen for its own special attributes. In contrast to many guides on the market, there is no charge whatsoever to the hotel to be included: our selections are based solely on what the hotel has to offer any guest. Because we are suggesting hotels that offer good value, cost naturally played a large part in our choices: those in the expensive and deluxe categories were immediately eliminated. After that, we considered many factors: old-fashioned ambiance, homely atmosphere, antique furnishings, comfort, location, size, and the warmth and friendliness of the owners. However, the hotels vary – each has its own personality. Please read the descriptions carefully to choose the style of hotel that is most to your taste. The appeal of a snug chalet tucked high in a remote mountain valley will beckon some while the glamour of a faded palace in the heart of Venice might appeal to others. We have indicated what each hotel has to offer so that you can make the choice to suit your personal preferences. We feel if you know what to expect, you will not be disappointed, so we have tried to be candid and honest in our appraisals.

Because the cost of a room varies dramatically from country to country, the basis for selection of hotels in relation to their cost per night does not fit into a standard structure. As an example, for a hotel room in Finland you might pay triple the price of a similar one in Portugal. The system we have used is to choose hotels which reflect good value for the country represented.

We would like to be able to say that our basis for selection included only those hotels which abound with the charm of antique decor, but this is not the case. Although some of the hotels chosen (even some of the most inexpensive ones) have a stunning collection of priceless antiques, we have not excluded hotels which have primarily modern furnishings – many of these make up for somewhat sterile interiors with their warmth of genuine hospitality. We have tried to indicate in the hotel descriptions what you can expect.

HOTEL RATES

A price is given for each hotel in the currency of the country (when you begin to plan your holiday, check with your bank for the conversion rate). Generally, this price reflects the approximate cost for two persons including tax, service and Continental breakfast. The main exceptions are in Britain and Ireland where the price is frequently 'bed and breakfast' (the price per person including accommodation and breakfast) and is so noted under the description. There are a few hotels where breakfast and one other meal (either lunch or dinner) are included in the rate and, if so, this too is noted. Please use the rates given only as a general guideline because each hotel has such a wide range of prices that it is impossible to quote comprehensive rates with accuracy. However, the price given will help you anticipate what the approximate cost will be.

The currency codes used for each country are as follows: *Austria: AUS (Austrian schilling); Belgium: BFR (Belgian franc); Denmark: DKR (Danish krone); Finland: FIM (Finmark); France: FFR (French franc); Germany: DM (Deutsche mark); Holland: DFL (Dutch guilder); Ireland: £ (Irish punt); Italy: Lire (lire); Luxembourg: LFR (Luxembourg franc); Norway: NOK (Norwegian krone); Portugal: ESC (Portuguese escudo); Spain: PTS (Spanish peseta); Sweden: SEK (Swedish krona); Switzerland: SFR (Swiss franc).*

HOTEL RESERVATIONS

People frequently ask, 'Do I need a hotel reservation?' The answer really depends on how flexible you want to be, how tight your time schedule is, in which season you are travelling, and how disappointed you would be if your first choice were unavailable. It is not unusual for the major tourist cities to be completely sold out during the peak season from June to September. Space in the countryside is a little easier. However, if you have your heart set on some special inn, you certainly should reserve as soon as your travel dates are firm. Reservations are confining. Most hotels will want a deposit to hold your room and frequently refunds are difficult should you change your plans. So it is a double bind: making reservations locks you into a solid framework, but without reservations you might be stuck with accommodation you do not like. During the height of the tourist season, some small hotels will accept reservations only for a minimum of three or more nights. However, many of the hotels which have this policy will take a last-minute booking for a shorter period of time if space is available.

For those who like the security blanket of each night preplanned, we recommend telephoning. The cost is minimal if you dial direct and you can have your answer immediately. If space is not available, you can then decide on an alternative.You can also ask about ways of saving money, such as the availability of weekly rates, family units, etc. Ask your local operator about the best time to call for the lowest telephone rates, bearing in mind the time in the country you are calling. Basically, the system is to dial 010 (the international code) followed by the country code, and then the city code (omitting the first 0) and the hotel telephone number which appears under each hotel listing.

The codes to use for each country are as follows: *Austria (43); Belgium (32); Denmark (45); Finland (358); France (33); Germany (49); Holland (31); Ireland (353); Italy (39); Luxembourg (352); Norway (47); Portugal (351); Spain (34); Sweden (46); Switzerland (41).*

TIPS ON HOW TO SAVE MONEY ON HOTELS

An important factor when travelling on a budget is to know in advance how much your hotel will cost each night. Therefore, it is of primary importance to check carefully when making your reservation (or when checking into the hotel) to determine what the total cost will be and what it will include. The following list will help you squeeze the most value out of each night's stay and give you suggestions for questions to ask when making reservations.

1) Avoid the cities (especially the tourist centres) and stay out in the countryside instead. This is one of the most dramatic ways to save money, and we cannot stress enough how much more value you will receive. You can live like a king in a castle in the countryside for what you would pay for a modest hotel room in the city.

2) Travel off season. Spring and autumn are usually lovely throughout Europe and the hotels often have bargain rates. Winter too can be beautiful and less expensive, although at ski resorts the prices are usually higher than in summer.

3) Travel agents can save you time and also offer suggestions on how you can save money. It costs no more to purchase your airline tickets through a travel agent who can sort out for you the complicated airline schedules, compare the costs, and help you find the best fares. However, because of the time and cost involved, most travel agents charge a fee when booking small hotels. Ask your travel agent what the service charges will be and determine which reservations to make yourself.

4) In the detailed information following each hotel description, you will note a few hotels that have a representative whom you can call to make a booking. However, if you are watching every penny, you will usually save money by making the reservation yourself because hotel representatives often make a charge for their services, reserve only the more luxurious rooms, or quote a higher price for the room to protect themselves against currency fluctuation and administrative costs.

5) Ask for a room without a private bathroom – many hotels have very nice rooms, usually with a washbasin in the room, but with the bathroom 'across the landing'. These rooms usually cost substantially less.

6) Ask about the difference in price between having a bathroom which has a shower versus a bathroom with the luxury of a bath. Usually the choice of a bath adds to the price.

7) Ask about the bed situation. It usually costs more to have a room with twin beds than with a double bed. However, bear in mind that rooms with twin beds are frequently larger than the less expensive double rooms.

8) Ask about the various choices of rooms rates. Usually within each hotel there is a wide range of prices. The hotel often automatically thinks you will want their nicest room. However, if money really matters, you might want to compromise by taking one of their smallest rooms without a view, etc. that costs less.

9) Ask if there is a special rate if you extend your visit – frequently hotels will offer a reduced price for guests staying a week or more.

10) Ask if there is a special price on a room designed for families if travelling with your children. Sometimes rooms are available with two rooms sharing a bathroom or one large 'family suite' with four beds within one room.

11) Ask about the cost of a single room if you are travelling alone or have a single person in your party. Usually the room is very tiny – space only for a bed and a dresser, but the cost is almost half of what a double room would cost.

12) Ask if breakfast is included in the price. The system for breakfast varies from country to country. As examples: throughout the countryside of Britain, a full English breakfast is usually included in the room rate while in Germany and Scandinavia a large buffet breakfast is often offered in the price. But at some hotels the price of breakfast is not always automatically included in the rate and when this is the situation, check what the breakfast costs and you might decide it is better value to purchase a cup of coffee and a roll at the corner café. We found this especially true in Italy where Continental breakfast was usually extremely expensive.

13) Ask about rates with meals included. If you are staying for three days or longer, many hotels offer a special rate including two or three meals a day.

14) Should your room have its own small mini-bar, avoid the temptation to use the supplies tucked inside. It will always be less expensive to buy your own from the local shop.

15) If you enjoy a cocktail in the evening, it is fun to join other guests in the bar. However, cocktails are very costly and, if you are on a tight budget, you might want to bring a plastic flask filled with your favourite beverage and have a quiet drink in your room before dinner.

16) Many travellers have been shocked to find out how expensive a long-distance phone call home can be when charged to your room. Ask the manager of the hotel what the surcharge will be before making any long-distance calls.

Austria

If the thought of slipping back through the ages and living in an authentic romantic castle appeals to you, then I highly recommend the Burg Bernstein. It has everything one dreams of in the castle department - enormous rooms, priceless antiques, a hilltop setting, towers, turrets, an old well, a prehistoric museum and even a resident ghost! The ghost is the wandering spirit of a beautiful young woman - the wife of a medieval owner of the castle. Her husband became grouchy when he discovered she was in love with her music teacher. For her indiscretion he promptly walled her up in her room to die. But she is a friendly ghost and you will never be bothered in the comfort of your bedroom - and what rooms they are. A few are just large bedrooms, but most of the accommodations are suites. Our suite consisted of a huge living room, a tiny sun room, an enormous bedroom PLUS a bathtub in the corner of the room artfully hidden behind a curtain hanging from an antique four-poster bed. Meals are served in the courtyard or in a splendid dining room where frescoed walls decorate the deeply recessed windows and ornate plasterwork enhances the ceilings. Sometimes dinner is accompanied by music - the night of our stay a talented group played chamber music.

BURG BERNSTEIN
Owner: Family Berger
Bernstein A-7434, Austria
No Telephone or Telex
10 Rooms - AUS 800
Open: Easter through September
Credit cards: AX DC
Wonderful hilltop castle
Located 100 km S of Vienna

The history of the Gasthof Gams dates back to 1648 when it was built as a homestead for the Feuerstein family, although its age could not be determined from the rather drab exterior. From the time of its first occupant the Gams has operated as a Gasthof and inside the atmosphere takes on the character and flavor of its past and the love its successive generations of innkeepers have lavished becomes readily apparent. On each side of the rather plain second floor entrance hall are a series of individually styled, superbly decorated dining rooms in antique decor. Happily, the cuisine is delicious and its excellence complements the beauty of its surroundings. At the rear of the hotel is a glass-enclosed terrace which overlooks a garden where lounge chairs are set out near the pool, beyond which are tennis courts. The inn has 40 bedrooms, which vary from modern to the more traditionally decorated rooms found in the older section of the hotel. The Gams is being renovated, modernized and restored on an ongoing basis. In 1904 the great festhall with its baroque ceiling designed by local artists was added. Although the original Feuerstein family name was lost through marriage in 1900 as there were no more heirs, the Nenning-Kaufmann family are direct descendants. The entire family takes pride in combining the modernization with the old tradition of the hotel.

GASTHOF GAMS
Owner: Family Nenning-Kaufmann
Bregenzerwald
Bezau A-6870, Austria
Tel: (05514) 2220 Telex: 59144
40 Rooms - Double AUS 680-1,040
Closed: Dec 1 to 15 and Apr 11 to 28
Credit cards: None accepted
Especially famous as restaurant
Located 70 km E of Feldkirch

The picturesque old village of Durnstein lies high above the Danube, surrounded by vineyards and watched over by the ruins of the castle where Richard the Lionheart was imprisoned by the Austrian Duke Leopold V. Legend has it that a wandering minstrel by the name of Sanger Blondel passed by the castle in search of Richard. The minstrel sat on a rock and commenced to sing Richard's favorite song and before he had finished the first verse, a voice from the dungeon of the castle joined in. Sanger Blondel knew it must be his king, and he subsequently procured English money to pay for Richard's release and return to England. The Gasthof zum Sanger Blondel keeps this story alive, and is a comfortable base from which to explore the surrounding historical wine-making region full of old castles, monasteries, churches and museums. Herr Schendl and his family are gracious hosts who speak good English and are happy to offer information and help in planning tours of the surrounding countryside. They are experts, as the Schendl family has been in Durnstein, and indeed in this house, for 300 years. Its cheerful yellow wisteria-covered facade in a small courtyard invites guests inside to lodge, or to enjoy one of the delicious meals or pastry specialties served in the congenial restaurant. Guest bedrooms are simple with modern furnishings in a country style, homey touches and private baths. The ambiance throughout the Gasthof is friendly and very Austrian.

GASTHOF BLONDEL
Owner: Johann Schendl
Durstein A-3601, Wachau, Austria
Tel: (02711) 253
16 Rooms - Double AUS 680-750
Open: All year, restaurant closed Mondays
Credit cards: None accepted
Restaurant with garden seating, bar
Located 90 km W of Vienna.

In every book there are a few favorites - inns that incorporate all the ingredients for a perfect little hotel. The Hotel Alpenrose is such an inn. One of the reasons this hotel is so special is the charm of the owner, Mrs Gutwinski, who orchestrates her establishment with grace and skill. She radiates charm and speaks excellent English. In addition to her friendly management, the hotel has many other attributes: it is conveniently located (on a small side street just a block from the heart of Feldkirch), it is very old (dating back to 1550), it is very small (only 16 bedrooms), and it has many antiques (most inherited from Mrs Gutwinski's grandmother who originally owned the hotel). The guestrooms are quite charming - not deluxe but furnished with loving care and with a few well chosen antiques. Each room is different, but each nice in its own way. As I walked around, it seemed as though I was visiting in a private home rather than staying in a hotel. There is a small square in front of the hotel; then, as you enter, an intimate lobby with a small breakfast room to the left. Breakfast is the only meal served - and I might add it is served splendidly on fine china. Lunch and dinner are no problem since there are many excellent restaurants close by. (A very famous restaurant, the Baren, is only a few blocks away.)

HOTEL ALPENROSE
Owner: Family Hefel Gutwinski
Rosengasse 6
Feldkirch A-6800, Austria
Tel: (05522) 22175
16 Rooms - Double AUS 600-730
Open: All year
Credit cards: MC VS
Beautiful small hotel
In the center of Feldkirch
Located near the Swiss Border

Walk back in time through the arched stone doorway leading to the interior courtyard of the Gasthof Deim Zum Goldenen Hirschen. Dating from 1442, and filled with antiques and artifacts, this is an atmospheric inn which overflows with character and history. Wolfgang Deim is the hospitable owner who oversees all aspects of the Gasthof Deim, as his family has done for three generations. We found him supervising the friendly, bustling restaurant where many local families were enjoying a late breakfast. Delicious meals and large steins of thirst-quenching beer are served here on wooden tables amidst stone pillars which support the low, arched and beamed ceiling. A particularly pretty old ceramic stove warms the restaurant on cold days, and in warm weather guests are served on the lovely garden terrace. Bedrooms are reached by walking through the flower-filled interior courtyard and hallways that are decorated with antiques and old prints. Good taste prevails in the rooms, which are furnished in a contemporary country style. Herr Deim's artistic flair and love of history are evident throughout, from strategically placed jugs of flowers to an old apple wine press and sauerkraut cutter displayed in a stone corridor. If you are visiting the historical walled town of Freistadt, the Gasthof Deim should not be missed.

GASTHOF DEIM ZUM GOLDENEN HIRSCHEN
Owner: Wolfgang Deim
Bohmergasse 8
Freistadt A-4240, Austria
Tel: (97942) 2258 or 2111
23 Rooms - Double AUS 700-1,000
Closed: 2 weeks end of January
Credit cards: DC
Restaurant with garden seating
Located 40 km N of Linz

Fulpmes is situated in a lovely, long and narrow Alpine valley located high above Innsbruck. Take the Brenner road out of Innsbruck, but do not take the freeway. Instead, enjoy the beautiful winding drive up through forested hillsides, opening up onto high meadowlands. The unfolding scenery will undoubtedly prompt many photos, for it is breathtaking and picturesque. Continue past the first part of Fulpmes, through a covered wooden bridge to the "Ortsteil Medraz". Signs will direct you to turn left to find the Hotel Pension Auenhof. The Auenhof is a newer chalet, but built in the old style. The guest sitting area contains appealing antique painted furniture, Oriental rugs, and a collection of clay pipes mounted on the wall. One can easily imagine skiers playing cards at the table in front of the fireplace after a day on the nearby slopes. The dining room is pretty, with carved wooden chairs and benches upholstered in muted tapestry colors, fresh flowers and plants and a spectacular view through picture windows of rolling hills, pine trees and an impressive glacier. Guests may choose from three set dinner menus, all appealing and offering regional cooking. The 24 bedrooms can be reached by elevator or the main staircase. These rooms all have private toilet and shower and are comfortable and functional in their furnishings. The highlights of this inn are its antique filled public areas and the surrounding Tyrolean countryside.

HOTEL PENSION AUENHOF
Owner: Karl & Edith Volderauer
Fulpmes-Medraz A-6166
Austria
Tel: (05225) 2763
24 Rooms - Double AUS 640
Open: All year except November
Credit cards: None accepted
Located 15 km SW of Innsbruck

Loving care shows through in every detail of the Hotel Seehof - such as family heirlooms artistically arranged in glass display cases, one with great grandmother's dirndl complete with hat and scarf, another with great grandfather's Sunday outfit complete with leather britches, fancy hat and marvelous old pipe. The oldest room in the house is a fabulous old paneled dining room, now used only for very special occasions. To the rear of the house there is a cheerful lounge, completely modern in decor, but bright and airy. The dining room is also modern. Under a large shade tree behind the hotel, tables and chairs invitingly dot the lawn which stretches down to a small lake where guests swim in summer. The bedrooms are all most attractive with stark white walls accentuated by charming watercolor prints by the Swedish artist Carl Larsson. Most of the bedrooms have modern furniture but my favorites were the few with antique handpainted chests and beds. The Schellhorn family has owned the inn for four generations. Mrs Schellhorn is the chef and a most talented one - the food is delicious. Should your holiday be in late June, you might be able to sample some tiny succulent fresh wild strawberries - freshly picked from the forest.

HOTEL SEEHOF
Owner: Family Schellhorn
Goldegg am See A-5622, Austria
Tel: (06415) 81370 Telex: 67672
27 Rooms - Double AUS 760-880
Open: Dec 1 to Mar 25, May 1 to Oct 25
Credit cards: DC MC VS
Swimming in small lake & skiing
Located 65 km S of Salzburg

Goldegg im Pongau is a jewel-like village nestled beside a lake and surrounded by green meadows, forests and high mountain peaks. Its graceful church spire and old stone castle rise above old wooden chalets, their windowboxes brimming with bright geraniums. This is a very unspoilt village, where the residents still go about their daily business in traditional Austrian dress, and hold to old customs. We arrived on a brilliantly sunny and crisp fall day to find the street into town blocked off due to wedding festivities. The square in front of the little white church was filled with women in colorful dirndls and men in loden suits. Tradition is also closely followed at the Gasthof Zum Bierfuhrer, a large old chalet which dates from 1480 and is chock full of antiques and olde worlde ambiance. The cozy wood paneled "stube" and dining room are favorites with the locals as well as with visitors. Both rooms display old paintings, antiques and other artifacts and offer a tasty, home-cooked Austrian menu. Fresh flowers and little candles warm the tables and one is tempted to linger in order to fully drink in the rustic atmosphere. The Gasthof Zum Bierfuhrer offers twelve guestrooms which all have private shower. The rooms are simple and spacious, decorated partly or entirely with painted antique furniture. Goldegg is a year-round paradise, offering miles of hiking in summer and many trails for skiing in the winter when the nearby hills take on a fairytale quality with a mantle of fresh snow.

GASTHOF ZUM BIERFUHRER
Owner: Family Burgler
Goldegg im Pongau A-5622
Austria
Tel: (06415) 8102
12 Rooms - Double AUS 500-560
Open: All year except November
Credit cards: DC VS
Located 65 km S of Salzburg

The quiet simplicity and artful decor of the Schlossberg Hotel in Graz is most refreshing. After the ornate, fussy antique furniture encountered in many hotels throughout Austria, the Schlossberg Hotel is like a breath of fresh air. The mood is set by the exterior which is two simple shuttered buildings, one French blue and one pink. Inside there is a small courtyard, a tiny bar, a comfortable lounge and two very cozy breakfast rooms. The owner, Mr Marko, is a retired race-car driver. His attractive wife owns an antique store, and it is her taste for simple, predominantly country-style antiques which creates the delightful ambiance. The walls are painted white, contrasting pleasantly with the antique wooden furniture, baskets of fresh flowers and colorful old oil paintings. The bedrooms maintain the country feel, most with antique accents such as beautiful armoires. The hotel's biggest assets are the hillside terraces reached by taking the elevator to the top floor. The view over the tiled rooftops across the river to the cathedral is spectacular. On one terrace level there is a small swimming pool. The hotel dining room serves only breakfast but there are many restaurants close by. Although the Schlossberg sneaks above what would normally be a "budget" category, we felt it important to be able to offer you a suggestion for the city of Graz and this was definitely the best value we could find.

SCHLOSSBERG HOTEL
Owner: Family Marko
Graz A-8010, Austria
Tel: (0316) 702 557
43 Rooms - Double AUS 1,350-1,600
Open: All year
Credit cards: All major
Lovely country antiques
Small pool in terraced garden
Located in the heart of Graz

Rarely have I found a more delightful small budget hotel than the Deutsches Haus am Almsee. Although tiny (only five bedrooms) and simple (none of the bedrooms has a private bathroom) the hotel is extremely charming. Its appeal begins outside - a small chalet-style building with a high pitched roof, a balcony encircling the second floor, flowerboxes at the windows and a small outdoor patio where meals are served in the summer. From the Deutsches Haus you look across the meadow to the shimmering green Almsee. Inside, the attractive restaurant has heavy beamed ceilings, cheerful red draperies, an antique ceramic tiled stove and country-style wooden chairs with heart-shaped carvings. Upstairs the bedrooms all have hot and cold water and share a bathroom down the hall. These guestrooms are cheerful, immaculately clean and cozy with down comforters plumped on the beds. This little inn exudes a quality of caring and careful management. The day I arrived, although everything looked spotless, the rugs were rolled up, the chairs set upon the tables, and the walls and floors were being scrubbed to a sparkling brightness. Grete Leitner owns this small chalet-style inn and it is her style and excellent taste which make the Deutsches Haus am Almsee so appealing.

DEUTSCHES HAUS AM ALMSEE
Owner: Grete Leitner
Grunau am Almsee A-4645
Austria
Tel: (07616) 802 118
5 Rooms - Double AUS 340
Credit cards: None accepted
Especially nice for price
No private bathrooms
Near lovely small lake
Located 125 km E of Salzburg

Hallstatt is a very ancient village, a tiny town clinging to the steep hills which rise from the waters of the Hallstattersee. In the center of the village is a charming little square enclosed by colorful houses. Tucked into one of the corners of the square, with its flower-laden balconies just peeking into view, is the Gasthof Zauner. You enter a tiny hallway and then go up a flight of stairs to the main lobby. Probably your genial young host and chef, Mr Zauner, will be there to greet you. Up another flight of stairs are the the bedrooms. Most are rather drab and the bathrooms tiny although a few have antique decor - I would definitely ask for one of these. Do not expect too much in the way of decor in your sleeping quarters. However, the dining rooms are quite charming, especially the corner one with its mellow paneled beamed ceiling, old hunting prints and hunting trophies. The food is excellent. The inn has been in Mr Zauner's family for many generations and he has maintained the professionalism one would expect to be handed down from father to son. Grilled specialties always highlight the menu, including of course fish fresh from the Hallstattersee.

GASTHOF ZAUNER
Owner: Family Zauner
Seewirt
Hallstatt A-4830, Austria
Tel: (06134) 246
24 Rooms - Double AUS 500
Open: December - October
Credit cards: All major
Charming town on Hallstattersee
Located 80 km SE of Salzburg

The resort of Heiligenblut, located just south of the summit of the world famous Grossglockner Pass, is popular with tourists both winter and summer. Just north of this beautiful little town set in a hillside meadow is the Haus Senger, a chalet-style hotel whose dark wood facade has three tiers of balconies overflowing in summer with brilliant geraniums. As you walk up the hill from the parking lot, you see children playing on the swings on the front lawn while their parents sit on the terrace enjoying the sun and the stunning mountain view. A feeling of warmth and welcome permeates the air. The owners are famous for their gracious hospitality and their excellent meals. Be sure to sample their apple strudel - mit schlagg (with whipped cream) of course. Inside the hotel is quite simple with a rustic mountain decor. Some of the furnishings seemed too gaudy for my taste, but overall the ambiance is most pleasant. The bedrooms are upstairs. Many of them are suites, very practical for families. The hotel is not old, but built in the traditional chalet mountain style. What is very special here is the fabulous view and the kindness and hospitality of the owners.

HAUS SENGER
Owner: Hans & Rosy Senger
Heiligenblut A-9844, Austria
Tel: (04824) 2215
4 Rooms and 6 Suites - Double AUS 580-860
Open: Jun - Sep and Dec - Apr
Credit cards: AX DC
Sauna, mountain view terrace
South of Grossglockner summit
Located 180 km S of Salzburg

Perched high in an unspoilt Alpine meadow above the town of Imst, the Alpenhotel Linserhof enjoys an idyllic setting. The small lake nestled in the meadow in front of the hotel invites peaceful contemplation or a quiet walk. Cared for with pride by the Linser family, the Alpenhotel Linserhof is a large structure of dark wood and white plaster built in chalet style. Charm is added by the numerous balconies overflowing with red geraniums. The restaurant is obviously a very popular dining spot, and its enclosed porch dining area affords lovely, peaceful views of the surrounding Alps. A varied menu offers traditional Austrian dishes as well as Italian specialties. A large flagstone terrace overlooking the Alpine panorama is a wonderful place to relax with an afternoon beer, the large Austrian flag flying overhead. On a cold or cloudy day, enjoy lunch or dinner in the warm, wood paneled dining room, decorated with paintings and drawings by a local artist, interspersed with numerous hunting trophies. Dramatic wrought iron accents and dark, beamed ceilings complete the typical Austrian ambiance. The 35 guest bedrooms all have private bath and are modern and functional in decor. Further guest amenities include an indoor, heated swimming pool, a library and a billiard room. This hotel is recommended primarily for its tranquil, picturesque setting and its restaurant.

ALPENHOTEL LINSERHOF
Owner: Family Linser
Imst A-6460, Austria
Tel: (05412) 2412
35 Rooms - Double AUS 820
Closed: October 15 to December 15
Credit cards: AX VS
Terrace, indoor pool, sauna, solarium
Located 40 km W of Innsbruck

The Romantik Hotel Post has the ambiance of a very deluxe hotel. It is deluxe in everything but price. From the moment you walk up a flight of stairs to the main lobby, the mood is of quality and refinement: tasteful antiques abound: most of the furniture is of the formal, somewhat stiff Biedermeir period except for one cozy little dining room which is decorated in a country flavor with rustic wooden furniture and paneled walls. The formality also disappears completely as you enter onto a romantic trellised veranda which sweeps around the side of the hotel. Here lunch and snacks are served overlooking the garden, the swimming pool and the mountains. Whether served on the veranda or in the main dining room, the food is delicious. The bedrooms are pleasantly furnished - not in antiques, but in a tasteful traditional style. Although the inn looks quite new, it dates back several hundred years with many additions over the centuries, the latest being a new wing and an indoor swimming pool. There is also a large, inviting garden.

ROMANTIK HOTEL POST
Owner: Family Pfeiter
Postplatz 3
Imst A-6460, Austria
Tel: (05412) 2554
40 Rooms - Double AUS 550-800
Open: December 15 through October
Credit cards: DC VS
Swimming pool, playground
Located 50 km W of Innsbruck

Winter or summer, the Hotel Pension Zur Linde is a delightful refuge where one can relax and be enveloped by Herr and Frau Patscheider's genuine hospitality. Their picturesque, gable-roofed and balconied house is located on a sunny corner in the small ski town of Hungerburg, 6 kilometers north of Innsbruck. In the early spring the front terrace and garden are filled with skiiers sunning themselves, as the Zur Linde enjoys an ideal location across the street from the gondola, open year round for hikers and sightseers. Inside, the aroma of baking apple strudel welcomed us to this Tyrolean treasure trove. The house is filled with family antiques, lovely old oil paintings by local artists, and hanging wood sculptures depicting the ancient legends of this mountainous region. If asked, Frau Patscheider is happy to relate these fascinating stories to guests in her excellent English and Herr Patscheider will proudly show his magnificent collection of rare old prints and documents relating to Austria's historic hero, Andreas Hofer. The four guest bedrooms and two suites are comfortable, containing antique or pine furniture and homey touches such as paintings on the walls and a good-night chocolate on the pillow. All rooms have balconies and sink areas, but only half have private bath. In the evening, we enjoyed a delicious, traditional Austrian meal in the cozy restaurant, topped off (of course) by fresh apple strudel.

HOTEL PENSION ZUR LINDE
Owner: Family Patscheider
Innsbruck-Hungerburg A-6020
Austria
Tel: (05222) 892345
6 Rooms - Double AUS 560-900
Credit cards: None accepted
Garden and terrace
Funicular from Innsbruck
Located 6 km N of Innsbruck

The Gasthof Zur Traube is a traditional country inn dating from 1313. Incredibly enough, the house has been in the Raitmayr family for 16 generations, and today is still a beloved family concern, managed by Hans Raitmayr, his pretty wife and his two brothers. The charm of this inn is not immediately apparent in the wide, somewhat cold, entryhall. But once through the wooden doors leading to any of the three cozy dining rooms, visitors are rewarded by the sight of low, beamed or carved wooden ceilings and warm pine paneled walls, all with a rich patina achieved only by time. Each of the dining rooms is slightly different: one has an old ceramic stove, another a collection of old pewter plates and mugs. Pretty tablecloths and fresh flowers dress the tables, and a wide variety of wines and carefully prepared dishes are offered. Upstairs, the wide hallways are a bit bare, but lead to comfortable rooms, all with private bath. The fresh, clean rooms are furnished in either contemporary knotty pine or picturesque antique painted furniture, in the Raitmayr family for generations. Most rooms have flowered balconies which look out to spectacular views of the surrounding Tyrolean scenery. A friendly gathering spot for locals and a haven for the Raitmayrs' faithful, returning clientele, the Gasthof Zur Traube is a historic, yet highly comfortable inn from which to explore the Innsbruck area.

GASTHOF ZUR TRAUBE
Owner: Family Raitmayr
Lans 9, A-6072
Austria
Tel: (05222) 77261
26 Rooms - Double AUS 780
Closed: Oct 10 to Nov 4
Credit cards: None accepted
Located 6 km S of Innsbruck

The setting of the Hotel Grunwalderhof is breathtaking - high on a plateau overlooking a beautiful green valley whose soft meadows are accentuated by a backdrop of gigantic rocky mountains. The favorite rendezvous for guests is the grassy terrace behind the hotel where chairs dot the green lawn - a perfect spot for soaking up the sun and the stunning view. A path leads off to a swimming pool in the garden which is an oasis on warm summer days. The view must have been the motivation of the Counts of Thurn when they chose this site to build their hunting lodge. The Hotel Grunwalderhof still embraces its past. This is not a fancy deluxe hotel, rather a comfortable "homey" lodge reflecting its hunting heritage. There are antiques accenting all of the rooms, but the basic decor is a sporty motif with antlers and hunting mementos decorating the walls. The bedrooms vary considerably in size and decor: most are quite simple although a few have some exceptionally nice antique furniture. It is the setting that makes this hotel so very special.

HOTEL GRUNWALDERHOF
Owner: Count Franz Thurn
Patsch A-6082, Austria
Tel: (05222) 77304
27 Rooms - Double AUS 560-1,080
Open: May to September 30
Credit cards: DC
Two swimming pools, tennis
Spectacular mountain vistas
Located 8 km S of Innsbruck

CLOSED

The Kruz family owns and manages the Gasthof Goldener Adler and lovingly tend to the needs of their guests. In their own words, "You and your family not only feel welcome as our guests, but as friends of the house as well." The entire Kurz family does their best to insure that everyone is having a good time: as a result the hotel exudes a feeling of comfort and hospitality. The hotel is on one of the main streets (just a block from a lovely, 18th-century parish church) in the small town of Ischgl. There are numerous ski-lifts in what is known as the Silvrette-Ski area. Although winter is the most popular season, summer too is perfect for long mountain hikes: Mrs Kurz leads hiking excursions along beautiful trails. The evening we were guests, the living room seemed more like a house party than a hotel as Mrs Kurz showed slides of the latest hiking adventures. Friendliness is not all the Gasthof Goldener Adler offers. It is an interesting historic building dating back to the 17th century. The Kurz family has lovingly restored it, incorporating antiques into every nook and cranny - old sleds, cradles, grandfather clocks, armoirs, wedding chests and displays of antique clothing. The bedrooms are modern in their decor, with simple new rustic wooden furniture, nice earth-tone carpets and homespun draperies.

GASTHOF GOLDENER ADLER
Owner: Family Kurz
Ischgl A-6561, Austria
Tel: (05444) 5217
30 Rooms - Summer Double AUS 560-660
Open: Dec to Apr, Jun to Sep 20
Hiking and skiing
Located 130 km SW of Innsbruck

Even among Austria's superb selection of castle hotels, the Schloss Kapfenstein is very special. Like most of the fortified castles, the Schloss Kapfenstein crowns the crest of a hilltop. As you drive up the road, the woods break into open fields where grapes are planted. These vineyards belong to the castle and yield a delicious wine. Just before reaching the crest of the hill, you pass a beautiful tall steepled church, then round one final curve and you are at the outer gates of the castle. You will probably be welcomed by a member of the gracious Winkler family. Mrs Winkler, who speaks excellent English (her grandmother was from England), efficiently sees to everyone's needs. The day we were there, she seemed to be everywhere at once - on the terrace serving glasses of wine, at the front desk managing the bills, in the kitchen overseeing the meal. The terrace, where she was serving the guests, is spectacular: tables are set out along the walls of the castle where below you stretches a stunning panorama of rolling hills, farmland, vineyards, forests and tranquil villages. Kapfenstein Castle is in the southeast corner of Austria so as you look to the right you see Yugoslavia and to the left Hungary. Whether served indoors or on the terrace, the kitchen prepares delicious cuisine, using only the freshest of local produce.

SCHLOSS KAPFENSTEIN
Owner: Family Winkler
Kapfenstein A-8353
Austria
Tel: (03157) 2202
*9 Rooms - Double AUS 800 **
** reduced rates for extended stays*
Closed: December to mid-March
Credit cards: None accepted
Beautiful hilltop castle
Located 60 km SE of Graz

The Hotel Strasshofer is located on the main street of the picturesque little town of Kitzbuhel, a colorful walled Tyrolean village dating back 700 years. The entrance to the Hotel Strasshofer does not hold much promise - just a little street-front hallway. It is not until you walk up a flight of stairs that you have any inkling of how nice this small hotel really is. Arriving on the second level, you find a small lobby and two very attractive little dining rooms: one has a hunting motif with antlers decorating white walls above wooden paneling; the other has light wooden chairs and pretty gay curtains. Another flight of stairs leads to the bedrooms. All of the guestrooms are pleasing in decor, but some are especially appealing, decorated in what is called "bauer mobel" motif (or farmer style furniture). These rooms cost a little more, but are really lovely with rustic-style canopied beds, light pine tables and chests, and colorful provincial print fabric used for the draperies and the slipcovered chairs and sofas. There is a sauna in the hotel for the use of guests; however, the nicest asset of this inn is the price - very reasonable for Kitzbuhel.

HOTEL STRASSHOFER
Owner: Franz Strasshofer
Kitzbuhel A-6370, Austria
Tel: (05356) 2285
20 Rooms - Double AUS 800-1,000
Open: January - October
Credit cards: None accepted
Good value for Kitzbuhel
Sauna, skiing
Located 120 km NE of Innsbruck

Built in 1806, the Hotel Drei Mohren is an atmospheric old hotel with the character of a mountain fishing lodge. Photos show many happy guests with their prize-winning catches from the hotel's exclusive fishing waters in two nearby lakes and the River Loisach. Delicious fresh trout dishes can be sampled in the Drei Mohren's Tyrolean restaurant which features fine dining and tableside preparation. For dessert, twelve kinds of Austrian strudel are proudly offered. The sitting room is an inviting spot for a before or after dinner drink. It has a beamed ceiling, a small fireplace, and picture windows framed by green plants which look out to a spectacular view of the Zugspitze. In warm weather, the hotel's large outdoor terrace offers guests the same magnificent vista. The 50 bedrooms, 40 of which have private bath or shower, are simply but adequately furnished, some with antiques. All are very clean and some have pretty mountain views. Thoughtful touches such as Tyrolean designs painted around all the bedroom door frames and antique furniture and paintings in the hallways add a certain refinement to this comfortable hotel. The light and airy breakfast room is a blend of crystal chandeliers and old, gilt framed oil paintings with homey, contemporary chairs and tables. Views of the mountain scenery can be enjoyed from every table as picture windows form one side of the room.

HOTEL DREI MOHREN
Owner: Family Kunstner
Lermoos A-6631, Austria
Tel: (05673) 2362 Telex: 55558
50 Rooms - Double AUS 500-730
Closed: November 15 to December 15
Credit cards: AX DC
Terrace, private fishing rights
Located 40 km NW of Innsbruck - 30 km SW of Garmisch

Burg Lockenhaus is a wonderful old castle on the top of a small mountain in the province of Burgenland, reached by a road that winds up through a densely forested hill. Just before attaining the pinnacle you go through the ancient doorway to a wonderful inner courtyard, on sunny days a hub of gaiety with wine and beer and good food being served at wooden tables. A door leads off to the right of the courtyard to a tavern-style dining room where excellent cold beer and hearty meals are served in cozy surroundings. The reception desk is in a small room close to the entrance and nearby stairs lead up to six freshly painted bedrooms, some with antique beds and beautiful views. Except for the wonderful old beds, the furnishings are not outstanding, but the views certainly are very special. (Rooms three and four are especially attractive.) There are also 29 rooms in an annex down the hill so, when making a reservation, be sure to specify a room in the castle. Some English is spoken by the staff who are gracious and helpful. The castle is also a museum so you can combine your night's stay with sightseeing.

BURG LOCKENHAUS
Owner: Family Keller
Lockenhaus A-7442, Austria
Tel: (02616) 2394
35 Rooms - Double AUS 766
Open: March - October
Credit cards: None accepted
Dramatic hilltop castle
Open to public as museum
Inner courtyard cafe
Located 120 km S of Vienna

The Hotel Post is a picture-postcard perfect chalet style inn, whitewashed with green shutters, painted detail around the windows and wooden balconies dripping with cheerful red geraniums. Inside, the lobby is simple but leading off to the left is a charming little dining room with mellow paneled walls, simple wooden chairs with rounded backs, comfy country print cushions and blue curtains at the windows. The bedrooms are furnished with simple wooden furniture, rag rugs on the floors and fluffy down comforters on the beds. I was told that some of the best guestrooms have antique wooden furniture - so when making a reservation be sure to request one of these. This is a very simple hotel - certainly nothing suitable for those seeking luxury. But the town of Lofer is extremely attractive and the Hotel Post is a most picturesque little inn. It is located on the main street just steps away from many beautiful small shops - many specializing in Tyrolean style clothing. The Moldan family owns both the Hotel Post and the Hotel Brau. The two hotels are located about a block apart. Both are charming on the outside, have appealing dining rooms and simple bedrooms. The Hotel Post is slightly less expensive.

HOTEL POST
Owner: Helmuth Neunteufel
Lofer A-5090, Austria
Tel: (06588) 3030 or 3040
30 Rooms - Double AUS 550-750
Open: Dec - Mar and May - Sep
Credit cards: None accepted
Beautiful old village
Surrounded by mountains
Located 48 km SW of Salzburg

The Hotel Garni Prem is a picturesque Tyrolean inn which is fastidiously looked after by the Prem family. Attired in her traditional dirndl, Rose Prem is an attractive and hospitable Austrian hostess who speaks very good English. Her family's pretty, 270-year-old chalet is found in a garden off a tiny side street in the heart of Mayrhofen. Bright red rose bushes border the lush green lawn, and fruit trees shelter the walkway to the front door. The lower windows are bordered by fresco paintings and the top two floors are ringed by light wood balconies and vari-colored geraniums. The Prem family is documented as having been in Austria since 1320, and many of their family antiques are displayed in the hotel. These painted chests and armoires, old paintings, prints and Oriental rugs add character to the public areas. The cozy wood paneled dining rooms invite guests to linger over a delicious breakfast before a day of winter skiing or summer hiking. A good night's rest is assured in the 28 functional, comfortable, and very clean bedrooms, all with private bath. All rooms also offer a romantic balcony for gazing out over the incomparable mountain scenery. In warm weather the tranquil back garden is a perfect setting for a leisurely game of cards, a good book, or quiet contemplation.

HOTEL GARNI PREM
Owner: Family Prem
Mayrhofen A-6209
Austria
Tel: (05285) 218
28 Rooms - Double AUS 600
Open: All year except November
Credit cards: None accepted
Garden
Located 70 km SE of Innsbruck

The Alpenrose is located high above the Millstattersee with a glorious panorama of rolling hills, small farms, villages, meadows and forests - with the highlight being the beautiful Millstattersee in the distance. At first glance I thought the Hotel Alpenrose was totally new, but it was so attractive and the view from the deck so outstanding, that I decided to investigate further. I found that although most of the building is new, olde worlde ambiance oozes from every nook and cranny of the inside and best of all - the center of this lovely hotel incorporates a 300-year-old farmhouse, complete with darkened, heavy-beamed ceilings, a snug fireplace, and a cozy breakfast nook in a sunlit bay window. The bedrooms follow the mood set by the dining and sitting rooms, with light pine rustic furniture and provincial prints. Another bonus is the food: everything is absolutely fresh and prepared in a gourmet fashion. The meals are truly outstanding - especially if you like the idea of healthy, hearty meals without the use of any preservatives or artificial ingredients - instead you will enjoy butter and cheeses from the farm, homemade breads, soups prepared daily and vegetables from the garden. This hotel is not inexpensive, but considering the quality of the meals included, a good buy.

ALPENROSE
Owner: Family Obweger
Obermillstatt A-9872
Austria
Tel: (04766) 2500
*32 Rooms - Double AUS 1,200-1,600 **
** Rate includes 2 meals*
Open: All Year
Credit cards: None accepted
Good value for excellent meals included
Swimming pool, on hillside above lake
Located 150 SE of Salzburg

The Hotel Plomberg-Eschlbock is one of my favorite types of hotels - a gourmet restaurant with rooms. What a joy to savor a feast of the finest food and wines, and then be able to push your chair from the table in contented bliss and to walk upstairs for a happy night's sleep. Food is the star attraction at the Hotel Plomberg. It is hard to imagine that this tiny hotel, tucked along the shore of the Mondsee, only a short drive from Salzburg, can offer what is considered by many experts to be the finest food in Austria. The owner, Karl Eschlbock, is also the chef and his culinary creations are not only delicious, but so artistically arranged on the plate that momentarily one hesitates to destroy the beauty of the design. There are four dining rooms, each stunning. There is also a charming little carved bar in a cozy nook with comfortable chairs, baskets of fresh flowers and an antique grandfather clock. There are only ten guestrooms. The rooms with a balcony have a beautiful view of the lake and the big linden tree in front of the house, but have the disadvantage of the road passing by which explains the price difference.

HOTEL PLOMBERG-ESCHLBOCK
Owner: Monika & Karl Eschlbock
Plomberg
Mondsee A-5310, Austria
Tel: (06232) 3166 or 3572
10 Rooms - Double AUS 619-1,800
Credit cards: AX DC VS
Some of finest food in Austria
400-year-old guest house
Across the street from Mondsee
Located 33 km E of Salzburg

The Gasthof Zum Stern is one of the prettiest inns in Austria. This 18th-century inn is just oozing with olde worlde charm - a faded ochre facade almost entirely covered with intricate paintings, windows framed with lacy designs, gay flowers spilling from pots on windowledges, and, over the front door, a fabulous projecting six-sided oriel window beneath which flowerboxes dance with red geraniums. When you come inside you might at first be disappointed because the lobby is starkly simple, but one of the three dining rooms offers all the charm promised by the exquisite exterior: the wooden walls are mellowed dark with age, a plump ceramic stove nestles in the corner, antique pewter plates line the shelves on the walls, rustic hand-carved antique chairs surround sturdy wooden tables. The dining room in the new wing of the hotel is much more modern in mood. The food is hearty and very good - prepared from the local fresh produce and fruits. There are twelve bedrooms located on the second floor: these are fairly large and immaculately clean, but do not expect too much decor - the furnishings are very simple and the bathrooms are made of one-piece molded plastic. However, these guestrooms are most satisfactory for a budget inn - especially one with such an appealing facade and lovely dining room.

GASTHOF ZUM STERN
Owner: Josef Griesser
Kirchwege 6
Oetz A-6433, Austria
Tel: (05252) 6323
12 Rooms - Double AUS 380
Open: All year
Credit cards: None accepted
Beautiful 18th-century inn
Located 50 km SW of Innsbruck

Pertisau is a town which is comprised mainly of hotels, pensions and gasthofs, all built to accommodate the large number of tourists who come here to appreciate its serene setting on the edge of the Aachensee. The drive approaching Pertisau winds through pretty rolling green hills, pastures and trees complemented by many tempting picnic spots along the way. However, if you can wait, the scenery along the banks of the Aachensee is even lovelier, with dramatic views of mountains plunging right down into the lake. The Pension Enzian offers traditional Tyrolean hospitality, not fancy, but very homey. The comfortable sitting room displays hunting trophies and an antique rifle mounted above the fireplace, as well as a bookcase full of books, pewter plates and tankards. It's a cozy room for a good book in front of the fire or a chat with friends. Meals are enjoyed in the cheerful restaurant with its rose toned Alpine upholstery and matching silk flower arrangements on the tables. Friendly waitresses dressed in pretty dirndls add to the warm atmosphere. Comfort and cleanliness rather than decor are the outstanding features of the 22 bedrooms. Furnishings are modern, yet tasteful, and all rooms have private bath and balcony. This modest pension is sure to charm those travellers seeking an informal, family atmosphere.

PENSION ENZIAN
Owner: Family Niederist
Pertisau 17 A-6213
Austria
Tel: (05243) 5265
22 Rooms - Double AUS 560
Closed: October 15 to December 15
Credit cards: MC
Located 50 km NE of Innsbruck

The Gasthaus Zur Goldenen Ente is an atmospheric little hotel in the heart of Old Salzburg. The building dates from 1300 and is recommended for the traveller seeking atmosphere more than modern comfort. The outstanding features of this hotel are its quiet, central location and charming traditional restaurant. The entry through an old arched doorway leads into an unprepossessing hallway between the kitchen and first floor restaurant, while a tiny old stone stairway or small elevator lead up to the second floor dining room and 17 guest bedrooms. Small in their proportions and simple in their furnishings, all bedrooms nevertheless have private bath or shower. The first floor restaurant is very "old Salzburg" with dark wooden beams, old prints on the walls and pewter tankards on the high shelves. Traditional cuisine is served on tables dressed with fresh flowers and pretty tablecloths. In the morning, an Austrian breakfast buffet is served for guests. The Goldenen Ente is found on the well-known pedestrian street, the Goldgasse, and is surrounded by tiny, exclusive boutiques. This location is very picturesque and convenient for sightseeing on foot, but a bit inconvenient for parking. Guests can bring cars close to the hotel to only load and unload, and must find long-term or overnight parking on nearby streets.

GASTHAUS ZUR GOLDENEN ENTE
Owner: J. Steinwender
Goldgasse 10
Salzburg A-5052
Austria
Tel: (0662) 845622
17 Rooms - Double AUS 640-820
Closed: Nov 1 to 15 and Feb 1 to 15
Credit cards: All major
Restaurant, elevator
Located near the center of Old Salzburg

The Pension Herbert is an immaculate and charming pension located about a 15-minute walk or short ride from the center of Salzburg. Herr Herbert Lindpointner is the solicitous host who speaks excellent English. He also owns the cozy cafe next door where delicious cakes and coffees are served as well as savory lunches and dinners. The pension is a plain but attractive building which has always been a guest house since it was built in 1880. A wide wooden staircase leads upstairs to the twelve tastefully furnished bedrooms, six of which have clean and modern private baths. Painted antique chests and armoires decorate the hallways, while the bedrooms feature Bavarian style reproduction furniture. Careful attention to detail is evident in the good lighting, complementing curtains, carpets and wallpapers, and atmospheric paintings which brighten all the bedrooms. Breakfast is served in the traditional dining room on the first floor which contains heart carved wooden chairs and fresh flower posies on each table. The original pine benches built around its perimeter add to the warmth of the room. Herr Lindpointner and his Pension Herbert offer comfortable accommodation at a reasonable price, perfect for the traveller seeking a more homey atmosphere in city accommodation.

PENSION HERBERT
Owner: Herbert Lindpointner
Nonntalerhauptstrasse 87
Salzburg A-5020, Austria
Tel: (0622) 841304
12 Rooms - Double AUS 750
Open: All year except February
Credit cards: AX
Garden, parking
Located 1 km from the Mozartplatz

A stay at the Pension Nonntal is truly like visiting friends in Salzburg. Otto and Anna Heumer enthusiastically offer their personalized, very Austrian hospitality at the Pension Nonntal. Cozy guest dinners are served in the "stube", a small dining room tucked away downstairs and decorated with country rose curtains and tablecloths. The three course meals are always festive occasions where Anna serves freshly prepared regional dishes and Otto introduces guests to a delicious variety of Austrian wines. A sumptuous morning buffet is served in the elegantly Austrian breakfast room, decorated with delicate white and gilt chairs with rose upholstery. Matching drapes frame the pretty view of the green gardens around the house. All of the guestrooms also enjoy a view of this peaceful garden. The 19 bedrooms, two apartments and one "honeymoon" suite all have private bath and are tastefully decorated and spacious. The suite is particularly atmospheric, furnished entirely in antiques. Its pretty sitting room has French doors which open onto a private terrace with a view of the Salzburg castle. The Heumans speak good English and are extremely accommodating and helpful. They will pick guests up from the airport or train station and in winter they are even known to lead guests on afternoon ski sojourns into the nearby mountains.

PENSION NONNTAL
Owner: Otto and Anna Heumer
Pfadfinderweg 6-8
Salzburg A-5020, Austria
Tel: (0662) 841427 or 846700
22 Rooms - Double AUS 950
Closed: November and December
Credit cards: AX MC VS
Handicapped access in two rooms
Located 1 km from the center of Salzburg

The Gasthof Zur Plainbrucke is a simple country inn on the outskirts of Salzburg offering low prices and traditional atmosphere. It is an inviting yellow, two-story building, its top floor windows framed by green shutters and healthy geraniums. A pretty guest garden is sheltered from the somewhat busy road by trees and is a popular dining spot in warm weather. Indoors, the typical Austrian dining room and "stube" are warmed by pine paneling and an old ceramic stove. Hunting trophies and old pewter are displayed on the walls while country print tablecloths adorn the tables. The menu is reasonably priced and offers hearty Austrian and Italian cuisine, plus special game dishes in October. The restaurant is a favorite with locals, and is thus a good spot to brush up on your German skills while enjoying a cool stein of beer. The Gasthof Zur Plainbrucke has a total of 22 bedrooms, 13 of which are located in a pretty farmhouse annex just up the road. Some rooms have antique painted furniture, but most have old style reproductions. Very friendly hosts Walter and Sophie Schweiger are understandably proud of their establishment, and happy to help guests in any way.

GASTHOF ZUR PLAINBRUCKE
Owner: Walter & Sophie Schweiger
Itzlinger Hauptstrasse 91
Salzburg A-5020
Austria
Tel: (06222) 72728 or 73883
22 Rooms - Double AUS 500
Closed: December
Credit cards: MC VS
Restaurant with garden seating
Located 3.5 km from center of Salzburg

Enter the Hotel Stadtkrug through the old arched doorway and up the long, sloped entryhall. This part of the hotel dates from 1287, and the entryway is the former horse entrance: hence the inclined floor instead of steps. It is fun to "go back in time" by imagining horses plodding up this stone hallway with its low, arched ceiling. Today guests are greeted in the wood paneled reception area by the friendly Lucian family. Locals and visitors alike frequent the cozy restaurant with its old stone arched ceilings, large lead glass window and antique accents. Forest green tablecloths are complemented by pretty print curtains and dark wood tables, chairs and benches. A traditional menu is served and prices are reasonable. Upstairs, the 25 bedrooms are a pleasant surprise for a city hotel, as they are homey and inviting with pretty print coverlets and sometimes antique painted furniture. All are very clean with private bath and phone as well as a compact little sitting area or desk. There is even a small garden in back of the hotel with tables and chairs for guests' use. The Hotel Stadtkrug is a very atmospheric, family run hotel which is really quite a bargain considering its central location and charm.

HOTEL STADTKRUG
Owner: Family Lucian
Linzer Gasse 20
Salzburg A-5020
Austria
Tel: (0662) 73545 or 79588
25 Rooms - Double AUS 880
Closed: February and March
Credit cards: All major
Restaurant, guest garden, elevator
Across the river from the Mozartplatz

The Gasthof Trumer Stuberl is more expensive than most Salzburg hotels recommended in this guide, but, for a few more shillings, it assures you of a high level of comfort in a central location. Gracious hosts are the young, energetic couple Hermann and Marianne Hirschbichler. They have completely updated the interior of this 600-year-old building, creating a very comfortable and tasteful city hotel. There are only 22 guestrooms, fostering an intimate and friendly feel to the Trumer Stuberl. Both Hermann and Marianne speak good English and are happy to help with guests' needs from laundry service to transportation for Salzburg's popular "Sound of Music" tour. All the bedrooms have private shower and toilet, good lighting and soundproofed doors. Furnishings are contemporary and tasteful with soft and restful colors. Breakfast is the only meal served in the hotel, but there are many fine restaurants nearby. The Trumer Stuberl is well located, near the center of the Old Town on a quiet side street. Its pretty facade is brightened by pink geraniums at every window of all five stories. A handful of foreign flags fly above the front door, welcoming visitors from all over the world.

GASTHOF TRUMER STUBERL
Owner: Marianne & Hermann Hirschbichler
Bergstrasse 6
Salzburg A-5020
Austria
Tel: (0662) 75168 or 74776
22 Rooms - Double AUS 920
Open: All year
Credit cards: AX
Across the river from the Mozartplatz
Near the center of Salzburg

Scharding is a postcard-pretty little village, looking more like a painted backdrop for an operetta than a "real" village. A fountain graces the central square which is encircled with gaily painted, narrow buildings whose roof lines step up in a wonderful assortment of shapes and designs. The effect is one of gaiety and charm. Every exceptionally pretty hamlet needs a good hotel and luckily Scharding has the Forstingers Wirtshaus, located half a block from the square. The facade is very old and quite simple: it is a boxy green building with an arched doorway. But within you are greeted with warmth, both from the cozy decor and from the owners. The attractive young Mrs Forstinger will probably be at the front desk to greet you - wearing an Austrian dirndl and her blond hair drawn back in a bun. If you are not staying the night, you might still want to stop for a meal in one of the series of dining rooms which stretch the length of the building. These are all attractive, one having an interesting collection of antique fishing gear (Scharding is famous for its fishing). The bedrooms are decorated in a variety of styles: some are quite modern in their decor; a couple have beautiful antique painted furniture. But my favorites were the rooms with new light pine furniture and traditional rustic style four-poster beds.

FORSTINGERS WIRTSHAUS
Owner: Family Forstinger
Unterer Stadtplatz 3
Scharding am Inn A-4780, Austria
Tel: (07712) 2302
Open: All year
Credit cards: None accepted
20 Rooms - Double AUS 640
Medieval town with painted houses
Near German border in NE Austria

The Hotel Krone's greatest fame is as a restaurant, and indeed there is a stunning restaurant with a decor so charming that you would love it even if the food were not outstanding - which it is! The room is completely enclosed in warmly hued wood - hardwood floors, intricate paneled walls, and a beautifully detailed ceiling. The windows, deeply set within the thick walls, are of bottle glass, accentuated by country print draperies. Around the wooden tables are beautifully carved rustic Alpine chairs. Cowbells, antique copper, old prints, Oriental rugs, and fresh flowers complete the picture of perfection. In summertime there is a terrace, adjacent to the inn, where meals are served beneath gay umbrellas. Although food is the principal attraction at the Hotel Krone, you might well want to consider staying for a few nights enjoying the picturesque village of Schruns. This is an especially attractive old village of many colorful buildings with a river rushing through the center. In winter Schruns is famous for skiing, in summer for hiking. If you want to linger, the Hotel Krone has some very reasonably priced bedrooms. They all vary in decor and many are exceptionally attractive with beautiful antique beds. The owner, Mr Mayer, personally oversees this small hotel. He is most gracious and speaks excellent English.

HOTEL KRONE
Owner: Robert Mayer
Schruns-Montafon A-6780, Austria
Tel: (05556) 2255
9 Rooms - Double AUS 560-760
Credit cards: None accepted
Wonderful old mountain village
Summer hiking, winter ski resort
Located in SW Austria - 13 km S of Bludenz

Steyr is an exceptionally charming old town whose central plaza is lined with rainbow-hued medieval houses, most of them tall and narrow with colorful red tiled roofs. Perfectly located, facing the main plaza in the heart of the old town, are two especially attractive three-story houses joined together with a series of suspended arches. Originally each house was a separate hotel - one called the "Inn to the Three Allies" and the other the "Inn of the Three Roses". Several years ago both hotels were renovated and cleverly joined together to form the Hotel Mader. Not that the hotel business is a new venture - for 300 years inns have occupied the two small houses. The recent renovation has produced an excellent modern hotel with each bedroom having its own private bath and direct dial telephone. Although the bedrooms are modern in decor, they are very attractive with nice wooden furniture, white walls, colorful print draperies, and crisp white curtains. There are two restaurants which, like the lobby and lounges, have some antique accents. One of the most appealing and unusual parts of the hotel is the inner courtyard - surrounded by arcaded walkways - where meals are served in the summer.

HOTEL MADER
Owner: Family Mader
Stadtplatz 36
Steyr A-4400, Austria
Tel: (07252) 23350 Telex: 28302
55 Rooms - Double AUS 650-840
Open: All year
Credit cards: MC VS
Located 40 km S of Linz

The Hotel Krone has all the right ingredients for a country inn - small, very old, with a beautiful facade, lovely antiques, good cooking, attractive bedrooms, large modern bathrooms, and, best of all, gracious owners who speak English. The combination is very hard to find, especially in inexpensive small inns in secluded valleys. The Hotel Krone is immediately appealing, a square box of a building ornamented in the corner with a fabulous multi-faceted bay window intricately decorated with bright colorful designs. There are shutters at some of the windows while others are outlined with painted designs. A whimsical gold sign dangles above the street suspended from a wrought iron brace. Outside tables are set for dining. Inside are several dining rooms, each a jewel of antique woods and provincial print curtains. On the second floor is a museum-quality room dating back to the 17th century now used just "for show". The third floor contains six nice bedrooms, not with antique furniture, but lovingly decorated by Mrs Marberger, some with painted furniture, others with classic wood furniture. Mr and Mrs Marberger recently took over the management of the hotel when his father retired. I asked the charming Mrs Marberger if the inn had been in her husband's family a long time. "No", she said, "only about 200 years."

HOTEL KRONE
Owner: Family Marberger
Umhausen A-6441, Austria
Tel: (05255) 5212 or 5202
6 Rooms - Double AUS 400-600
Closed: April
Credit cards: None accepted
Excellent value, lovely inn
Located 60 km SW of Innsbruck

Our stay here was a very special one, highlighted by an imaginative and delicious six course gourmet dinner in the Altwienerhof's authentic old Viennese "winter garden". Popularized at the turn of the century in wealthy Vienna townhomes, the "winter garden" is a glassed-in room which looks out into a walled garden. In the summer, guests are treated to a view of a flower-filled bower, while in the winter the garden becomes a fairytale landscape as snowflakes drift down in the soft light of gas lamps. The room is fresh and inviting, filled with an assortment of plants and flowers among the white wrought iron chairs and tables. Gleaming silver, china and glassware complete the picture of this unusual "garden". Guests may also dine in the atmospheric, cherry paneled dining room, which offers subdued candlelight and an elegant ambiance of a bygone era. It is important to note that the budget prices of the rooms are not reflected in the restaurant prices: some of the finest cuisine and wine available in Vienna are offered here and are priced accordingly. Rudolf Kellner is the head chef, and he and his wife Ursula are very proud of the fact that the Altwienerhof has recently been classified as one of the twenty best restaurants in the entire country of Austria. The bedrooms at the Altwienerhof vary from large, impeccably furnished suites to simple, modern bedrooms which share a bath.

ALTWIENERHOF
Owner: Rudolf & Ursula Kellner
Herklotzgasse 6
Vienna A-1150, Austria
Tel: (0222) 837145
23 Rooms - Double AUS 760-925
Open: All year
Credit cards: AX
Restaurant, garden, elevator
Located near the Schonbrunn Palace

This atmospheric pension began as a small, luxury hotel in 1913. Although it is now considerably scaled down in size, one can easily imagine its former grandeur from the abundance of fine antiques still in evidence. Entering the Pension Franz is like discovering a lovely pearl inside an oyster shell as the building is very unprepossessing from the outside. In addition, one must pass through a rather drab entry and climb a flight of stairs before being rewarded by the sight of the rich cherrywood paneling and fine antiques in the guest lounge and reception area. It is a great temptation to just sit and rest in the warm red tapestry chairs, under the pretty brass chandelier which lights up the wood beamed ceiling. A lace covered table with a bouquet of fresh flowers completes this charming room. All of the 24 bedrooms have bath or shower, but not all have a private toilet. The rooms are prettily furnished with white and gilt reproductions, old oil paintings, vases and Oriental rugs. Some traffic noise might be heard from the front rooms, but the views of the Gothic cathedral across the street and the ornate town hall a block or so away are a wonderful sight for visitors to Vienna. We were surprised by the intimate, yet elegant, breakfast room that greeted us the morning of our stay. A lovely little stained and leaded glass window let in morning light as we took our places at a lace covered table. Large oil paintings of the 1800s and oversize antique vases set a mood of days gone by.

HOTEL PENSION FRANZ
Owner: Alice Gesmbh
Wahringerstrasse 12
Vienna A-1090, Austria
Tel: (0222) 343638 or 343639
24 Rooms - Double AUS 890-990
Open: All year
Credit cards: AX DC VS
Located 3 blocks N of the town hall

The Hotel Zur Wiener Staatsoper offers reasonably priced rooms and a wonderfully old-fashioned atmosphere right in the heart of Vienna. The pretty, white baroque facade welcomes guests with a selection of international flags flying over the front door. A filigree wrought iron door leads into the gilt and crystal lobby area where your host, Walter Ungersbock, extends his greeting. The Hotel Zur Wiener Staatsoper is located on a pedestrian street, thus quiet prevails in the high ceilinged guestrooms. Delicate flower print wallpapers, matching curtains, crystal chandeliers, and reproduction white furniture create a fresh, feminine feeling in the rooms. All rooms have a private shower, w.c. and telephone. There is no restaurant at the Zur Wiener Staatsoper, but a satisfying Continental breakfast is served. The breakfast room is pretty and inviting, with rose toned tapestry chairs and old prints on the walls. Take advantage of the marvelous location of the Zur Wiener Staatsoper and go on foot to visit the many nearby coffeehouses and tempting shops along the Kartnerstrasse. The hotel offers no parking, but spots can usually be found without too much difficulty on neighboring streets.

HOTEL ZUR WIENER STAATSOPER
Owner: Walter Ungersbock
Krugerstrasse 11
Vienna A-1010
Austria
Tel: (0222) 5131274
22 Rooms - Double AUS 850
Open: All year
Credit cards: None accepted
Close to the Opera House
Located near the Kartnerstrasse

The Hotel Schoneben is truly a perfect example of an Austrian country inn, inside and out. Perched on a grassy hillside amidst spectacular mountain scenery, it is made up of two white plaster chalets, accented by dark wood balconies overflowing with bright geraniums. Inside, one finds a Tyrolean treasure chest of antiques, warm wood paneling, beamed ceilings and fresh flowers. It is as if the German term "gemutlichkeit" were invented to describe this inn. Pretty Alpine print fabrics adorn the dining room windows and bench upholstery, while carved wooden chairs and tables grace the warm tile floors. Dinner on the terrace or in the cozy dining rooms is a romantic treat. A rustic elegance pervades this inn, whose oldest part dates from 1604. Host Stefan Schneider offers 17 lovely bedrooms and 4 apartments, all with private bath and phone. Most of the rooms and all the apartments have either a balcony or a garden terrace, and all are filled with carved pine furniture. Special touches such as fresh flowers, lace curtains, and old framed prints add warmth and charm. The apartments are newer, but care has been taken to maintain the hotel's rustic flavor with beamed ceilings, pine furnishings and soft colors. A visit here is a memorable experience, as Stefan Schneider's great love of Austria, her culture and people is expressed in every detail of the Hotel Schoneben.

HOTEL SCHONEBEN
Owner: Stefan Schneider
Wald im Pinzgau A-5742, Austria
Tel: (06565) 82890
21 Rooms - Double AUS 640
Open: All year except November
Credit cards: None accepted
Restaurant, cafe
Located 75 km SE of Innsbruck

The Raffelsbergerhof is an especially attractive hotel located just a short stroll from the River Danube in the heart of the Wachau wine district of Austria. The hotel was originally the home of the controller of the river traffic: it must have been a lucrative job because his home is outstanding. The outside is extremely appealing - looking much more like a French manor house than an Austrian inn. The hotel is two mansard roofed buildings joined by a two-story walkway punctuated with a series of arches. You enter through heavy wooden doors into an inner courtyard formed by the two sections. The staircase to the right leads to private living quarters and the staircase to the left leads up to the second floor where the hotel reception desk is located. When I visited the hotel the reception was extremely gracious and the hotel was immaculate and attractive with antique chests, old sleds, wrought iron light fixtures and fresh flowers providing an inviting atmosphere. The bedrooms are spacious, clean and attractive although their furnishings are modern rather than antique. On the outside of the hotel an enormous grapevine is cleverly espaliered across the length of the building - a most appropriate decoration for a wine village inn.

RAFFELSBERGERHOF
Owner: Hubert Anton
Weissenkirchen A-3610
Austria
Tel: (02715) 2201
12 Rooms - Double AUS 650-900
Open: May 1 to October 31
Credit cards: MC
Lovely 16th-century manor
Near the dock for ferry
Located on Danube 96 km W of Vienna

The Sporthotel Alpenhof, a 300-year-old farmhouse renovated into a modern hotel, is definitely stretching the upper limits of "moderately priced": however, considering the fabulous food and refreshing country ambiance, it is still a good value. Plus, how could one possibly resist a hotel that gives you not only a key to your room, but also a key that unlocks what looks like a post-office box in the henhouse where you will go each morning to collect the fresh egg laid by your very own hen (Claudia, Susie, Monika, Olga, etc). Returning to the terrace, you will be served an exquisite breakfast buffet - a feast of fresh cheeses, farm butter, home-made jams, piping hot breads, country ham, fresh orange juice - plus, of course, your egg cooked to your special taste. All the food is sensational: with 180 acres, the farm is able to provide almost all of the food for the kitchen. The Alpenhof is nestled in a beautiful meadow which gently slopes down to the shimmering green Weissensee. The rooms at the Sporthotel Alpenhof vary tremendously. Many are family suites with special little nooks for the children, others have new wooden furniture painted with an Alpine motif, one is "Grandfather's Room", furnished with his original furniture. None of the bedrooms are "cutesy pretty" but all are outstanding in their comfort. If you are travelling with children, especially consider splurging - your little ones will be enchanted.

SPORTHOTEL ALPENHOF
Owner: Family Zohrer
Naggl 4
Weissensee A-9762, Austria
Tel: (04713) 2107 Telex: 48267
*28 Rooms - Double AUS 1,350-2,010**
** Rate includes 2 meals*
Open: May - October and December - Easter
Credit cards: None accepted
Located 170 km S of Salzburg

Gralhof Pension, a delightful small inn, is located across the road from the emerald green Weissensee. It has its own grassy lawn stretching down to the lake where a wooden pier is available for swimming, boating or fishing. The hotel is a farmhouse dating back 500 years - one of the oldest farmhouses in the valley. The lower part of the building is of white stucco and the upper portion constructed of wood. Wooden balconies with carved banisters and windowboxes overflowing with red geraniums encircle the inn. The inside is immaculate. Most of the light pine furniture is new but there are accents such as an antique cradle, antlers, deer skins, wedding chests, red checked curtains and family portraits giving a country flavor. The food is country-simple and delicious. Mrs Knaller, who is young and gracious, and speaks English very well, was cooking dinner when we arrived. The smells from the kitchen were enticing and she explained that her husband is a farmer and all the milk, butter, cheeses and vegetables are fresh. Before dinner you might want to take a short walk down the road and board one of the ferries which circle the lake.

GRALHOF PENSION
Owner: Family Knaller
Neusach
Weissensee A-9762, Austria
Tel: (04713) 2213
*18 Rooms - Double AUS 720-820**
** Price includes breakfast and dinner*
Closed: mid-Oct to mid-Dec, end Mar to end Apr
Credit cards: All major
Exceptionally nice budget hotel
500-year-old farmhouse
Boating and swimming in the lake
Located 170 km S of Salzburg

Benelux Countries
Belgium - Holland - Luxembourg

Brugge is the romantic gem of Belgium, with lazy canals spiderwebbing through this charming city. A half-hour boat trip on the canals, winding past the characterful buildings, the waterway shaded often by wispy trees and the span of numerous arched bridges, is a wonderful introduction to Brugge. The picturesque canal trip will also glide you under the windows of the lovely Hotel de Orangerie. A handsome 16th-century building, the De Orangerie was renovated and remodeled as a hotel under the artful direction of Madame Beatrice Strubbe. The hotel is set off a quiet street at the heart of old Brugge, with ivy framing a multitude of back windows that overlook the waterway. The interior decor is inviting: fresh flowers are displayed in abundance, public areas are spacious and stylish and soft pink and green pastels warm and color the halls. Most of the hotel's nineteen bedrooms overlook the canal and vary from a large wedding suite with a secluded courtyard, a spacious double room with a private fireplace to a lovely loft apartment set under painted beams whose dormer windows overlook the maze of Brugge's rooftops. The hotel does not have a restaurant but there is, however, an intimate bar and an attractive large breakfast room and delightful terrace. Although the Hotel de Orangerie is priced higher than most hotels found in this guide, Brugge is an expensive city and the De Orangerie is an excellent value for a first class hotel.

HOTEL DE ORANGERIE
Owner: Dirk & Beatrice Strubbe
Kartuizerinnestraat, 10
8000 Brugge, Belgium
Tel: (050) 34 16 49 Telex 82433
19 Rooms - Double BFR 4,500-7,800
Open: All year
Credit cards: All major
No restaurant, lovely canal hotel
Located 96 km NW of Brussels

We discovered this hotel when searching for an inexpensive but well located spot for our own two-day sojourn in the delightful city of Amsterdam. With a detailed city map in hand we had no trouble locating the Hotel Agora as it is just a block from the colorful flower market (Bloemen Markt). At the heart of old Amsterdam, amidst its bustle and activity, parking near the hotel is difficult to find, but secure a temporary spot near the hotel, unload your luggage and then either Giorgio or Pierre, the owners, will offer a recommendation as to street or garage parking. Housed in a lovely old canal house, the Agora proves a delightful and convenient hotel. Very reasonably priced, simple but well and personally managed, the Hotel Agora attracts a wide range of guests - from very sophisticated couples to budgeting students. The entry hall doubles as the only lobby of the hotel and its walls are a display of tourist information and appreciative notes and cards of previous guests. Beyond the lobby is a long narrow dining room where individual tables are set each morning with flowers and a bountiful breakfast served on decorative china. The hotel is limited to twelve bedrooms, all found up a narrow staircase. The rooms are very basic in comfort, not all with private bath. The Hotel Agora is a very comfortable and convenient base from which to explore Amsterdam, but one remembers the Agora for its charming owners who are ever-present to make their guests welcome.

HOTEL AGORA
Owner: Giorgio Campeggi & Pierre Giauque
Singel 462
1017 AW Amsterdam
Holland
Tel: (020) 27 22 00 and 27 22 02
12 Rooms - Double DFL 120-144
Open: All year
Located at city center, near the flower market

On the outskirts of Markelo, in a region of farmland, the setting of the In de Kop'ren Smorre is inviting and quiet. Markelo is a town well known for its folklore and historic arts and crafts. The Lammertink family endeavor to preserve the pride and tradition of the region in their restaurant-hotel. Dating back to 1472, this farm became an inn in 1958. The barn is now the beautiful restaurant, "De Delle", where waiters and waitresses serve you graciously, dressed in local costume. Lovely wall tiles, a stone floor, heavy old beams and a warming fire combine to give a rustic charm. Regional specialties are the feature of the menu, with dishes prepared using only the freshest ingredients and seasoned with herbs from the hotel's garden. In keeping with the name and tradition of the inn, coffee is served at your table in copper pots set above a flame. Breakfast, light meals and afternoon teas are offered in the "De Eenskamer", a spacious, bright room under old beams with copper pieces, antiques and samplers adorning the walls. In 1980, simple but comfortable rooms (six double, three single - not all with private bath) were added for the convenience of dinner guests. "De Gastenhof" is a modern annex of additional bedrooms located across the herb garden.

IN DE KOP'REN SMORRE
Owner: Arend-Jan Lammertink
Holterweg 20
7475 Markelo, Holland
Tel: (05476) 1344
9 Rooms - Double DFL 90-140
Open: All year
Restaurant closed Sunday & Monday
Credit cards: All major
Located 125 km E of Amsterdam

The Kasteel Wittem is a superbly renovated castle hotel in absolutely tip-top condition. The owner, Mr Ritzen, has directed the meticulous restoration over the last seventeen years, and recently completed the finishing touch: the restored crest of this stone fortress was mounted on the tower. With a sparkle in his eye Mr Ritzen sees to every detail and the comfort of each guest - the hotel industry is lucky to have such a fine hotelier to set their standards by. What fun it is to sleep in a castle turret, protected by yard-thick walls and luxuriate in an enormous tiled bathroom whose floor to ceiling windows open up to the surrounding expanse of grounds. The hotel's twelve bedrooms are all grand in their furnishings and in keeping with the mood of the castle. The restaurant, although popular with day guests and travellers from across the German border, is small and intimate and often able to accommodate only overnight guests. It is very elegant in its setting and a crew of professional waiters serve the menu selections which change every week and vary with the seasons and the availability of fresh game, fish and produce. The chef offers his recommendations for either a four course menu or a seven course dinner. With the fixed menu you can purchase wines by the glass so that you can enjoy an appropriate wine with each course.

KASTEEL WITTEM
Owner: P. Ritzen
Wittemerallee No. 3
6286 AA Wittem, Holland
Tel: (04450) 1208
12 Rooms - Double DFL 200
Open: All year
Credit cards: All major
Located in S Holland, near Belgium & Germany

Set against a backdrop of vineyards, on the banks of the Moselle River, facing Germany on the opposite shore, the Hotel Simmer is a wonderful base from which to explore Luxembourg and the Moselle wine district (of both Luxembourg and Germany), and a convenient stopping point when enroute to or from the region of Alsace in France. Set on the main road, with a plain, stucco facade, the Hotel Simmer offers simple rooms that open up to views of the Moselle and the endless stream of barge traffic. Millim Schammo, who has inherited the position of innkeeper from her father, openly describes the accommodations as basic, but comfortable, very reasonable in price and, in contrast, uses only superlatives when discussing the Restaurant Simmer. A team of six chefs under the guidance of Bernard Lambert perform miracles in the kitchen. Serving guests since 1863, the excellence of the menu draws an impressive list of clientele, amongst them diplomats and royalty from countries worldwide. The massive stone fireplace, original to the hotel, is the focal point of the restaurant's intimate, soft yellow decor. The excellent cuisine and the owners, Jean and Millim Schammo, are responsible for a contented and loyal guest list. Having travelled extensively, they are well versed hosts and delighted and proud to welcome their international guests.

HOTEL SIMMER
Owner: Jean & Millim Schammo
117 Rue du Vin
5416 Ehnen, Luxembourg
Tel: 76030
23 Rooms - Double LFR 1,260-2,592
Open: March 9 to January 5
Credit cards: All major
Located 20 km S of Luxembourg

England

The Old Vicarage stands out as a home that offers exceptional accommodation to visitors to this tranquil part of the country which Thomas Hardy immortalised in his novels. Standing next to the old village church, surrounded by green lawns and neatly clipped hedges, this fine Georgian house is Michael and Anthea Hipwell's pride and joy. Their home is beautifully furnished with antiques. The sitting room has big French windows opening onto a terrace overlooking the garden - it is here that guests can take their breakfast on sunny summer mornings. Breakfast is the only meal that Anthea prepares - but she has a long list of wonderful places where you can eat in the surrounding villages. Upstairs the bedrooms have pretty wallpapers and are furnished in character with the house. There is lots to see and do in the area: Cerne Abbas with its thatched cottage and giant carved into the hillside is the Casterbridge of Hardy's novels, and historic Dorchester, Salisbury and Shaftesbury are nearby. From Dorchester take the A35 northeast for 5 miles to Tolpuddle (this is the village where the six martyrs met to fight starvation farmworkers' wages) where you turn left for Affpuddle (1 mile).

THE OLD VICARAGE
Owner: Michael & Anthea Hipwell
Affpuddle
Dorchester
Dorset DT2 7HH, England
Tel: (0305) 84315
3 Rooms, 1 with private bathroom
From £13 to £14 per person B & B
Open: All year
Credit cards: None accepted
Country home
Located 50 miles SW of Southampton (6 miles NE of Dorchester)

Surrounded by soft, pretty countryside, the picturesque village of Barrowden is far from the usual tourist path, deep in the Rutland countryside. (Rutlanders appear to be ignoring the bureaucratic edict that Rutland is now part of Leicestershire.) This traditional English village (consisting of a school, farms, houses and a pub - the "Exeter Arms") is grouped around a village green. At the far end of the village, by the duck pond, is the quaint, charming thatched house that is Pepperday Cottage. Watch your head. Low-beamed ceilings abound in the small, comfortably furnished cottage rooms. By arrangement, Beryl, a cookery teacher, will be happy to provide dinner and serve it on the fine old farmhouse table before the inglenook fireplace. Upstairs are three cottage-style bedrooms. This is a no-smoking home, where Beryl and Tony welcome visitors and enjoy giving advice on what to see and do in the area. Barrowden is located off the A47 between Leicester and Peterborough - 8 miles west of the junction of the A1 and the A47.

PEPPERDAY COTTAGE
Owner: Mr & Mrs A. Maxwell
Church Lane
Barrowden near Uppingham
Leicestershire LE15 8ED, England
Tel: (057 287) 874
3 Rooms with private bathrooms
£20 per person B & B
Closed: November to Easter
Credit cards: None accepted
Country home
Located 30 miles E of Leicester near Uppingham

Bath is a most interesting town with its Georgian squares, Roman baths, museums and shops, and Bathford lies a 15-minute drive or bus ride away. Isolated by its own large garden, this listed Georgian country house is one of the many lovely homes in the village. The four high ceilinged bedrooms are unusually spacious and most attractively decorated - all with bathroom, TV and large windows overlooking the garden. The large sitting and dining rooms are equally attractive and full of period furniture. Guests are encouraged to bring their own wine to accompany the three course dinner such as: melon, fillet of sole and plum crumble. Guests can play croquet and badminton on the lawn. Leave the M4 motorway at junction 18 and follow the A46 south to the A4 (signposted Chippenham), turn right onto the A363 and first left, at the Crown Pub, into Bathford and The Orchard is half way up the hill on your right.

THE ORCHARD
Owner: John & Olga London
Bathford
Bath
Avon BA1 7TG, England
Tel: (0225) 858765
4 Rooms with private bathrooms
£39 Single, £39 Double
Open: March to October
Credit cards: None accepted
Country home
Located 4 miles E of Bath

Willmead Farm is the most endearing thatched cottage nestled in a sheltered glen - my idea of idyllic. Willmead offers visitors a simple, informal and relaxed holiday. The farmhouse has only three simply decorated bedrooms grouped around a minstrels' gallery that overlooks the entrance hall. They share the facilities of a bathroom and separate shower room. Low beamed ceilings and old-fashioned board doors with metal latches add to the appeal of this adorable house. Comfortable sofas and chairs are grouped around the fireplace in the sitting room and beyond is the dining room where guests gather in the morning around the large table. A scrumptious farmhouse breakfast that includes wonderful homemade jams is the only meal that Hilary serves. For a sinfully rich Devon cream tea, detour round the duck pond and follow the path that heads past the barn to the thatched hamlet of Lustleigh. Guests can select where they would like to dine from the book of local restaurants' menus that Hilary has compiled. For those who seek something special, Willmead Farm and Hilary will find a place in your heart. To find Willmead Farm take the A382 from Bovey Tracey in the direction of Mortenhampstead (2 miles) then take the first narrow lane to the left after you pass the Hawksmoor Hospital.

WILLMEAD FARM
Owner: Hilary Roberts
Bovey Tracey, near Newton Abbot
Devon TQ13 9NP, England
Tel: (064 77) 214
3 Rooms sharing a bathroom
£16 per person B & B
Open: All year
Credit cards: None accepted
Bed & breakfast
Located 14 miles SW of Exeter

Built over a century ago, Chilvester Hill House is a solidly constructed Victorian home isolated from the busy A4 by a large garden. John and Gill Dilley retired here and subsequently unretired themselves: John, a physician, now works as an occupational health consultant and Gill entertains guests and breeds beef cattle. Gill enjoys cooking and a typical dinner might consist of smoked trout, lamb noisettes with vegetables from the garden, fruit fool and cheese and biscuits. They have a short wine list with over 20 French and German wines. Guests do not have to eat at the house and Gill is always happy to recommend pubs and restaurants in nearby villages. A soft pastel decor, treasured antiques and a cleverly displayed collection of commemorative plates make the large, high-ceilinged drawing room the most elegant room in the house. The bedrooms are spacious, high-ceilinged rooms, each individually decorated with flowery Sanderson wallpaper - all have mineral water, tea and coffee tray, and TV. The house is unsuitable for children under 12. Guests can enjoy the heated swimming pool during the summer months. Close by are Castle Combe, Lacock and the Avebury Neolithic circle. Bath, Oxford and Salisbury are an easy drive away. From Calne take the A4 west towards Chippenham. After half a mile turn right (signposted Bremhill) and immediately right into the drive of Chilvester Hill House.

CHILVESTER HILL HOUSE
Owner: John & Gill Dilley
Calne, Wiltshire SN11 0LP, England
Tel: (0249) 813981
3 Rooms with private bathrooms
From £30 single to £45 double
Open: All year
Credit cards: AX MC VS
Country home
Located 20 miles E of Bath

Just up the hill from the delightful Dartmoor town of Chagford is the former rectory that is now Bly House, a very English family-run hotel. I was pleased by the excellent value for money that it offers. The house is packed with Victorian furnishings: Mrs Thompson's extensive collections of Victorian china and delicate glassware are displayed throughout the house. As a result of this, small children are understandably not encouraged as guests. The lounge, with its view of the garden, provides you with a comfortable retreat and lots of collectables to admire. The spacious bedrooms are a perfect backdrop for the large furniture and bathrooms have been added into the corner of many. Room 1 has a four-poster bed and room 4 a half-tester. Because Bly House was a rectory it is unable to be licensed for the sale of alcoholic beverages, but guests are encouraged to bring their own wine to accompany Mrs Thompson's home-cooked food. An additional discount is given for stays of over six nights. From Exeter take the A30 to Whiddon Down, then turn left for Chagford (5 miles).

BLY HOUSE
Owner: Mr & Mrs G. B. Thompson
Nattadon Hill
Chagford
Devon TQ13 8BW, England
Tel: (06473) 2404
8 Rooms, 5 with private bathroom
From £12 single to £32 double
Closed: November to mid-January
Credit cards: None accepted
Guesthouse
Located 17 miles SW of Exeter

We covered quite a few miles exploring the quaint villages of the Yorkshire Dales in search of an inn that would reflect the atmosphere of the region. Coxwold is considered by some to be one of the most charming villages in the area and we happily ended our search here. The Fauconberg Arms is a 17th-century stone inn with olde worlde charm, oak beams, a warm character and a friendly atmosphere. It has a popular pub and good restaurant which is frequented by a very jovial crowd. Dick and Tricia Goodall are your hosts and they have carefully decorated four snug bedrooms (two double and two twin) with dainty prints in matching wallpapers and fabrics. One bedroom has a private shower. Travel west to the next tiny village of Kilburn and watch hand carvers make beautiful oak furniture, each piece incorporating a small carved mouse as a symbol of quiet industry. Eight miles farther is the old market town of Thirsk, now known as the place where James Herriot and his wife Helen lived at Skeldale House. Wander the lanes to the east and visit Castle Howard where "Brideshead Revisited" was filmed. From York take the A19 - Coxwold is between Easingwold and Thirsk.

FAUCONBERG ARMS
Owner: Mr & Mrs Richard Goodall
Coxwold
Yorkshire Y06 4AD, England
Tel: (03476) 214
4 Rooms, 1 with private shower
From £36 single to £38 double
Open: All year
Credit cards: None accepted
Historic inn
Located 24 miles N of York

Michael Nightingale is an actor and his easy welcoming manner and warm personality make you feel a valued guest at his country home, the Thatched Cottage, which is an adorable 16th-century cobb cottage with the most superb views across rolling farmland to Haytor and distant Dartmoor. With its blackened beams and low ceilings the sitting room offers a country-cozy welcome. The bedroom in this very old part of the cottage has an adjacent private bathroom. The remaining two bedrooms are cleverly incorporated into a 20th-century extension: downstairs a light and airy twin room and up a steep open-tread stairway a large family room tucked under the eaves. Children are made very welcome and the Nightingales have a crib, high-chair and extra folding bed on hand. Daphne cooks dinners by special arrangement: they may include fish, steak, roast lamb or beef as a main course. You are encouraged to bring your own wine. Guests select their breakfast on the previous evening and Daphne has it waiting for them at their chosen breakfast time. Every room has an extensive list of recommended restaurants, pubs, museums, stately homes and special places of interest to children. Crediton is 8 miles northwest of Exeter. The Thatched Cottage is 2 miles northwest of Crediton on the A377 (Barnstaple road) at Barnstaple Cross.

THE THATCHED COTTAGE
Owner: Michael & Daphne Nightingale
Barnstaple Cross, Crediton
Devon EX17 2EW, England
Tel: (03632) 3115
3 Rooms with private bathrooms
From £13.50 to £16 per person B & B
Open: January to November
Credit cards: None accepted
Bed & breakfast
Located 10 miles NW of Exeter

Overflowing with charm, this small inn is hidden away in the village of Doddiscombleigh. The inn derives its name from a legend that in the 1500s an owner closed the door of the inn, refusing hospitality to weary travellers. With no response to their repeated knocks, the visitors continued to believe that there was "nobody in" and the title "Nobody Inn" has remained since then. However, contrary to the legend, today you are assured a warm welcome. This popular inn always bustles with activity and people who seek its atmosphere and hospitality. Low ceilings, blackened beams and an imposing stone fireplace create a relaxing mood in both the pub area and adjoining restaurant. There is an extensive wine list and the well-stocked bar offers 130 brands of whisky. Upstairs the bedrooms are simply decorated, clean and comfortable and, please note, are within earshot of the gaiety and noises of the social gathering below. To find Doddiscombleigh turn right off the A38 at Haldon Racecourse (signposted Dunchideock) and follow the signs 3 miles to the Nobody Inn.

NOBODY INN
Owner: Mr N. F. Borst-Smith
Doddiscombleigh near Exeter
Devon EX6 7PS, England
Tel: (0647) 52394
7 Rooms with private bathrooms
From £10 single to £30 double
Open: All year
Credit cards: VS MC
Restaurant closed Sundays and Mondays
Historic inn
Located 6 miles SW of Exeter

John Budd gave up a high powered executive job in Brussels to buy this run-down 17th-century mill deep in the Dorset countryside. He moved in with his wife, Tina, and three children, and they set about transforming The Old Mill. Now it is a lovely home - the Budds have kept the mellow feel of the old building while adding fitted carpets, modern bathrooms and central heating. Guests have a large sitting room where a cheerful log fire blazes on chill evenings. A pine dresser holds the bar and guests help themselves, noting down their drinks on the honor system. Arrangements of little square tables topped with pink and white tablecloths each decorated with a fresh bouquet of flowers add an air of romance to the dining room where Tina serves a three course dinner. On the night of our visit cream of celery soup, coq au vin and chocolate log were being served. There are over 50 wines on the wine list. One of the bedrooms boasts a four-poster bed and spacious sitting area. All of the guestrooms have a tea and coffee tray, TV and modern bathroom. The Old Mill is ideal for a few days away from it all in the quiet countryside that Thomas Hardy made famous in his novels. From Yeovil take the A37 for 2 miles and turn right to Halstock (5 miles) where you follow signs for Chedington and after half a mile turn right to The Old Mill.

THE OLD MILL
Owner: John & Tina Budd
Halstock
Dorset BA22 9SJ, England
Tel: (093 589) 278
4 Rooms with private bathrooms
From £19 to £21 per person B & B
Open: mid-March to mid-October
Credit cards: MC VS
Country home
Located 30 miles SE of Taunton (5 miles SW of Yeovil)

No longer a farm, this 17th-century house is the adorable home of Mike and Sheila Edwards. Chintz covered chairs gathered before a blazing fire in the inglenook fireplace, mullioned windows set into thick walls, blackened beams, an antique dresser displaying china and an old polished table set for dinner create the picture of country-cozinesss that awaits you at Ford Farm House. Upstairs is a comfortable sitting room with lots of games and a TV. The bedrooms are particularly inviting: Louise's Room is a sunny single with lots of books, the Patchwork Room has a patchwork quilt on its double bed and a private bathroom, the Flower Room has watercolor prints of flowers, flowery curtains and shares a large bathroom with Louise's Room. For self catering accommodation the Edwards can offer two adorable cottages across the courtyard. Mike and Sheila previously owned a restaurant so you can be assured of good cooking: our delicious dinner was avocado and prawn salad, the tenderest of roast lamb with a mustard, garlic and herb sauce and nectarines in brandy. Ford Farm House is a most delightful place. Take the A38 round Exeter, the A384 to Totnes where you take the A381 Kingsbridge road to your right on the outskirts of town. At the top of the hill turn right to Harberton and Ford Farm is the first old house in the village.

FORD FARM HOUSE
Owner: Mike & Sheila Edwards
Harberton, near Totnes
Devon TQ9 7JS, England
Tel: (0803) 863539
3 Rooms, 1 with private bathroom
From £13.50 to £15 per person B & B
Open: All year
Credit cards: None accepted
Guesthouse
Located 24 miles SW of Exeter (2 miles SW of Totnes)

Combe House Hotel is located in the Quantocks, a beautiful coastal region of Somerset, on the outskirts of the quiet village of Holford. Once a tannery and still retaining its water wheel, this soft-pink toned, rectangular cottage reflects the peace and quiet of the surrounding countryside. The resident proprietors, the Richard Bjergfelt family, see that their guests are pampered. The rooms are simply but tastefully decorated with delightful prints and warm colors. The bar and lounge are also very attractive and the restaurant offers a very tasty set dinner menu. This is walking and riding country, with riding stables nearby. Tennis courts are in the grounds. A delightful Scandinavian-style log chalet houses a heated swimming pool, sauna and solarium. Your local explorations should include the medieval village of Dunster with its cobbled streets, yarn market, shops and famous castle, the nearby picturesque villages of Porlock and Porlock Weir and the villages of Lynton and Lynmouth with their connecting cliff railway.

COMBE HOUSE HOTEL
Owner: Richard Bjergfelt
Holford near Bridgwater
Somerset TA5 1RZ, England
Tel: (027 874) 382
16 Rooms, 10 with private bath
From £22 single to £50 double
Closed: mid-November to mid-February
Credit cards: All major
Small hotel
Located 15 miles N of Taunton

Lacock was once a prosperous medieval wool town, and now it is preserved by the National Trust as one of the most picturesque of British villages - its streets lined with splendid old houses and cottages. Next to the church King John's Hunting Lodge is an olde-English tea shop serving thick slices of homemade fruit cake and fluffy scones topped with Jersey cream as accompaniments to piping hot pots of tea. Fortunately for visitors the lodge offers two delightful bedrooms sharing the facilities of one bathroom. The large front bedroom has a delightful old four-poster bed and a romantic window seat while the adjoining dressing room has two single beds suitable for children. Next door the very prettily decorated Church Room overlooks the churchyard. There are several places in the village that serve evening meals (though you can do no better than the traditional roast dinner offered by the adjacent At The Sign of The Angel). A short stroll away is Lacock Abbey. This abbey was converted from a religious establishment to a mansion in the 16th century but still retains its 13th-century cloisters. The barn houses a display of Henry Fox Talbot's early photographs, apparatus and letters. If you are arriving from London exit the M4 at junction 17 and take the A350 Melksham road south to the village.

KING JOHN'S HUNTING LODGE
Owner: Bob & Jane Woods
21 Church Street, Lacock
Wiltshire SN15 2LB, England
Tel: (024973) 313
2 Rooms sharing 1 bathroom
From £12.50 to £15 per person B & B
Open: All year
Credit cards: None accepted
Bed & breakfast
Located 25 miles E of Bristol

Prospect Hill Hotel has that "end of the earth" feel to it, though it is only 9 miles from the M6 motorway. Just outside the picturesque village of Kirkoswald, John and Isa Henderson have creatively restored an 18th-century farmhouse and outbuildings, converting them into a delightful, original, country hotel that offers exceptional value for money. John and Isa's love and enthusiasm for Prospect Hill is infectious and reflected in the number of guests who return again and again. John's fascinating collections of "domestic bygones" and farm implements are displayed throughout the hotel. The bar was the 1700 cow byre; the dining room was the 1770 hay barn and features an intricate oak-timbered roof. The bedrooms, of varying size, are all decorated with country style furnishings. Only four bedrooms have private bathrooms - of these "Woodend" and "Park View" have lovely antique brass beds. Several rooms are located across the courtyard in the annex. Ample information on interesting walks and the local area is provided in all rooms. If approaching from the south leave the M6 at junction 41 onto the A6 to Plumpton, turn right onto B6413 through Lazonby and Kirkoswald up a steep hill and the hotel is on your left.

PROSPECT HILL HOTEL
Owner: Isa & John Henderson
Kirkoswald near Penrith
Cumbria CA10 1ER, England
Tel: (076883) 500
10 Rooms, 4 with private bathrooms
From £16 single to £44 double
Closed: February
Credit cards: All major
Country hotel
Located 15 miles S of Carlisle

The Gables is a quaint, thatched guesthouse near one of the most beautiful stretches of the Somerset coastline. Tucked away into a corner of the picturesque village of Porlock, the Gables has a charm all its own. There are some distinct advantages to staying in a guesthouse rather than a traditional hotel: one such is that with Mr and Mrs Crick as your hosts, you will be thoughtfully cared for, graciously welcomed and assured a comfortable, spotlessly clean bedroom. The bedrooms on the second floor share a bathroom while the twin-bedded first floor bedroom has its own private bathroom. Linger in the morning to enjoy a delightful country breakfast and the charm of this small inn. From The Gables it is only a few minutes' drive to the picturesque fishing village of Porlock. As you turn inland the beauties of Exmoor unfold. This area of river torrents plunging through wooded valleys and of herds of wild ponies galloping free is where R. D. Blackmore set his famous novel "Lorna Doone". Overnight parking is in the public car park next to the Porlock Information Centre - you will find the Gables a short walk behind the car park. Porlock is 6 miles west of Minehead on the A39.

THE GABLES
Owner: Mr & Mrs D. Crick
Porlock
Somerset TA24 8PB, England
Tel: (0643) 862552
7 Rooms, 1 with private bathroom
£11.50 per person B & B
Open: All year
Credit cards: None accepted
Bed & breakfast
Located 7 miles W of Minehead

Shearings is an adorable 16th-century thatched cottage sitting beside a winter stream in one of the prettiest villages in Hampshire - right on the edge of the New Forest. Shearings is positively oozing with olde-worlde charm, with its blackened oak beams, large inglenook fireplaces and sloping floors - one of the most charming prospects of a stay here is the fact that there is not a straight wall or even floor in the house. Colin (a retired army brigadier) and Rosemary Watts "adopt" guests into the family, joining their guests for pre-dinner drinks in the drawing room, dining with them and joining them for coffee and conversation around the fireplace afterwards. A cocktail, wine and coffee are included in the cost of the three course dinner. Rosemary aims to provide good English cooking and you can expect such things as roast lamb and lemon meringue pie. The bedrooms are very pretty: one has a bathroom en suite and a single and double room share a bathroom. A small sitting room is packed with information for guests to plan their visits to the surrounding area - Salisbury is a short drive away and Stonehenge and the New Forest within easy reach. From Salisbury take the A354 towards Dorchester and after Combe Bissett (5 miles) turn left for Rockbourne. Shearings is on your left in the village, reached by a little bridge that spans the stream.

SHEARINGS
Owner: Colin & Rosemary Watts
Rockbourne, Fordingbridge
Hampshire SP6 3NA, England
Tel: (07253) 256
3 Rooms, 1 with private bathroom
From £16 to £18.50 per person B & B
Open: February to November
Credit cards: None accepted
Home stay
Located 8 miles S of Salisbury

Atop the quaint cobbled streets of Rye is the ancient church and churchyard of St Mary's surrounded by a square of delightful old houses. Fortunately for visitors to this picturesque town, one of them, The Old Vicarage, is run as a welcoming guesthouse by Ernest and Ruth Thompson. The walls of the small sitting area and the large sunny dining room are covered with interesting pictures and prints, all of which are for sale and whenever the oak refectory table is not in use for breakfasts it displays additional prints and pictures. Upstairs are three large bedrooms (one king size and two with reproduction four-posters), two of which have private showers. In the attic are three additional small double bedrooms with sloping ceilings. All guestrooms are prettily decorated and have armchairs and televisions but I am concerned that there are only two loos for the six bedrooms. On summer weekends the Thompsons offer a traditional afternoon tea in the garden. Overnight car parking is provided across the square in a residents only parking area and the Thompsons will send you a map on just how to find them amongst the maze of Rye's narrow cobblestoned streets. Rye is on the A259 between Folkestone and Hastings.

THE OLD VICARAGE GUEST HOUSE
Owner: Ernest & Ruth Thompson
66 Church Square
Rye
East Sussex TN31 7HF, England
Tel: (0797) 222119
6 Rooms, 2 with private shower
From £15 to £19 per person B & B
Closed: for Christmas
Credit cards: None accepted
Guesthouse
Located 27 miles SW of Folkestone

Stratford Lodge is tucked down a quiet lane overlooking a large park just a few minutes' drive from the center of Salisbury. Jill Bayly runs the house as a home rather than a traditional guesthouse: guests have the use of a large sitting room and the adjacent entrance hall is lined with books galore, including a great many that are useful in planning your sightseeing adventures. Pretty wallpapers and fabrics, pastel color schemes, antiques, flowers and family mementos combine to give the bedrooms a romantic charm - all have a tea tray and biscuits, TV, and private bathroom. Jill provides imaginative meals. A typical dinner might consist of baked pears with Roquefort, roast duckling in a black cherry and port sauce, apple strudel with clotted cream, and then cheese. Fruit from the garden is usually offered for breakfast and instead of the usual bacon and eggs you might like to try mushrooms on toast or smoked haddock kedgeree. Plan on using this exceptional guesthouse as a base - in addition to Salisbury's old streets and cathedral, Stonehenge and Avebury's megalithic monuments are close at hand while Bath, the New Forest, Winchester, Southampton and Bournemouth are easy daytrips. As you enter Salisbury on the A345, from Amesbury, take the first righthand turn (at the shop) and you are on Park Lane.

STRATFORD LODGE
Owner: Jill Bayly
4 Park Lane off Castle Road
Salisbury, Wiltshire SP1 3NP, England
Tel: (0722) 25177
5 Rooms with private bathrooms
£15 per person B & B
Closed: for Christmas & New Year
Credit cards: None accepted
Bed & breakfast
Located 5 mins from the center of Salisbury

Near Tintagel Castle (claiming the honor of being King Arthur's birthplace) is the tiny town of Tintagel, bustling in summer with tourists. However, only a few miles south of Tintagel is the Old Millfloor, a blissful oasis of serenity. You will see the sign as you drive south from Tintagel towards the fine sandy beaches of Trebarwith Strand. Park your car at the top of the hill and wind your way down the steep path to the whitewashed Old Millfloor, nestled amongst the trees beside the mill stream. (Due to the steep climb, this hotel is not for those who have difficulty walking.) The three guestrooms in this cozy converted mill share a bathroom, yet each has delightful amenities such as hairdryer, talcum powder, hand cream, bath oil and even Malvern bottled water. Your day begins with piping hot tea or coffee brought to your bedside. Then, upon arising, you are served a delicious full English breakfast. Your pampering continues in the afternoon when tea arrives with hot scones, jam and clotted cream. Guests can select what they desire to eat for dinner from a tempting menu prepared by Janice. This idyllic little inn is not only a romantic hideaway, but also excellent value. From Camelford (A39) take the B3266, then the B3263 towards Tintagel and turn off for Trebarwith Strand.

THE OLD MILLFLOOR
Owner: Janice Wadden Martyn
Trebarwith Strand near Tintagel
Cornwall PL34 0HA
Tel: (0840) 770234
3 Rooms sharing 1 bathroom
£12 per person B & B
Open: Easter to November
Credit cards: None accepted
Bed & breakfast & restaurant
Located 63 miles W of Exeter (1 mile S of Tintagel)

Holdfast Cottage Hotel is set in a charming garden surrounded by miles of farmland. Here you will find a simple country hotel offering visitors good food and accommodation at excellent value. The Victorian exterior of the house surrounds a much older interior evidenced by the beamed entrance hall, the old wooden doors and the low-beamed ceilings. Furnishings are comfortable and homely - the lounge contains the well-worn leather sofa and chairs that Diana and Dennis bought at a local auction. The dining room is large and sunny with views across the garden: Old English as well as conventional fare is offered on the menu. The bedrooms vary in size from large twin and double rooms to a small single tucked into the eaves of the house. The rooms are furnished with an eclectic variety of auction "finds" and priced according to size. A warm welcome is given to children and there is a large garden where they can play. According to Diana, many guests visit the Royal Worcester Porcelain factory in Worcester, 15 miles away. You must make an appointment to tour the factory where you can also purchase "seconds" at bargain prices. Holdfast Cottage also offers a four-day Christmas program. Take junction 1 off the M50 and turn north on the A38. After 2 miles turn left on the A4104 for 4 miles to Holdfast Cottage Hotel.

HOLDFAST COTTAGE HOTEL
Owner: Dennis & Diana Beetlestone
Welland near Malvern
Worcestershire WR13 6NA, England
Tel: (0684) 310288
9 Rooms with private bathrooms
From £18 to £20 per person B & B
Open: All year
Credit cards: None accepted
Small countryside hotel
Located 15 miles SW of Worcester

The splendors of Blenheim Palace and the charms of the neighboring town of Woodstock merit an overnight stay. The opening of The Blenheim on the palace's doorstep provides the charming, reasonably priced accommodation that holidaymakers have craved. Visitors who have a sweet tooth will find the Blenheim especially appealing as downstairs is divided between a traditional sweet shop and an old-fashioned tea shop. Sprigged flowered wallpaper, groupings of tables and chairs and a cake trolley loaded with scrumptious cakes make the tea shop my idea of a delightful place to spend the latter part of an afternoon. Apricot gateau, carrot cake with cream cheese and hot apple cake are among a few of the tempting selections. In addition, patrons choose between nine varieties of tea for their cuppa. The accommodation is above the shops, reached by a narrow staircase. The family room has three single beds and a bathroom with shower. The large double room has a splendid antique bed and a bathroom with shower. The twin-bedded room has its bathroom across the hall. There is no sitting room but there are many restaurants and pubs nearby. Woodstock is 9 miles northwest of Oxford on the A34.

THE BLENHEIM
Owner: David & Jenny Macrae
Audrey Speller
17 Park Street, Woodstock
Oxfordshire OX7 1SJ, England
Tel: (0993) 811467
3 Rooms with private bathrooms
From £21.50 single to £32 double
Open: All year
Credit cards: None accepted
Bed & breakfast & Tea shop
Located 9 miles W of Oxford

France

Transected by the sweeping Rhone, Arles is a beautiful city, rich with Roman and medieval monuments. Just 50 kilometers to the sea when following the path of the Rhone, Arles has long guarded a strategic location. It is also convenient to all of Provence and an ideal base for exploring the region. The Hotel d'Arlatan is tucked off one of the small streets in the center of Arles near the Place du Forum within easy walking distance of all the city's major sights. In the 12th, 15th and 17th centuries the Hotel d'Arlatan belonged to the Counts of Arlatan de Beaumont and served as their private home. It is now the pride of Monsieur and Madame Roger Desjardin who offer you an ideal retreat with charming accommodation and service. This is a quaint hotel, ornamented with antiques and pretty fabrics. Many of the hotel bedrooms overlook a quiet, inner courtyard or garden. Although the hotel does not have a restaurant, a delightful breakfast can be enjoyed in the inviting salon or on the patio. For those travelling by car it is also wonderful to note that the hotel can offer secure parking in their private garage.

HOTEL D'ARLATAN
Owner: M & Mme Roger Desjardin
26, Rue du Sauvage
13200 Arles, France
Tel: 90 93 56 66 Telex: 441203
46 Rooms - Double FFR 444-566
Open: All year
Credit cards: All major
No restaurant
Patio, garden
Region: Provence
Located 30 km SE of Nimes

Le Moulin des Ruats is a charming, wood-shingled cottage set on the river's edge, in the shade of the surrounding lush greenery. Located on a scenic stretch of road as it winds along the banks of the Cousin, between the town of Avallon and the hilltop, medieval village of Vezelay, the setting of this renovated mill is quite peaceful. Monsieur and Madame Bertier are a lovely couple and very involved with the management of their inn. In the afternoons they are present in the lobby to welcome their guests and at mealtimes either in the restaurant or on the terrace to offer menu suggestions. When the weather cooperates, breakfast is quite memorable when enjoyed under a canopy of trees on the edge of the rushing Cousin river. The setting is quite peaceful and affords a good night's rest. The accommodations are not luxurious: they are decorated in simple prints, and are almost motel-like in their furnishings, but are moderate in price. Not all of the hotel's 20 bedrooms have private baths, but the rooms are quiet and clean. The Moulin des Ruats is an inviting hotel and Avallon, a reasonable drive from Paris, would serve as an ideal overnight destination en route to the Burgundy wine region. Be sure not to venture too far, however, without first visiting the neighboring village of Vezelay and with its acclaimed Romanesque basilica.

LE MOULIN DES RUATS
Owner: M & Mme Bertier
Vallee du Cousin, 89200 Avallon, France
Tel: 86 34 07 14
20 Rooms - Double FFR 200-360
Open: Mar 3 to Oct 30, Restaurant closed Mon
Credit cards: AX VS DC
Region: Burgundy
Located 4.5 km from Avallon

Nestled along the river's edge with a terrace banked by flowers in the lovely valley of the Cousin, Le Moulin des Templiers offers a peaceful night's rest at an inexpensive price. The rooms are all very simple in their decor, very few with private bath, small and sparse in furnishings, but fresh, clean and carefully tended to by a charming Madame Hilmoine. Sound the horn in the snug reception area and she will appear to offer a smile and a welcome. The setting here is idyllic. The bedrooms, although not overlooking the rushing Cousin, open up to the sounds of the cascading river, and a small farmyard of roosters, chickens, goats and one lone, lazy boar. If you are blessed with warm sunshine, enjoy either afternoon drinks or breakfast of fresh bread, jam and hot coffee at white wrought-iron tables set along the water's edge. With a number of outstanding restaurants as neighbors (Marc Menau's L'Esperance at St Pere Sous Vezelay is located just a few miles away in the direction of Vezelay) it is a welcome fact that Le Moulin des Templiers does not have a restaurant where one feels obligated to dine. This is a dear little hotel, quite inexpensive in price and convenient to exploring Vezelay and a perfect overnight en route to Burgundy.

LE MOULIN DES TEMPLIERS
Owner: Mme Robert Hilmoine
Vallee du Cousin, Pontaubert
89200 Avallon, France
Tel: 86 34 10 80
14 Rooms - Double FFR 225-282
Open: March 15 to November 2
Credit cards: None accepted
No restaurant
Region: Burgundy
Located between Avallon and Vezelay on the Route de la Vallee du Cousin

The Hotel Bois Joli is a roadside inn, set on the hill, surrounded by trees just as the road winds away from the river into the resort town of Bagnoles de l'Orne. Very pretty, almost gingerbread in appearance with its red timbered beams and windowboxes, the Bois Joli is a favorite of many who frequent this charming town. I am certain there are other hotels in town whose accommodations equal those of the Bois Joli, and yet no other can boast the same warm and genuine welcome. An extraordinarily lovely hostess, Madame Gabriot, a young, exuberant and handsome woman, is responsible for the hotel's friendly atmosphere as well its fresh new decor. All of the hotel's 20 bedrooms have been refurbished in a traditional French country style. Pretty, colorful wallpapers and prints have been selected and decorate each of the rooms. Accommodations are spotlessly clean and I noticed many thoughtful, feminine touches, such as a spray of fresh heather on a bedside table. The dining room is very inviting and the food which is served in ample portions is quite good. Many guests use the Bois Joli as a base for exploring the region and take advantage of the offered pension plan (room with meals).

HOTEL BOIS JOLI
Owner: Mme Chantal Gabriot
Avenue Philippe du Rozier
61140 Bagnoles de l'Orne
France
Tel: 33 37 92 77 Telex: 171782
20 Rooms - Double FFR 300-400
Open: April 1 to November 1
Credit cards: All major
Region: Normandy
Located 50 km NE of Laval

Monsieur and Madame Auregan are your charming and helpful hosts at this lovingly restored Normandy townhome in Bayeux, a picturesque city known for its outstanding tapestry museum. A large courtyard and stone, semi-circular staircase lead up to the front entry of their hotel, the Hotel d'Argouges, and to a warm welcome. Off the entry hall, French doors in the beautiful and gracious salon-library lead out to the quiet back garden and terrace. Sheltered behind its main gate, the Hotel d'Argouges manages to retain the feeling of a quiet country home while its address is, in actuality, downtown Bayeux. Looking out over the beautiful garden or front courtyard, the bedrooms all have exposed beams and comfortable furniture as well as private shower or bath and phones. There are also two charming suites which have a small extra room for children. Next door the Auregans have begun renovating another very old home and some of the bedrooms are found there. Breakfast can be enjoyed in the privacy of one's room, in the intimate, elegant breakfast salon, or on the back garden terrace overlooking Madame Auregan's vivid flowers. A veritable haven for travellers visiting Bayeux, the Hotel d'Argouges offers good value in lovely surroundings plus gracious hosts who have great pride in their profession.

HOTEL D'ARGOUGES
Owner: Marie-Claire & Daniel Auregan
21, Rue St Patrice
14400 Bayeux, France
Tel: 31 92 88 86 Telex: 170234
25 Rooms - Double FFR 250-350
Open: All year
Credit cards: All major
Garden, no restaurant
Region: Normandy
Located 28 km NW of Caen

Perfect for those on a budget who prefer a countryside setting to the city of Chinon, La Giraudiere is a modest hotel offering excellent value, a rural setting and a pleasant welcome. Travel the D749 north from Chinon in the direction of Bourgeuil. At Bourgeuil watch for signs that direct you to "Hotel" and follow them along the V6 in the direction of Savigny en Veron. Set back off a country road, La Giraudiere is a 17th-century farmstead consisting of a cluster of buildings set around a central courtyard. The reception area and restaurant (breakfast only) are located in a separate building from the hotel's 24 bedrooms which are housed in neighboring buildings of the complex and back on to open farmland. These are furnished with reproduction as well as a few effectively placed antiques and a number of them are very picturesque with old beams and stone fireplaces. All the bedrooms have private bath or shower and we were told that twelve are equipped with kitchenettes. Breakfast can be enjoyed either in the room, in the restaurant or on the terrace in the shade of the tranquil courtyard. Much frequented by British tourists, this inn is recommended for its calm, rural setting and bargain rates.

LA GIRAUDIERE
Route de Savigny
Beaumont en Veron
37420 Avoine, France
Tel: 47 58 40 36
24 Rooms - Double FFR 200-285
Open: All year
Credit cards: All major
No restaurant
Rural countryside setting
Region: Loire Valley
Located 5 km N of Chinon

L'Auberge de l'Abbaye is a very pretty, Norman, half-timbered inn in an equally charming village. Le Bec Hellouin is a cluster of half-timbered and thatched buildings set around a medieval abbey, nestled along a trickling stream, a peaceful setting removed from the main road (D39). When we entered the cozy, low ceilinged restaurant of the 18th-century L'Auberge de l'Abbaye we were greeted by the sight and aroma of a large, freshly baked apple tart. We were told by the welcoming owner, Madame Sergent, that her restaurant is renowned all over the world for apple tarts. Grand Marnier, a specialty of the region, is also featured here, with large bottles present on each table. Madame Sergent has owned the inn for a quarter of a century and her taste and feminine touches are apparent throughout. Lace curtains at the windows, polished copper and faience ornamenting the walls, and pretty fabrics enhance the decor of the inn. The stairway leading to the inn's ten bedrooms is flanked by former exterior walls whose heavy old half timbering add character to this charming auberge. The bedrooms are simple, yet pretty in their furnishings and all have private bath or shower. The rooms either overlook the inn's interior courtyard or look out over a shaded town square. Inside and out this inn is truly what one imagines a simple, country French inn should be.

L'AUBERGE DE L'ABBAYE
Owner: Sergent family
2780 Le Bec Hellouin, France
Tel: 32 44 86 02
10 Rooms - Double FFR 340-360
Open: February 28 to January 10
Credit cards: VS MC
Lovely half-timbered inn
Region: Normandy
Located 42 km SW of Rouen

Soon after the publication of the first edition of this guide, I was directed to the Hotel Bonnet and have since returned for repeated visits. Serenely located on a bend of the Dordogne, in the shadow of the impressive Chateau de Beynac, the Bonnet is indeed a "gem". The bedrooms are simple in decor, but the restaurant setting, either indoors with large windows looking onto a river panorama or on the vine-covered terrace, encourages one to linger for hours. The Dordogne meanders through the Perigord, a region whose products have attracted the recognition of true gourmets. Turkeys, ducks, geese, foie gras, crepes, a variety of truffles, plentiful vegetables and fruits (particularly strawberries and raspberries) are all found in abundance. Chef Monzie was trained in Perigord and his excellent cuisine reflects the regional specialties. With the vineyard regions of Bordeaux, Bergerac and Cahors nearby, the Restaurant Bonnet is able to offer you a fine selection of wines to accompany your meal. Generations of the Bonnet family have managed this inn for almost a century and today Mademoiselle R. Bonnet is in residence to act as gracious host. Stay here for a minimum of three nights and take advantage of the fantastic pension rates. This is a reasonably priced, simple, but delightful, inn with an incomparable riverside setting.

HOTEL BONNET
Owner: Bonnet family
Beynac et Cazenac
24220 St Cyprien, France
Tel: 53 29 50 01
22 Rooms - Double to FFR 244
Open: April 1 to October 15
Credit cards: VS
Terrace restaurant, riverfront setting
Region: Dordogne
Located 64 km SE of Perigueux

The village streets of the picturesque town of Biot are narrow, a bit difficult to negotiate, and parking is limited, but the effort will be rewarded once you reach the Place des Arcades and the inviting Hotel Galerie des Arcades. Cafe tables monopolize the sidewalk in front of the arched doorways of this little inn. The indoor cafe-bar is always a-bustle with local chatter and usually a member of the Brothier family is found here tending the bar. The Brothiers welcome numerous artists, photographers and models as their guests. The inn focuses around the three rooms that Monsieur Brothier opened as a gallery and provincial restaurant more than 30 years ago. Rooms on the upper floors were renovated and offered to overnight guests a decade later. Steep, old tile stairways climb to a maze of rooms that are like an extension of the gallery as they are hung with an array of abstract, original art. The bedrooms are moderate in price and those with private terraces that look out over the rooftops of Biot are a real bargain. Many of the rooms are equipped with private bath, shower, washbasin and toilet. The decor is a bit bohemian in flavor and arrangement, with heavy armoires and often four-poster beds. Facing onto a quiet, picturesque square, the Hotel Galerie des Arcades is a friendly gathering spot and it is easy to transcend time and envision the likes of Van Gogh and Gaughin frequenting the Cafe des Arcades.

HOTEL GALERIE DES ARCADES
Owner: Brothier family
16, Place des Arcades
06410 Biot, France
Tel: 93 65 01 04
12 Rooms - Double FFR 150-280
Open: January to November 20
Credit cards: None accepted
Region: Riviera
Located 15 km NW of Nice

We truly felt that we'd discovered a special little inn when we happened upon the Hotel le Cheval Blanc. Facing the Place de l'Eglise, Le Cheval Blanc is easy to spot with its lovely timbered facade and wrought iron sign of a white horse. Dating from the 17th century, this was once an annex for the neighboring church. Now filled in, an old stone archway that once opened onto a passageway to the stables stands as evidence of its earlier history. After the revolution, the building was converted to a cafe-bar and remained a popular, local spot for almost two centuries. It was just a few years ago that Michel and Micheline Bleriot converted the cafe into one of the most charming, most reasonably priced inns in the Loire Valley. The restaurant's decor is charming in its simplicity; a pretty wallpaper covers the walls and wooden chairs and tables dressed with crisp white linen are set beneath dark beams. An inner courtyard latticed with vines and set with white outdoor tables is a delightful spot for breakfast. The bedrooms are unbelievably attractive, particularly when one considers the bargain rates. Each room has its own private bath or shower and overlooks either the central courtyard or a quiet back street. Located just west of Chenonceaux and south of Amboise, Blere is a convenient base from which to explore the castles of the Loire Valley and Le Cheval Blanc is a reasonably priced, delightful inn.

LE CHEVAL BLANC
Owner: Michel and Micheline Bleriot
Place de l'Eglise
37150 Blere, France
Tel: 47 30 30 14
13 Rooms - Double FFR 210-230
Open: All year, closed Sun & Mon (except Jul & Aug)
Credit cards: VS
Region: Loire Valley
Located 27 km SE of Tours

When searching for a luncheon spot for my first tour group to France I was thrilled to discover the enchanting village of Bourdeilles. Tucked 10 kilometers farther up a quiet valley from the larger town of Brantome, the setting of Bourdeilles is idyllic. In this old village, crowned by a castle, the Hotel des Griffons clings to a narrow bridge. The hotel met and surpassed my every wish and expectation. Madame Denise Deborde manages the hotel, supervises the restaurant and personally pampers her guests. Her command of the English language is limited, but she and her husband always sport a welcoming smile. Bedrooms dressed in pretty fabrics and tucked under old beams are charming and many overlook the quietly flowing river. The restaurant is intimate and inviting with windows opening up the soothing sound of cascading water. Tables are set on the terrace on warm summer nights - the outdoor setting is romantic and perfect for enjoying wonderful Perigord specialties. The food is excellent: beautifully presented and very reasonably priced. Monsieur Deborde heads off each week to the market and purchases only the freshest ingredients. The Hotel des Griffons is a delightful inn and an excellent value on the northern boundaries of the Dordogne.

HOTEL DES GRIFFONS
Owner: Mme Denise Deborde
Bourdeilles, 24310 Brantome
France
Tel: 53 03 75 61
10 Rooms - Double FFR 300-350
Open: April to October 10
Closed Tuesdays April 10 to July 1
Credit cards: VS DC MC
Region: Dordogne
Located 24 km NW of Perigueux

Paul and Jenny Dyer came to the Dordogne Valley from England in search of a country setting in which to raise their two daughters. They discovered this wonderful, 18th-century farmhouse, abandoned and in a state of ruin, and spent their time and savings to literally rebuild and restore it. In its fourth season, the Auberge du Noyer, named for the large walnut tree that fronts it, is a warm and inviting inn. Guests have only glowing reports and praise for the accommodation, the food and the hospitality of the hosts. The auberge's intimate dining room has a large, open fireplace and orange and brown tablecloths which blend warmly with the stone walls and sienna tile floors. The Dyers have plans for a veranda to front the home and extend the seating area for morning breakfasts, or dinner on a balmy night. A lovely swimming pool sits on a hill behind the farmhouse. The inn has ten bedrooms all decorated beautifully in Laura Ashley prints and all with private bath or shower. The inn is open later in the season than most of the hotels of the region. Guests return when the weather turns a bit cooler to sit before the large fire, read or don wellingtons and walk the countryside lanes. The atmosphere at the Auberge du Noyer is very relaxed and comfortable and the presence of the Dyers' darling, blond daughters, who leave school bags about, add to the feeling of being "at home".

AUBERGE DU NOYER
Owner: Paul & Jenny Dyer
Le Reclaud de Bonny Bas
24260 Le Bugue, France
Tel: 53 07 11 73
10 Rooms - Double FFR 280-380
Open: Palm Sunday to December
Credit cards: MC VS
Region: Dordogne
Located on D703, 41 km S of Perigueux

Chambord is the largest of the castles of the Loire Valley and very impressive in size and appearance. The castle stands dramatically on a large open expanse of lawn, bounded by forest. Although almost bare of furniture, it retains its grandeur and enchantment, especially at sunset or shrouded in the morning mist. Staying at the Hostellerie Saint Michel provides an opportunity to explore the expanse of grounds surrounding Chambord either before you begin your day's adventures or at its end. It is one of the very few hotels in the Loire Valley that enjoys such a marvelous, close proximity to one of its castles. The Hostellerie Saint Michel has an inviting terrace restaurant where many, hotel and chateau guests alike, enjoy a refreshing drink and snack. Indoors is an attractive restaurant and comfortable entry salon. Accommodation is surprisingly inexpensive. The rooms are simple in their country prints, basic in furnishings, but comfortable. Of the 40 rooms a choice few look out through the surrounding lacy trees to the Chateau de Chambord. Of these, the corner rooms are the largest and should definitely be requested as they are no more expensive than the other rooms with a view.

HOSTELLERIE SAINT MICHEL
Le Meur
Chambord
41250 Bracieux
France
Tel: 54 20 31 31
40 Rooms - Double FFR 240-360
Closed: November 12 to December 22
Credit cards: VS MC
Faces the Chateau de Chambord
Region: Loire Valley
Located 18 km E of Blois

On the main road, opposite the gates to the Chateau de Chaumont, is the lovely Hostellerie du Chateau. An attractive, timbered building, the location of the hotel is its largest drawback, as it is hard to shut out the traffic noises from the rooms that overlook the road. But for the Loire Valley the prices are moderate and from the moment you enter the hotel you will be charmed by the wood beamed interior, the glowing fire, the beautiful dining room, quaint salons and Madame Desmadryl's hospitality. On a warm summer day tables are spread out under the trees in the front garden and provide an inviting spot to rest and enjoy a refreshing drink. The hallways leading to the upstairs bedrooms are in need of some fresh paint, but the rooms are still quite attractive. The least expensive rooms fall into the moderate price range and are smaller in size and overlook the road. The more expensive rooms are worth a splurge as they are more commodious and overlook the hotel's back garden and pool and enjoy views of the passing Loire River. All the rooms are decorated in warm and attractive colors and the bathrooms are modern. The Hostellerie du Chateau is a well-located hotel for exploring the castles of the Loire. Accommodations are not luxurious, but comfortable and well priced.

HOSTELLERIE DU CHATEAU
Owner: M Bonnigal, Manager: Mme Desmadryl
Chaumont sur Loire, 41150 Onzain, France
Tel: 54 20 98 04
15 Rooms - Double FFR 360-544
Open: March to end November
Credit cards: MC VS
Pool
Region: Loire Valley
Located 41 km NE of Tours

Standing proud with its castle turret is the Hotel du Manoir. Newly constructed, the hotel is set on the main road of Chenonceaux, opposite the Hotel Bon Laboureur et du Chateau and just a short distance from the town's beautiful castle. Opened as a hotel just a few years ago, the Hotel du Manoir definitely radiates a pride of ownership. A lovely couple, the Mazzellas offer a warm welcome and the character of the inn reflects the heritage of its Italian owners. Vivid colors, heavy patterns and garish paintings abound and there is a lot of detail in the furnishings. The entry salon is comfy, with inviting large overstuffed chairs. A handsome, wide stairway leads up from the lobby to the hotel's seven bedrooms. The restaurant is intimate and charming in its decor: in the evening, candlelight from the individual tables reflects off the room's stone walls and vaulted ceiling. The menu boasts a number of Italian specialties, such as "lasagne a la maison". Afternoon tea is served at tables set round an old well at the center of the flagstone terrace. One can also relax in the shade of a garden that extends out at the back of the hotel. The Hotel du Manoir is a delightful inn because of its endearing owners.

HOTEL DU MANOIR
Owner: M & Mme Carlo Mazzella
1, Rue La Roche
37150 Chenonceaux
France
Tel: 47 23 90 31
7 Rooms - Double FFR 280-560
Open: March to November
Credit cards: Unknown
Region: Loire Valley
Located 35 km SE of Tours

Chinon is a pretty riverside town with narrow cobblestoned streets which climb to the ruins of its crowning castle. This is where Jeanne d'Arc met Le Dauphin and is an interesting stop for any Loire Valley itinerary. The Hotel Diderot is well located just off the Place Jeanne d'Arc in a residential district of town. The Hotel Diderot is owned and managed with care by Theo Kazamias and his family who came to France from Cyprus ten years ago in search of a new life. He purchased and completely renovated the home, installing bathrooms and decorating with a homey touch. Off the entryway, a breakfast room set with country tables and chairs before a large 15th-century fireplace, is where one enjoys breakfast complete with homemade jams and the chatter and good spirits of the many British travellers who frequent this hotel. An old wooden stairway and hallways with exposed walls and beams lead to eighteen of the bedrooms. Another room is found in the pavilion, and three additional rooms, converted from the stables, are located at street level and are equipped for handicap access. All of the bedrooms are furnished with a mixture of antique and contemporary pieces with bathrooms that are adequate and spotless. The Hotel Diderot offers simple comforts and moderate prices. Your host is a kind and very interesting man who genuinely cares about his guests.

HOTEL DIDEROT
Owner: Theo Kazamias
4, Rue Buffon, 37500 Chinon, France
Tel: 47 93 18 87
22 Rooms - Double FFR 200-350
Closed: Christmas holidays
Credit cards: MC VS
No restaurant
Region: Loire Valley
Located 48 km SW of Tours

A converted mill, this ivy-covered complex of buildings is situated along the River Orne just downstream from the old stone bridge. It is an idyllic setting ablaze with masses of flowers and the sound of the river tumbling past the former mill is quite soothing. The Moulin du Vey has a lovely terrace set with tables and shaded by a lacy willow tree. If you choose to dine indoors, the restaurant is in an adjacent building. Twelve bedrooms tucked away in the former mill could use a little sprucing up but they are comfortable and equipped with either private bath or shower. Three kilometers from the mill is the Relais de Surone, an annex, where seven additional bedrooms are offered. The Relais is an old home built in the style of a church or a priory. Although away from the river and without a restaurant, the rooms of the Relais are more attractive and spacious than those of the Moulin. Breakfast can be taken in the salon, in the bedroom, or, on a nice day, in the front garden. Clecy le Vey is the capital of the beautiful district referred to as Swiss Normandy. The Moulin du Vey is located 2 kilometers east of Clecy in the village of Le Vey. The Relais is located on the other side of Clecy le Vey, just off the road that travels between Caen and Domfort (route D962).

LE MOULIN DU VEY
Owner: Mme Leduc
14570 Clecy le Vey
France
Tel: 31 69 71 08
12 Rooms (Mill) - 7 Rooms (Relais)
Double FFR 360-460
Open: Moulin du Vey - February to December
Le Relais - Easter to October
Credit cards: AX DC VS
Region: Normandy
Located 37 km S of Caen

The medieval village of Conques overlooks the Dourdou Gorge. Tucked off the beaten track, the village is glorious in the gentle light of evening or in the mist of early day. Conques' pride is an 11th-century abbey, directly across from which is a simple hotel, the Ste Foy. The shuttered windows of our room opened up to the church steeples and we woke to the melodious sound of bells. The decor is neat and attractive and one can't fault the location. The restaurant is reserved exclusively for guests of the hotel and is open for breakfast and dinner. The interior restaurant is lovely and rustic in its decor, the walls hung with an exhibition of French, English and American paintings and on warm summer nights dinner is served family-style on a sheltered courtyard terrace. One can order a la carte or select from a well-chosen three or four course fixed menu at a very reasonable price. The restaurant offers a number of regional dishes. The Roquefort cheese produced in the area is exceptional and the house "salade verte aux noix et roquefort et huile de noix" is a perfect first course to any meal. A wide selection of fine French wines from the various provinces comprise the wine list. The hotel's finest feature is Madame Cannes, whose charm, welcoming smile and eagerness to please create the wonderful atmosphere of the Ste Foy.

HOTEL STE FOY
Owner: M & Mme Jean Cannes
and Mme Garcenot
Conques, 12320 St Cyprien
France
Tel: 65 69 84 03
20 Rooms - Double FFR 260-424
Open: April 10 to October 6
Region: Lot
Located 37 km NW of Rodez

An alternative for travellers who would like to avoid the crowds on the island of Le Mont Saint Michel, the ivy-clad, grey-stone Manoir de la Roche Torin is a lovely hotel. This stately manor was a private residence for 25 years before it was converted to a hotel. A short tree-lined drive past an ancient chapel on the front lawn leads to the front steps. The highlights of this hotel are the mix of antique furnishings in the public rooms and the magnificent view from the dining room where one looks out over sheep grazing on the tidal grasslands to Le Mont Saint Michel. The regional specialty known as "pre-salted lamb", sheep who have grazed on the salty grass, is roasted over a large open hearth in the restaurant. Two stately grandfather clocks watch over the dinner guests. It is important to note that hotel guests are expected to dine in the Manoir's restaurant. The twelve bedrooms of the Manoir de la Roche Torin are furnished with modern pieces and sometimes overly bright colors have been chosen for their decor. The rooms, however, are clean, cheerful and reasonably priced. All but one room is equipped with private bath. Considering its location, priceless views and the warm welcome extended by the Barraux family, this hotel is a bargain and a tranquil haven near an otherwise congested tourist destination.

MANOIR DE LA ROCHE TORIN
Owner: M & Mme Barraux
50220 Courtils
France
Tel: 33 70 96 55
12 Rooms - Double FFR 260-440
Open: March to December
Credit cards: All major
Region: Normandy
Located 9 km E of Le Mont St Michel

The Dordogne River makes a panoramic journey through a rich valley studded with castles. The ancient village of Domme has for centuries stood guard 1,500 feet above the river, and commands a magnificent panorama. The town itself is enchanting, with ramparts that date from the 13th century, and narrow streets that wind through its old quartier and past a lovely 14th century Hotel de Ville. At the center of town under the old market place one finds access to some interesting stalactite and stalagmite grottos. But most visitors come to Domme for its spectacular valley views and the best vantage point is from the Terrasse de la Barre. Very near to la Barre, facing the church, is a hotel which enables you to savor the village long after the tour buses have departed: Monsieur and Madame Gillard extend a warm and friendly greeting at the Hotel de l'Esplanade. Rene Gillard is both your host and chef. In the dining room he'll propose some excellent regional specialties that feature the delicious cepes, truffles, foie gras and local fish. There are two restaurants to choose from, both attractive and very country in decor. The hotel's 20 rooms, all with either bath or shower, are located in the main building or in a neighboring annex that was once a building of the church and dates from the 17th century. The bedrooms are simply decorated, reasonably priced and commodious.

HOTEL DE L'ESPLANADE
Owner: M Rene Gillard
24250 Domme, France
Tel: 53 28 31 41
20 Rooms - Double FFR 240-420
Open: Dec to end Jan & Mar to end Oct
Credit cards: AX MC VS
Region: Dordogne
Located 75 km SE of Perigueux

The Chateau de Fleurville is a less expensive alternative for travellers with a longing to stay in a castle. Conveniently located for touring the Burgundy and Rhone wine regions, this 16th- and 18th-century farmstead chateau is found on D17 between Beaune and Macon. Although set in a pleasant garden, the chateau still suffers from some traffic noise as it is separated from the main road only by a stone wall. Ask for a room nearer the pool to be assured of a quieter stay. The fourteen bedooms (two with handicapped access) and one small apartment are comfortable but not luxurious; the color schemes and wallpapers do not always make up an entirely pleasing ensemble. However, all are clean and equipped with private bath or shower. The dining room is decorated in a simple country French style: stone walls surrounding the wooden chairs and tables set with pretty pottery before a large open fireplace. Simple fare is offered at a reasonable price, so wine, dine and enjoy the hospitality of the Naudin family. An after dinner brandy can be enjoyed in the tile-floored salon with its tapestry chairs and couches and old marble fireplace. A good choice for a family, complete with three sweet-tempered collie dogs to romp with on the front lawn, this modest chateau is for those seeking homey rather than elegant accommodation.

CHATEAU DE FLEURVILLE
Owner: Naudin family
71260 Fleurville, France
Tel: 85 33 12 17
15 Rooms - Double FFR 330-(Apt)620
Closed: November 15 to December 26
Credit cards: All major
Park, pool
Region: Rhone Valley
Located 17 km N of Macon

Located just around the corner from the Chateau de Gace, a small chateau dating from the 1200s and 1400s on a green town square, Le Morphee is set behind tall iron gates and a driveway that circles a fountain from an ancient spring. This stately brick manor has two stories and our spacious room was tucked cozily under the eaves. It was extremely attractive with exposed dark wooden beams and was papered in a pink floral print with matching rose bedspreads and curtains. The bathroom was spotless and contained all the modern conveniences as well as thoughtful touches such as a small traveller's sewing kit. Downstairs we found an intimate dining room with a beautifully restored paneled ceiling. Request a window seat if eating breakfast downstairs, as the garden view is pretty. The sitting room across the main hall from the billiard room is jewel-like, with another beautifully restored ceiling, a chandelier, decorative plaster relief work on the walls, a lovely parquet floor and a small piano. The fortunate traveller will be treated to selections played by Madame Lecanu. Lavish praise for Le Morphee in the guest book attests to the main attraction of this hotel, the hospitality of its owners, the Lecanus.

LE MORPHEE
Owner: M & Mme Lecanu
2, Rue de Lisieux
61230 Gace, France
Tel: 33 35 51 01
10 Rooms - Double FFR 250-310
Open: March 1 to January 1
Credit cards: All major
No restaurant
Region: Normandy
Located 46 km NE of Alencon

Gordes is a very picturesque village whose terraced buildings cling to a rocky hillside that is dominated by its church and chateau. Located less than 20 miles east of Avignon and in the heart of Provence, this medieval village is worth a detour for a visit regardless of one's base of exploration. Since 1970 the Vasarely Museum (closed Tuesdays), which focuses on the evolution of painting and cinema art, has been installed inside the walls of the old chateau. The narrow streets stumble through town and shelter a number of interesting art and craft shops. Should you decide to stay in Gordes, La Mayanelle is a moderately priced hotel and enjoys a central location at the heart of this medieval village. Monsieur Mayard extends a warm welcome: he is your host as well as chef for the hotel's lovely restaurant. La Mayanelle's ten bedrooms are small (room number four being the largest), but comfortable and pleasing in their decor. Since the hotel is perched on the side of the village, the bedrooms whose windows open out to the Luberon Valley enjoy some magnificent views. I was here at the time of a festive wedding reception and had the only room not occupied by a wedding guest.

LA MAYANELLE
Owner: M Mayard
84220 Gordes
France
Tel: 90 72 00 28
10 Rooms - Double FFR 186-350
Closed: January and February
Restaurant closed Tuesdays
Credit cards: All major
Region: Provence
Located 38 km E of Avignon

Honfleur is one of the world's most picturesque port towns and I am certain that you will want to spend time here. On the outskirts of town, in a residential district, I have recommended the moderately priced Hotel l'Ecrin and just outside of town, the very expensive and excellent La Ferme St Simeon. Should these hotels be full, or if your budget needs some monitoring, there is an alternate, budget selection, the Hotel du Dauphin. Off St Catherine's Square just near the port, the hotel has a central location, but the port is teeming with activity so a quiet night's sleep is not guaranteed. The rooms of the hotel are very simple and spartan in their decor, but clean and inexpensive. A maze of stairways and confusing double doors ramble through the building and lead to the various rooms. Flowerboxes adorn the timbered facade. The Hotel du Dauphin has an informal bar and cafe, but no restaurant: however, there are numerous cafe-restaurants that specialize in fish bordering the scenic harbor. The Hotel du Dauphin offers basic, clean and inexpensive accommodation at the heart of picturesque Honfleur.

HOTEL DU DAUPHIN
Owner: Philippe Alfandari
10, Place Pierre Berthelot
14600 Honfleur
France
Tel: 31 89 15 53
30 Rooms - Double FFR 262-287
Closed: January
Credit cards: VS
No restaurant
Region: Normandy
Located 63 km E of Caen

Winding through the foothills of the Vosges Mountains, the wine route of Alsace is extremely picturesque. It meanders through delightful towns and is exposed to enchanting vistas of a countryside carpeted with vineyards and dotted by neighboring towns clustered around their church spires. The village of Itterswiller, nestled on the hillside amongst the vineyards, is a wonderful base from which to explore the region and the Hotel Arnold is a charming country hotel. The accommodation and restaurant are in three separate buildings. Although the color wash of the individual buildings varies from white to soft yellow to burnt red, each is handsomely timbered and the windowboxes hang heavy with a profusion of red geraniums. Most of the 28 bedrooms are located in the main building of the Hotel Arnold set just off the road on the edge of the village. The bedrooms are at the back of the hotel and look out over the surrounding vineyards. On the town's principal street, standing next to the hotel's restaurant, the Winestub Arnold, is a selection of lovely rooms in La Reserve. Set under lovely old beams with provincial cloths and decorative flower arrangements adorning the tables, the Winestub Arnold is an appealing place to dine on regional specialties and the estate's wines.

HOTEL ARNOLD
Owner: Gerard Arnold
Route du Vin, Itterswiller
67140 Barr, France
Tel: 88 85 50 58 Telex: 870550
28 Rooms - Double FFR 310-465
Open: All year
Restaurant closed Sundays & Mondays
Credit cards: VS
Region: Alsace
Located 41 km SW of Strasbourg

Kayersberg is one of Alsace's greatest splendors. The village sprawls up the hillside and the Hotel l'Arbre Vert is tucked away along a street in Haut Kayersberg. This delightful country inn whose facade is colored by boxes of overflowing geraniums has been a family business for three generations. The Hotel l'Arbre Vert is a simple, comfortable inn, rustic in its decor and reasonably priced. The atmosphere is friendly and the Kieny and Wittmer families extend a personal welcome. Monsieur Kieny who supervises the kitchen offers a number of interesting Alsatian specialties that are complemented by the regional wines. Even if the cuisine weren't such a gastronomic delight it would be a memorable treat to dine in the charming, country restaurant. The hotel also has a cozy wine cellar where one can sample some of the famous as well as local Alsatian wines. Should the Hotel l'Arbre Vert be full, the Hotel la Belle Promenade (tel: 89 47 11 51), directly across the square, is also attractive, a bit more modern in decor, but benefiting from the same gracious and hospitable management.

HOTEL L'ARBRE VERT
Owner: Kieny & Wittmer families
Rue Haute du Rempart
68240 Kayersberg
France
Tel: 89 47 11 51
23 Rooms - Double FFR 210-290
14 Rooms (Annex - Belle Promenade)
Closed: January 5 to March 5
Credit cards: None accepted
Region: Alsace
Located 11 km NW of Colmar

Levernois is a country village located a five-minute drive on D970 from Beaune. Here the ivy-clad Hotel le Parc offers a countryside alternative for those travellers seeking to guard their pocketbook as well as avoid city noises. Monsieur and Madame Moreau-Tanron own and manage their hotel with pride and care. Actually, Monsieur Moreau-Tanron informed us that he mainly tends to the flower garden and small park, while his wife scrupulously handles all facets of the hotel. The 20 rooms are almost always full with returning clients, who also enjoy congregating before dinner in the convivial bar near the cheerful entry salon. Prettily papered hallways lead to the simple, but charming bedrooms, all but one of which have their own spotlessly clean bath or shower. Antique pieces are strategically placed throughout the hotel, especially in the breakfast room which boasts an old country hutch filled with colorful plates, a large antique mirror and matching wooden tables and chairs which look out through French doors onto the flower-filled courtyard. Reserve early in order to be able to enjoy the warm hospitality of the Moreau-Tanrons in this tranquil setting. Travel 5 kilometers southeast of Beaune on Route de Verdun sur le Doubs D970 and D111.

HOTEL LE PARC
Owner: M & Mme Moreau-Tanron
Levernois, 21200 Beaune, France
Tel: 80 22 22 51
20 Rooms - Double FFR 166-220
Closed: February 28 to March 16 and
November 22 to December 11
Credit cards: None accepted
No restaurant
Region: Burgundy
Located 5 km SE of Beaune

It was late in the day, but we were spurred by a sense of adventure to follow a small inviting sign for the Manoir de Caudemonne. One sign led to another, tempting us deeper and deeper into the pastoral, picture-perfect Normandy countryside. The old timbered farmhouse cluster of the Manoir de Caudemonne suddenly appeared before us, immediately transporting us back to a simpler place in time. As we approached past tumble-down outbuildings we came upon the two guests of the manor, an English couple engaged in a leisurely game of cards on the front lawn. The only audible sound was the occasional squawk of geese or hens. Madame Dudouit greeted us at the front door under an ancient turret and amiably ushered us inside her rustic farm inn. It was easy to imagine a country banquet of long ago in the dining hall furnished with its one long heavy trestle table before a massive stone fireplace with open hearth. Madame led us up the steep and narrow curved staircase to the very simple and basic guestrooms. The two rooms share facilities and in fact adjoin, so two parties would almost be sharing a room. A farm-country breakfast is included in the cost of an overnight stay, so this country homestead is a real bargain. A family-style restaurant with rooms, Le Manoir de Caudemonne is for the traveller who seeks not modern comfort, but rather an evening in an ancient, peaceful, pastoral setting.

LE MANOIR DE CAUDEMONNE
Owner: Edith Dudouit
La Chapelle Haute Grue
14140 Livarot, France
Tel: 31 63 53 74
2 Rooms - Double FFR 170
Open: All year, Restaurant closed Wednesdays
Credit cards: Unknown
Region: Normandy
Located 10 km N of Gace

For 1,500 years the Manoir de Montesquiou was the residence of the Barons de Montesquiou. With the canyon walls at its back the Manoir de Montesquiou faces onto the street in the small town of La Malene at the center of the Tarn Canyon. This is a moderately priced chateau hotel, not luxurious but very traditional in furnishings. The welcome and service are warm and friendly. The Manoir de Montesquiou serves as a delightful and comfortable base from which to explore the spectacular beauty of the Tarn Canyon, "Gorges du Tarn". Here you can enjoy a wonderful meal and then climb the tower to your room. All the bedrooms are with private bath and those that overlook the garden at back are assured a quiet night's rest. Each bedroom is unique in its decor, some with dramatic four-poster beds, and the carvings on the headboard in room six are magnificent. Although the setting and accommodation of the Manoir de Montesquiou are not as spectacular as the Chateau de la Caze, it is a less expensive alternative and well located at the heart of the Tarn Canyon. With the Manoir de Montesquiou as a base, you can venture out by day to boat, fish, hunt, explore and walk.

MANOIR DE MONTESQUIOU
Owner: M Bernard Guillenet
La Malene
48210 Ste Enimie
France
Tel: 66 48 51 12
12 Rooms - Double FFR 258-450
Open: April to October
Credit cards: DC
Region: Tarn
Located 42 km NE of Millau

Timbered houses, windowboxes colored with geraniums, and sloping vineyards are typical of the Alsace region of France. Marlenheim is praised as a typical Alsatian village and the Hostellerie du Cerf represents the typical Alsatian inn. It is in fact an old coaching inn at the start of the Route du Vin d'Alsace. Settle in one of its nineteen pleasantly furnished bedrooms or in one of the three more spacious apartments. Dine indoors in the cozy elegance of the restaurant or in the sheltered courtyard, bordered by a multitude of flowers, under the skies that bless the region's grapes. This reasonably priced hostelry highlights local specialties. Both father and son, Robert and Michel, supervise the kitchen and their recommended "carte de marche", a menu that changes daily based on the freshest produce, meats and fish available, is always enticing. Both the hotel and restaurant are closed on Mondays and Tuesdays, but breakfast, lunch and dinner are served the rest of the week. Family pride and the desire to maintain a tradition of fine Alsatian cuisine inspire Robert and Michel Husser to keep an excellent kitchen. The Hostellerie du Cerf is a charming roadside inn and a perfect base from which to explore the vineyards of Alsace.

HOSTELLERIE DU CERF
Owner: Robert Husser
30, Route du General de Gaulle
67520 Marlenheim, France
Tel: 88 87 73 73
22 Rooms - Double FFR 250-350
*Open: All year **
** but closed on Mondays and Tuesdays*
Credit cards: AX VS
Region: Alsace
Located 20 km W of Strasbourg

The village of Millac is nestled on the river bank near the prettiest and most dramatic bend in the River Dordogne, "la Cingle de Tremolat". On the river's edge, set in the shadow of a small bridge, is the engaging Hotel de la Poste. We were so thrilled to "discover" this true French country inn and are now very proud to recommend it. It is simple, spotlessly clean, unpretentious and has been family-run for generations. Madame Mirabel Courtey takes pride carrying on the standards of service and hospitality established by her family and it shows. Glistening polished copper pieces adorning the walls, unrivalled flower arrangements taking central focus in the salon or dining room, and crisp clean sheets are all indications of her efforts. Very popular with locals, the large, airy dining room is charmingly decorated with country tables and chairs, and red checkered tablecloths - all set under heavy beams. Multicourse menus are offered at amazingly low prices (55F, 65F, 90F, 110F) and boast regional specialties such as "pate maison", "melon au Montbazillac" and "ris de veau sur canape". The bedrooms are very simply decorated, a few have private bath, some have only toilet, but they are clean, comfortable, inexpensively priced and eight enjoy river views.

HOTEL DE LA POSTE
Owner: Mme Mirabel Courtey
Mauzac
24150 Lalinde, France
Tel: 53 22 50 52
18 Rooms - Double FFR 200-280
Open: March to end October
Credit cards: AX VS MC
River setting
Region: Dordogne
Located 63 km S of Perigueux

In the heart of the Burgundy wine region, between the prestigious wine towns of Nuits St Georges and Gevrey Chambertin, this family-run hotel is off a quiet street in the village of Morey St Denis and right next door to a small wine making cooperative. Madame Jarlot and her family take great care to preserve a feeling of the past with their many antique furnishings, paintings and other memorabilia. From the cozy, low-ceilinged bar and reception area, to the television salon with its comfy couches, this is an unpretentious inn known locally for its cuisine. The dining room is a pleasant hodge-podge of many tables, tapestry chairs, antiques, plants and other cherished family knickknacks. The bedrooms are all located either in the main, 18th-century manor house or in the older annex, a former church and monastery dating from the 12th and 13th centuries. All rooms have private bath or shower except one. Do not expect luxury, merely comfort and atmosphere in this family-run country inn. To find the Castel de Tres-Girard, take N74 north through the vineyards from Beaune to Morey St Denis and then follow signs and backstreets in town to this endearing hotel.

AUBERGE LE CASTEL DE TRES-GIRARD
Owner: Herve Jarlot family
Morey St Denis
21220 Gevrey Chambertin
France
Tel: 80 34 33 09
13 Rooms - Double FFR 250-370
Open: All year
Credit cards: All major
Region: Burgundy
Located 16 km S of Dijon

Ideally situated on the tourist route that winds through the chalky plains of the "Haute de Cote de Nuits", just northwest of the center of Nuits St Georges as you travel the Route de Meuilley for one and a half kilometers, La Gentilhommiere is a charming and very reasonably priced hotel. The hotel can be seen set just a short distance off the road, but as it is built in the pale grey stone so typical of the region it blends beautifully with the landscape. The reception, restaurant and bar are found in the former 16th-century hunting lodge. Staged handsomely, the upstairs restaurant is lovely. Tapestries cover the dramatic stone walls and high-back tapestry chairs set round heavy wood tables add character to the decor. The bedrooms are in a newly constructed wing that stretches along a trout stream, behind the former lodge. All the rooms are identical in style and size and vary only as to whether they have a double or twin beds. The furnishings are simple, functional, but pleasant. The rooms, although not spacious, are comfortable and all are equipped with private bath. The Gentilhommiere is a pleasant inn set on the wine route of Burgundy, offering travellers an excellent location, a scenic setting and attractive rates.

LA GENTILHOMMIERE
Owner: Jack Vanroelen
Route de Meuilley O
21700 Nuits St Georges, France
Tel: 80 61 12 06 Telex: 350401
20 Rooms - Double FFR 330-350
Open: All year
Restaurant closed Mondays
Credit cards: AX DC
Region: Burgundy
Located 17 km N of Beaune

PARIS FAMILY HOTEL First Arrondissement Map: IV

This a budget hotel whose location alone could demand a higher price. On the Rue Cambon, just a few blocks off the Rue de Rivoli, the Family Hotel offers very simple accommodation. With the exception of one ground floor apartment, the 25 rooms of the hotel are basic in their decor, not all have private bath, but are clean and adequate. This hotel's greatest attributes are its location, price, clean accommodation and personal management.

FAMILY HOTEL
35, Rue Cambon, 75001 Paris, France
Tel: (1) 42 61 54 84, Open: All year
25 Rooms - Double FFR 300-500, Credit cards: Unknown

PARIS HOTEL DEUX ILES Fourth Arrondissement Map: IV

The quaint and charming Hotel Deux Iles is converted from a 17th-century house. Interior decorator Roland Buffat, responsible for the already popular Hotel de Lutece, has employed cheerful prints, bamboo and reed in the furnishings; made an open fireplace an obvious reason and focal point for a cozy retreat or rendezvous and expanded a central area into a garden of plants and flowers. The result, an unusual and harmonious blend of color, furnishings and an inviting atmosphere. Paris has once again profited from the talents of Roland Buffat.

HOTEL DEUX ILES
Owner: M Buffat, 59 Rue St Louis en L'Ile, 75004 Paris, France
Tel: (1) 43 26 13 35, Open: All year
17 Rooms - Double FFR 475-585, Credit cards: None accepted

PARIS GRAND HOTEL JEANNE D'ARC Fourth Arrondissement Map: IV

This is another hotel chosen as a budget entry. The Grand Hotel Jeanne d'Arc is tucked off a small side street near the Place des Vosges. It is a clean, simple hotel run by a lovely couple and their lounging dog. A pretty salon and breakfast room are found just off the hotel's narrow entry hall. In the public areas the furnishings are decorative, lace curtains soften the windows and plants are an attractive backdrop. The upstairs bedrooms are basic in their decor and comforts, all have private bath or shower.

GRAND HOTEL JEANNE D'ARC
3, Rue Jarente, 75004 Paris, France
Tel: (1) 48 87 62 11, Open: All year
38 Rooms - Double FFR 250-290, Credit cards: Unknown

PARIS HOTEL ST LOUIS Fourth Arrondissement Map: IV

This is a small hotel with atmosphere located on the Ile de St Louis, near antique and pastry shops. The rooms are not large, but they are simple and nicely furnished. A few choice accommodations: rooms 51 and 52 are doubles with bath and 53 is a double with shower. Mme Record describes her hotel "as if in another era ... 50 years behind - no TV, no telephone, no lift!". Guests leave only praises in the register with vows to return. The presence of the Records is a welcome advantage as they are efficient and very caring of their guests. Their hospitality far exceeds any other on the island.

HOTEL SAINT LOUIS
Owner: Andree & Guy Record, 75, Rue St Louis en L'Ile, 75004 Paris, France
Tel: (1) 46 34 04 08, Open: All year
25 Rooms - Double FFR 450-700, Credit cards: None accepted

Facing onto the Place du Pantheon, the Hotel des Grands Hommes is a haven in Paris. Small and quiet, the lobby abounds with fresh flower arrangements, has an interior court garden and inviting leather couches and chairs adorning its marble floors. A delicious "cafe complet" can be savored at small wooden tables paired with tapestry chairs all set under the light stone arches of the house's original cellar. The bedrooms are found up a spiral staircase (or elevator) and are beautiful in their decor of warm colors, fabrics, antiques and exposed beams. The beds are firm and the bathrooms lovely and modern. This is a delightful hotel, a bargain for its price, owned and managed by a very gracious and attentive Madame Brethous. She and her staff are friendly and speak wonderful English, yet they are courteous if you would like to practice your French. No restaurant.

HOTEL DES GRANDS HOMMES
Owner: Mme Brethous, 17, Place du Pantheon, 75005 Paris, France
Tel: (1) 46 34 19 60 Telex: 200185, Open: All year
32 Rooms - Double FFR 500-650, Credit cards: All major

PARIS RESIDENCE DU PANTHEON Fifth Arrondissement Map: IV

This hotel is located next door to the Hotel des Grands Hommes and is also owned and managed by Madame Brethous. Identical in feeling and decor, both 18th-century houses have been attractively converted and the Pantheon's 34 bedrooms all profit from Madame's excellent taste and are furnished in period style. Although there is no restaurant, the vaulted basement cellar is now used as a breakfast room or you can enjoy morning coffee and croissants in the privacy of your own room looking out to the Pantheon.

RESIDENCE DU PANTHEON
Owner, Mme Brethous, 19, Place du Pantheon, 75005 Paris, France
Tel: (1) 43 54 32 95 Telex: 206435, Open: All year
34 Rooms - Double FFR 500-650, Credit cards: All major

PARIS HOTEL DE VARENNE Seventh Arrondissement Map: IV

The Hotel de Varenne is recommended as a budget, left-bank property. A long, narrow courtyard leads to the hotel's entry. The reception is friendly and off the lobby are two comfortable sitting areas. A stairway (no elevator) leads up to the Hotel de Varenne's very simple, but clean rooms. Furnishings are sparse, but colors used in the decor are tasteful - soft colors and delicate prints, no loud colors. The Hotel de Varenne has only 24 rooms, and its attraction is a quiet setting, clean accommodation and inexpensive prices.

HOTEL DE VARENNE
44, Rue de Bourgogne, 75007 Paris, France
Tel: (1) 551 45 55 Open: All year
24 Rooms - Double FFR 350-550, Credit cards: AX VS

Bright, overflowing windowboxes hung heavy with red geraniums caught my eye and tempted me down a small side street just off the Place de Madeleine to the Hotel Lido. My small detour was greatly rewarded. The Hotel Lido is a "gem". Tapestries warm the heavy stone walls and Oriental rugs adorn the tile floors. Copper pieces are set about and wooden antiques dominate the furnishings in the entry lobby, an intimate sitting area and cozy bar. Downstairs breakfast is served under the cellar's stone arches. The hotel was full, but we were able to see what was described as one of the more basic rooms, yet we found it to be extremely charming with a delicate lace bedspread and inviting antique decor.

HOTEL LIDO
Owner: M & Mme Teil, Tel: (1) 42 66 27 37
4, Passage de la Madeleine, 75008 Paris, France, Open: All year
32 Rooms - Double FFR 500-630, Credit cards: AX VS

It is always a pleasure to visit the endearing Auberge du Vieux Puits. Although set on a main road in the town of Pont Audemer, its lovely timbered facade shelters a melange of charming rooms in which to dine and a back wing of rooms that overlook an oasis of "Shakespearean" garden. L'Auberge du Vieux Puits translates to mean the inn of the old well and is a typical Normandy home dating from the 17th century. It was used as a tannery in the 19th century, was converted to an inn in 1921 and has been in the Foltz family for three generations. Madame Foltz is an attractive and gracious hostess and Monsieur Foltz has established himself as a highly acclaimed chef. The restaurant is divided into a multitude of alcoves where tables are set under low, heavy beams, before a large open fireplace and surrounded by copper, paintings and antiques. A large portion of the inn was destroyed in World War II and only eight of the original twenty bedrooms were able to be salvaged. These eight rooms are small, modest, yet extremely charming. Five of the bedrooms have showers. In 1985 another timbered wing was renovated to accommodate six bedrooms, slightly more contemporary in decor, all with private bath. It is a treat to be awakened with a tray of fresh coffee, hot rolls, homemade jams and country fresh butter.

AUBERGE DU VIEUX PUITS
Owner: M & Mme Foltz
6, Rue Notre-Dame du Pre
27500 Pont Audemer, France
Tel: 32 41 01 48
14 Rooms - Double FFR 240-390
Open: Jan 23 to Jun 26 & Jul 7 to Dec 18
Restaurant closed Mondays and Tuesdays
Credit cards: VS
Region: Normandy
Located 52 km SW of Rouen

Chez Melanie, located on a street in the small town of Riec sur Belon, is a simple white, three-story building with three rows of shuttered windows hung with a bounty of colorful flowerboxes. Once an "epicerie" or local grocery store, it was converted to a restaurant in 1920. Over the years a few upstairs rooms were remodeled to accommodate guests and it has remained over the decades a very popular "restaurant with rooms". Considered one of the finest local restaurants of the region, the Chez Melanie offers a beautiful dining room where you can feast on seafood specialties. Waitresses dress in festive, regional costume and their intricate lace hats and aprons add a touch of elegance to the service. The first time I visited the Chez Melanie it was owned and managed by a very gracious Madame Trellu. On a recent visit I felt fortunate to meet a handsome young couple, the Tallecs, who only two weeks earlier had acquired the hotel. I feel confident that this dear inn will only blossom under their care. The restaurant will change little: platters of "les huitres fines Belon" and "le homard Melanie a la creme", to mention just a few of the house specialties, will still appear on the menu. The Tallecs do, however, plan to slowly refurbish the hotel's simple bedrooms. Not all rooms are with private bath, but they are very commodious, clean and offer a comfortable as well as inexpensive night's rest.

CHEZ MELANIE
Owner: M & Mme Tellec
Place de l'Eglise
29124 Riec sur Belon, France
Tel: 98 06 91 05
7 Rooms - Double FFR 210-275
Open: March to October, Restaurant closed Tuesdays
Credit cards: AX DC
Region: Brittany
Located 13 km SW of Quimperle

Monsieur Kubons has recently retired from Paris and restyled his country home in a tiny half-timbered hamlet into a charming country inn. Across the country lane from the old cemetery and church, the Auberge du Prieure is a former rectory. Its thatched roof, half-timbers, windows hung heavy with geraniums, odd angles and interesting sections dating from the 13th century lend much character to this peaceful inn. The low-ceilinged dining hall offers a wide variety of Madame Kubons's gourmet specialties. The centuries-old aroma of a log-burning fire mingles with the mouth-watering scents from the kitchen. One sits in the restaurant, which is very rustic in decor, on pew benches and tapestry chairs at long trestle tables placed in the firelight. In the morning, one is tempted to join the flock of ducks and geese in the lush back garden that faces the rose-covered stone wall of the auberge. Monsieur Kubons proudly showed us all of his seven bedrooms including one commodious duplex. The accommodations all have spotless and modern bathroom facilities (no easy task in a building of its age), large comfortable beds and dark beamed ceilings and are accented by handsome antique furnishings. Colors are muted earth tones and there is a very masculine touch to the decor. We felt very fortunate to have happened on the Auberge du Prieure and only wish our schedule had permitted us to stay longer.

AUBERGE DU PRIEURE
Owner: M & Mme Kubons
St Andre d'Hebertot
14130 Pont l'Eveque, France
Tel: 31 64 03 03
7 Rooms - Double FFR 325-480
Open: All year
Credit cards: None accepted
Region: Normandy
Located 11 km SE of Deauville

Beyond the ruins of a medieval arched gateway, the Hotel de la Pelissaria, nestled at the foot of St Cirq Lapopie, is an engaging inn whose character is enhanced by its artistic owners, the Matuchets. With only six rooms, it is a fortunate few who can enjoy a stay here. Fresh and simple in its decor, the inn's whitewashed walls contrast handsomely with dark wooden beams and sienna tile floors - strikingly reminiscent of the Mediterranean. Thick stone walls and shuttered windows frame the idyllic scene of St Cirq Lapopie perched high above a wide band of the meandering Lot River. The restaurant is limited in seating, so it is wise to make reservations well in advance in order to savor Marie-Francoise's delicious and fresh regional cuisine - one can select from a reasonably priced menu or order a la carte. It is incredible how efficient and creative Marie-Francoise can be in the confines of her small kitchen. Francois's talents are in the field of music. A piano and string instruments decorate the intimate, candlelit restaurant, and his own recordings stage a romantic mood. St Cirq Lapopie is truly one of France's most picturesque villages. With only 44 year-round residents, this hamlet of steep, narrow, winding cobbled streets, sun-warmed tile roofs, mixture of timber and stone facades, and garden niches is a postcard-perfect scene. It is wonderful to find an inn which so perfectly complements the beauty of this village.

HOTEL DE LA PELISSARIA
Owner: Francois & Marie-Francoise Matuchet
St Cirq Lapopie
46330 Cabrerets, France
Tel: 65 31 25 14
6 Rooms - Double FFR 340-360
Open: Apr to Nov, Restaurant closed Mon
Credit cards: DC VS MC
Region: Lot
Located 33 km E of Cahors

The Auberge du Sombral is a small country inn facing onto the main square of the picturesque village of St Cirq Lapopie. In such a small, remote village it was amazing to learn that editors of *Gourmet* and *Le Figaro* had already discovered the auberge and praised it for its restaurant. It is owned by the Hardevelds, with Monique a charming hostess and Giles the acclaimed chef. Cafe tables are set on the front porch and provide an inviting spot to linger and enjoy a cool drink after an afternoon of exploring the narrow and steep cobbled streets of the village. Inside, the restaurant is furnished with a melange of country tables and chairs set on a warm tile floor, watercolors that paint country scenes and a glorious, enormous, central arrangement of flowers. Offered are a number of well priced menus or a tempting a la carte selection. Specialties feature regional gastronomic delights such as "terrine de foie de canard frais" and "omellette aux truffes". The wine list highlights excellent regional wines. The inn's ten bedrooms are found at the top of a wooden stairway. All are with bath or shower and they are clean, basic and many look out over the rooftops of St Cirq Lapopie. During high season (May through September) the Hardevelds offer rooms on a demi-pension basis only. The Auberge du Sombral is a little inn with a stone facade and simple accommodations offering both moderately priced rooms and superb country French cuisine.

AUBERGE DU SOMBRAL
Owner: M & Mme Gilles Hardeveld
St Cirq Lapopie
46330 Cabrerets, France
Tel: 65 31 26 08
10 Rooms - Double FFR 240-310
Open: March 15 to November 11
Credit cards: VS
Region: Lot
Located 33 km E of Cahors

The wine town of St Emilion was introduced to us in all its splendor. It was a day that the town was dressed with banners, filled with music and laughter and visited by all the dignitaries of the region. It was a warm day in late September, a day to commence the "vendage" - the beginning of the wine harvest. The day was captivating and we fell in love with the town. Crowning a hillside with vistas that stretch out to the surrounding vineyards, St Emilion is a medieval village of tradition, long considered the capital of the Bordeaux wine region. The Hotel Plaisance opens on to the square, in the shade of the church, and its walls have echoed over the centuries the first church bells commemorating the start of the wine harvest. To stay here one could not be more central to the activity and town's events. The hotel has only twelve rooms, most of which were understandably occupied at the time of our visit. All are individual in decor and from their windows views extend out over vineyards and the maze of tile rooftops. The dining room is lovely and extremely popular, with tables set against windows whose views appear to plunge over the valley. Service is gracious and accommodating. La Plaisance is the place to stay in town and St Emilion is the most charming town of the Bordeaux wine region.

HOTEL LA PLAISANCE
Owner: Louis & Samira Quilain
Place du Clocher
33330 St Emilion, France
Tel: 57 24 72 32
12 Rooms - Double FFR 260-620
Open: All year
Credit cards: AX VS
Region: Dordogne
Located 39 km E of Bordeaux

This authentic, 18th-century mill has been lovingly converted into a true French country inn. Family-run and far from the closest town, Moulin d'Hauterive is located in a peaceful country setting, soothed by the sound of an adjacent rushing stream and surrounded by miles of unspoilt French countryside. The bedrooms of the mill are not overly large, but all have private bath, television and mini-bar, are furnished individually in soft colors and profit from the feminine touch of Madame Moille. The restaurant consists of two charming stone, low-ceilinged rooms, where intimate tables are dressed with pretty china and silver and silver plate covers are proudly displayed. Dining here, one is as likely to meet out-of-towners and international guests as well as locals, since the kitchen is known for its refined cuisine in this pastoral setting. To find this uncut jewel in the countryside of Burgundy, travel south from Beaune on D970 towards Verdun sur les Doubs until the turnoff to St Gervais en Valliere on D183. Look for signs as you continue deeper into the countryside and you'll see the ivy-covered inn on your left.

MOULIN D'HAUTERIVE
Owner: M & Mme Moille
71350 St Gervais en Valliere
France
Tel: 85 91 55 56 Telex: 801395
19 Rooms - Double FFR 260-360
3 Apts at FFR 550
Closed: December 1 to January 2
Credit cards: All major
Pool, tennis, sauna
Region: Burgundy
Located 20 km SE of Beaune

Le Hameau is an old farm complex set on the hillside just outside the walled city of St Paul de Vence. The whitewashed buildings, tiled roofs aged by years of sun, shuttered windows, arched entryways, heavy doors and exposed beams all create a rustic and attractive setting. The bedrooms of this inn are found in four buildings clustered together amidst fruit trees and flower gardens. Each building has its own character and name: L'Oranger, L'Olivier, Le Pigeonnier and La Treille. Three of the largest bedrooms have a small room for an infant and the attraction of their own balcony (rooms one and three with twin beds and two with a double bed). Of the rooms, eleven, with antique twin beds and a lovely view onto the garden, was my favorite. I was very impressed with the quality of this provincial inn. Monsieur Xavier Huvelin is a charming host and is graciously attentive to the needs of his guests. Le Hameau does not have a restaurant but a delicious country breakfast can be enjoyed in the garden or in the privacy of your room. I highly recommend Le Hameau as a wonderful inn and a great value.

LE HAMEAU
Owner: M & Mme X. Huvelin
528, Route de la Colle
06570 St Paul de Vence, France
Tel: 93 32 80 24
16 Rooms - Double FFR 260-390
Apt FFR 440-480
Credit cards: AX VS
Open: February to November 15
No restaurant, terraces, gardens
Region: Riviera
Located 20 km NW of Nice

The true French meaning behind their saying "chez soi" can be defined and experienced at the Hostellerie du Levezou. This is a simple hotel housed within the walls of a 14th-century chateau and lovingly run and managed by the entire Bouviala family: parents, sons, daughters and the dog. The Bouvialas do not boast a hotel of luxurious comfort, but rather a place where one can enjoy good food and comfortable accommodations at a reasonable price. Monsieur Bouviala's pride is his restaurant. Inviting in its decor the dining room is lovely and, when the weather permits, outdoor seating is set on a terrace that extends out in front of it. The focal point of the restaurant is a large fireplace where Monsieur Bouviala grills his delicious specialties. The 30 bedrooms of the Hostellerie du Levezou are basic, cheerful in their decor, a few with private bath or shower and all extremely reasonable in price. At the heart of the ancient fortified village of Salles Curan, with a beautiful view over Pareloup Lake and the countryside, the Hostellerie du Levezou, once the medieval summer residence of the Bishops of Rodez, offers a friendly welcome and good-value lodging.

HOSTELLERIE DU LEVEZOU
Owner: M Bouviala
12410 Salles Curan, France
Tel: 65 46 34 16
30 Rooms - Double FFR 150-300
Open: April 1 to October 15
Restaurant closed Sunday evenings & Mondays
Credit cards: All major
14th-century chateau
Region: Tarn
Located 37 km NW of Millau

Nestled in the area bordering Spain, the Hotel Arraya has captured the tradition and rustic flavor of this Basque region. Long ago the hotel was founded to provide lodgings for pilgrims on the road to Santiago de Compostela. Today it accommodates guests who have fallen in love with this dear inn and return time and again. The Hotel Arraya is decorated with an abundance of 17th-century Basque antiques and is a comfortable and hospitable country manor. The entry, lobby and breakfast nook are charming. Cozy blue and white gingham cushions pad the wooden chairs that are set round a lovely collection of antique tables. The restaurant offers regional Basque specialties and you must stay long enough to sample them all: "foie de canard frais poele aux poires", pigeon with salami sauce, country hams, goat cheese made by the mountain shepherds and "pastiza", a delicious Basque almond cake filled with cream or black cherry preserve. The bedrooms are all individual in decor and size but are attractive with their white-washed walls, exposed beams and pretty fabrics. The hotel is managed by Paul Fagoaga who welcomes his guests as friends in the traditional way, round the "zizailua", or bench near the fire.

HOTEL ARRAYA
Owner: M Paul Fagoaga
Sare, 64310 Ascain
France
Tel: 59 54 20 46
21 Rooms - Double FFR 250-420
Open: May 11 to November 2
Credit cards: AX VS MC
Region: Basque
Located 24 km SE of Biarritz

This has proven to be a popular spot for our readers to stay in while exploring the Champagne district. The Bernard family who lovingly manage the Hotel du Cheval Blanc consider it principally a "restaurant with rooms". With fresh flowers, linen, china and silver dressing the tables, the restaurant is very attractive. The menu features regional specialties and the wine list is impressive in its selection and presentation of French wines. On a warm day, one can enjoy a before- or after-dinner drink in a garden setting at tables in front of the restaurant. The bedrooms of the Cheval Blanc are actually located in a separate building across the road. The location proves to be an advantage, as one is removed from the late-night chatter of the restaurant guests. There are 21 rooms, only a few of which are original to the inn: the newer rooms are found in a modern, though very tasteful, extension - one hardly notices the transition from the old to the new wing. All the bedrooms are decorated with pretty print wallpapers, matching bedspreads and antique reproduction furniture. The nicest feature of the hotel is that the rooms are surrounded by an expanse of garden. Guests spend many a leisurely afternoon lounging in the grounds or playing tennis on the hotel's clay court. The Cheval Blanc is not a luxurious hotel, but is comfortable, the restaurant has an excellent reputation and the setting is rural and tranquil.

HOTEL DU CHEVAL BLANC
Owner: Robert Bernard
51400 Sept Saulx, France
Tel: 26 03 90 27 Telex: 830885
21 Rooms - Double FFR 270-486
Closed: mid-January to mid-February
Credit cards: All major
Park, tennis
Region: Champagne
Located 20 km SE of Reims

On a recent trip to France I discovered the Hotel des Rohan just around the corner from Strasbourg's stunning cathedral. On a pedestrian street, this charming hotel has a lovely foyer and a salon where breakfast is served. The 36 beautiful rooms have either private bath or shower, direct dial phone, radio, television and mini-bar. The hotel is decorated in 17th- and 18th-century style. Tapestries adorn the walls, and in the bedrooms the style is either Louis XV or rustic. The location is quiet, ideal for exploring Strasbourg on foot. The narrow streets are a maze that winds in the shadow of leaning, timbered buildings and in the shade of the lacy trees that grow beside the river. The shops are delightful with their beautiful displays of Alsatian specialties such as wines, foie-gras, sausages and costumes. The Hotel des Rohan is without a restaurant and so one is free to investigate the numerous sidewalk cafes and cozy restaurants that Strasbourg is famous for. Being at the heart of the city's old quarter is also the hotel's one drawback - one must park elsewhere. Nearby parking areas convenient to the hotel are at the Place du Chateau, the Place Gutenberg (underground) and the Rue du Viel Hopital (except on Wednesdays and Saturdays when there is a flea market).

HOTEL DES ROHAN
17-19, Rue du Morquin
67000 Strasbourg, France
Tel: 88 32 85 11 Telex: 870047
36 Rooms - Double FFR 480-540
Open: All year
Credit cards: VS
No restaurant, city hotel
Region: Alsace
Located at the center of town

A picturesque farm converted to hotel and restaurant, La Verte Campagne can offer you a delicious meal in a room with a cozy fireplace and comfortable accommodation. The dining room is intimate and charming. Under heavy beams, worn copper and decorative plates adorn the exposed stone walls of this 18th-century Normandy farmhouse. Tables huddle around the warmth of the room's large open fire. In centuries past the fireplace served as the stove and it was here that large kettles of food were cooked. La Verte Campagne has only eight bedrooms, most of them quite small, but then so is the price. Room seven with twin beds and bath, and six with a double bed and bath, are the largest bedrooms. Room one, on the other end of the scale, is the smallest; tiny in fact. It has a delicate pink print wallpaper and just enough room to sleep. Room three, one of the medium-sized rooms, is the one I liked most. It has one bed and is decorated with bright red and white checks. The hotel is a bit difficult to find, which is also the nature of its charm: travel southeast of Trelly, one and a half kilometers on D539.

LA VERTE CAMPAGNE
Owner: Mme Meredith
Hameau Chevalier, Trelly
50660 Quettreville, France
Tel: 33 47 65 33
8 Rooms - Double FFR 170-300
Closed: January 10 to end February
*Restaurant closed Sunday Dinner **
** in low season*
Credit cards: AX VS
Charming restaurant, small farmhouse
Region: Normandy
Located 12 km S of Coutances

Vence is a quaint little town of narrow streets, intriguing passageways and tempting craft and specialty shops. Located in the hills above the resort towns of the Riviera, Vence enjoys a quieter setting and medieval ambiance. It is a perfect base from which to explore neighboring hilltop villages such as the fortified St Paul de Vence and its Maeght Foundation, the perfume center of Grasse, and the charming Biot which has recently earned a reputation for fine glassware. Look for the largest tree in Vence and there you will find L'Auberge des Seigneurs. This is a delightful inn, located on a quiet side street at the center of Vence. The inn is charming in its decor and country ambiance: heavy old beams are exposed in the ceilings and walls are whitewashed. Copper plates, pans and bedwarmers adorn the walls, while provincial prints cover the tables and lovely antique pieces are used handsomely. Wooden doors, rich in their patina, a large stone fireplace and striking flower arrangements complete a scene in the restaurant and salon that is intimate and cozy. Up a creaking stairway are ten delightful, small rooms. Inexpensive in price, the bedrooms are a true bargain - comfortable and simply decorated with pretty country prints.

L'AUBERGE DES SEIGNEURS ET DU LION D'OR
Owner: M Rodi
Place Frene
06140 Vence
France
Tel: 93 58 04 24
10 Rooms - Double FFR 254-274
Closed: mid-October to end November
Restaurant closed Tuesdays
Region: Riviera
Located 22 km NW of Nice

The Dordogne, a favorite region of France, has an abundance of small country inns. It is difficult to isolate a favorite hotel as each has an individual style, charm and appeal. Since each deserves special attention, the only "sensible" solution is to make repeated visits to the Dordogne in the hopes of savoring them all. As a result I have one more "gem" - the Manoir de Rochecourbe. It is with special pleasure that I include and recommend it, as the wife of the owner, Madame Roger, is also the sister of Madame Bonnet of the delightful Hotel Bonnet in Beynac. The Manoir de Rochecourbe, a dainty chateau with its one single turret, belonged to Madame Roger's grandmother and most of the furnishings are original or from Monsieur Roger's family. Surrounded by its own lacy garden, it seems appropriate that each of the seven rooms is named after a flower. Climb the turret to your chamber. Only the smallest room does not have an en-suite bathroom. Although the hotel does not have a restaurant, simple meals are sometimes prepared by request and served in the small, intimate dining room. This is indeed a lovely hotel and the welcome is delightfully consistent and characteristic of this gracious family.

MANOIR DE ROCHECOURBE
Owner: M & Mme Roger
Vezac, 24220 St Cyprien, France
Tel: 53 29 50 79
7 Rooms - Double FFR 265-434
Open: April 18 to November 1
Credit cards: VS
No restaurant
Region: Dordogne
Located 64 km SE of Perigueux

Considered to be one of France's most picturesque villages, Vezelay is a "must" today just as it was in the Middle Ages when it was considered an important pilgrimage stop. Perched on the hillside overlooking the romantic valley of the Cousin, Vezelay is a wonderful place to spend the afternoon, enjoy a countryside picnic, or, if afforded the luxury of time, to linger and spend the evening. A popular choice for a hotel is the Poste et Lion d'Or, a hillside inn that sits just outside the village gates and walls. Poste et Lion d'Or is believed to have existed as a post house in the Middle Ages, accommodating those who awaited the opening of the village drawbridge. Throughout the hotel there are remembrances from times more recent than the days of knights in armor. The bedrooms in the main building are lovely and decorated with handsome antiques. The furniture has been collected piece by piece since the current owner's grandmother purchased the inn almost 60 years ago. An ivy-clad annex is surrounded by a sprawling English garden. Here the rooms are quiet but the decor is modern. Like the hotel, the restaurant has an intriguing blend of old and modern decor. The Danguy family are on the premises to welcome you and expertly manage this comfortable hillside inn.

HOTEL POSTE ET LION D'OR
Owner: Danguy family
Place du Champ de Foire
89450 Vezelay
France
Tel: 86 33 21 23 Telex: 800949
45 Rooms - Double FFR 270-564
Open: April 18 to November 3
Credit cards: AX VS
Region: Burgundy
Located 15 km W of Avallon

I was pleased to discover that the potential of this little inn has been realized under the direction of Monsieur Garnier. In the 16th century the walls of L'Atelier sheltered fabric workshops. The front room has been converted into a lovely sitting room with a tapestry chairs set on an Oriental rug before a large fireplace. A central stairway that led to the individual workshops in what was once an outdoor courtyard - exterior balconies remain as evidence on each of the floors - now climbs to the hotel's nineteen bedrooms. No two rooms are alike, but each is with private bath, charming and very reasonably priced. Old wooden ceiling beams have been re-exposed, walls are papered or freshly painted to contrast with supporting timbers, antiques contribute handsomely to the furnishings and a few rooms have a fireplace. One room is unique in that its top floor location and skylight window affords a view out over rooftops, across the river to the City of the Popes in Avignon. Sheltered in back is a delightful, quiet courtyard where one can enjoy a breakfast of croissants and "cafe au lait" and also two additional rooms of the hotel, each with a private terrace. If you have an afternoon at leisure, climb the old, exterior stone stairway off the courtyard to a peaceful terrace that overlooks the walls of the fort and village rooftops - a perfect spot to hide away with a book.

L'ATELIER
Owner: M Garnier
5, Rue de la Foire
30400 Villeneuve les Avignon, France
Tel: 90 25 01 84
19 Rooms - Double FFR 230-340
Closed: January
Credit cards: All major
No restaurant
Region: Provence
Located 3 km N of Avignon

Germany

Assmannshausen is a lovely little village on the Rhine, relatively unspoilt by any overabundance of postcard or tourist shops, as is the unfortunate case in nearby Rudesheim. Its scenic main street along the river offers several hotels, but the best bargain for the location is the Hotel Anker. Wisteria winds around the arched windows on the ground floor of this cheerful yellow hotel. Built in 1666 by Johann Jung, the Hotel Anker is still owned and managed with much pride by the Jung family. Guests are warmly welcomed into this charming hotel by Herr Jung who speaks good English, as well as French and Italian. The Anker's restaurant has two inviting dining rooms with dark beamed ceilings, rose tablecloths and a collection of old prints, paintings and pewter. The splendid view of the Rhine is seen from all tables through the large windows framed by pretty forest green and rose print drapes. The menu here offers an imaginative variety of dishes complemented by the special wines produced in the area. The 50 bedrooms all have clean private baths and are tastefully furnished with contemporary furnishings, flowered wallpaper and pictures on the walls. A few antique pieces adorn the halls and a beautiful old stained glass window is found on the stairwell. This comfortable hotel is recommended for its charm, value, and solicitous host.

HOTEL ANKER
Owner: Family Jung
Rheinuferstrasse 5
6224 Assmannshausen am Rhein, Germany
Tel: (06722) 2912
50 Rooms - Double DM 98-128
Closed: mid-November to February
Credit cards: MC VS
Elevator
Located 60 km W of Frankfurt

Set a country road's distance from the city of Bayreuth is a lovely castle hotel where one is treated more as "royalty" than simply as "Gast im Schloss". Intimate in its size, the Jagdschloss Thiergarten is an old hunting castle that has converted nine rooms to accommodate overnight guests. You can retire to a bedchamber and then choose from one of two lovely dining rooms. The Kamin Restaurant is small with just a few elegantly set tables warmed by a dramatic fireplace, and hence its name: "Kamin" translates as fireplace. The Venezianischer Salon's focus is on a very intricate Venetian glass chandelier that dates back approximately 300 years. The Barocksaal, used for banquets or weddings, is found in the imposing rotunda, open to a detailed ceiling and second floor balcony. When the hotel was a hunting lodge, guests actually shot from the vantage point of the balcony. In warm weather tables are set out on a stretch of grass behind the castle, under the blossoms of cherry and apple trees. The bedrooms are furnished appropriately for an old fortress, handsome in furnishings but a bit worn. Open as a hotel for approximately 40 years, the Schloss Hotel Thiergarten provides a lovely retreat from the neighboring city of Bayreuth.

SCHLOSS HOTEL THIERGARTEN
Owner: Kaiser Harald
8580 Bayreuth, Germany
Tel: (09209) 1314
9 Rooms - Double DM 126
Open: All year
Credit cards: All major
Located 230 km N of Munich

This is certainly an old family business: Mrs Lipmann, her son Goachim and her daughter Marion are the sixth and seventh generations of the family to run this inn and tend the family vineyards that rise steeply above the banks of the Moselle river. This small hotel is especially appealing because it is located at the heart of the prettiest village along the Moselle. With its picturesque medieval buildings, church and ruined castle, Beilstein is a gem. The dining rooms are just as quaint as the exterior: you may find yourself in a small farmhouse-style room before an old fireplace, in the warm paneled main dining room or feasting in the knights' hall surrounded by collections of old weapons. When weather permits, you can move out of doors to the terrace and watch the life on the gentle Moselle river glide by as you dine, then wind your way up through the narrow cobbled streets to enjoy the view from the church before returning to the square for a glass of wine in the 400-year-old wine cellar. None of the guestrooms offer much charm, but the rooms in the old inn have more appeal than those in the modern annex set amongst the vineyard. The two "choice" rooms have balconies and river views. Additional very simple rooms are found in a house next to the river road. The town's wine festival takes place during the first weekend in September.

HOTEL HAUS LIPMANN
Owner: Family Lipmann
5591 Beilstein, Germany
Tel: (02673) 1573
25 Rooms - Double DM 55-79
Open: April to October
Along the Moselle River
Located 150 km NW of Frankfurt

The atmospheric Hotel Watzmann is centrally located in Berchtesgaden across from the Franziskaner Kirche on the main road through town. It was originally built as a beer brewery in the 1600s and is now a family-run hotel filled with antiques, memorabilia and charm. The yellow facade with its green shutters and bright red geraniums is set back from the road behind a large terrace filled with tables, umbrellas, and, on a warm day, many patrons. The public areas and two dining rooms contain plenty of old prints, painted antique furniture and hunting trophies, as well as beamed ceilings and old ceramic stoves. Menu selections are traditionally Bavarian, featuring delicious pork and game dishes. The hotel has 38 bedrooms, only 17 of which have private baths, and none of which are equipped with phones or televisions. Bedrooms are comfortable, clean, and well appointed with reproduction Bavarian style furniture, and large family suites are also available. The upstairs hallways are decorated by door panels painted with Bavarian floral designs and a collection of colorful old archery targets. Antique chests, armoires, and paintings are also displayed in abundance. This is a very warm Bavarian inn, owned and managed with personal care by the English speaking Piscantor family.

HOTEL WATZMANN
Owner: Family Hinrich Piscantor
Franziskanerplatz
8240 Berchtesgaden, Germany
Tel: (08652) 2055
38 Rooms - Double DM 63-96
Closed: October 15 to December 23
Credit cards: None accepted
Restaurant, parking
Located 120 km SE of Munich, near the Austrian border

Elly Lange owns and manages the Pension Dittberner and lovingly tends to the needs of her guests. The atmosphere is homey and her guests consider this their home in Berlin. Located on a quiet side street just off the surging Kurfurstendamm, you enter into a dimly lit lobby and climb long flights of stairs to the third floor. Thankfully this need only be done once as Elly will give you a key to the charming old-fashioned elevator and explain its mysterious workings to you. An elaborate chandelier graces the lobby-lounge where guests gather to discuss and plan their sightseeing. Discussions continue in the adjacent breakfast room whose large Oriental rug and chandelier add an elegant touch. The walls and hallways display Elly's eclectic art collection, from Javan puppets to French posters and a modern sculpture or two for good measure. The bedrooms are freshly painted in bright shades: the furnishings plain with white linens and plump eiderdowns on the beds. Twelve rooms have showers with toilets across the hall, while the four choice rooms have private bathrooms. This bed and breakfast inn far outshines the other small hotels that I visited in Berlin.

PENSION DITTBERNER
Owner: Mrs Elly Lange
Wielandstrasse 26
1000 Berlin, Germany
Tel: (88164) 85
20 Rooms - Double DM 84-115
Open: All year
Charming pension
Located in the city center

Bernkastel is the most charming of the larger towns along the Moselle. Fronting the river are large turn-of-the-century hotels, but venture behind them and you find winding, cobblestoned streets lined by 400-year-old half-timbered houses. In amongst these side streets is found the Doctor Weinstuben. Named after the local tax collector, Doctor Wein, who lived here in the 17th century, the house went on to become a wine room and in 1974 became a hotel when a modern block of rooms was built across the courtyard. While an effort was made to put an olde worlde exterior on the annex, the accommodations are modern, functional hotel rooms. Their decor is clean and bright but far from memorable. Each room has a private bathroom. By sharp contrast, the hotel has put a great deal of effort into making the restaurant in the old wine room reflect the atmosphere of this pretty little wine town. A large hay wagon stands as a decorative centerpiece and around it the lofty room has been divided into intimate dining nooks with beams and dark wood.

HOTEL DOCTOR WEINSTUBEN
Hebegasse 5
5550 Bernkastel, Germany
Tel: (06531) 6081
15 Rooms - Double DM 85-125
Open: January to October
Credit cards: All major
Lovely River Moselle town
Located 75 km SW of Koblenz

The Hotel Zur Post is lovingly and professionally looked after by owners Frau and Herr Rossling. True hoteliers, the Rosslings do a superb job and are always striving to improve their charming hotel. Located slightly away from the center of town and right on the banks of the Moselle, the Zur Post has a mustard colored facade which is complemented by dark green shutters and windowboxes of red geraniums. In the oldest part of the Zur Post, dating from 1827, guests climb a narrow old stairway to rooms which do not all have private baths, but are spotlessly clean. A new annex has recently been added to the hotel, but so skillfully done that from the exterior the entire ensemble looks original. The newer rooms combine modern appointments with tasteful decorating, adding up to a level of comfort that is truly a treat. The Zur Post's excellent kitchen serves a generous breakfast buffet as well as savory lunch and dinner specialties. Guests may choose to dine in any one of the three warm dining rooms. The informal restaurant has walls and ceilings entirely of carved pine complemented by dried flower arrangements and bright tablecloths. Usually full of fun-loving guests, the restaurant is also a cozy spot for an afternoon sampling of the crisp, white regional wines. The other two dining rooms offer a slightly more refined atmosphere with tableside service and attentive waiters.

HOTEL ZUR POST
Owner: Family Rossling
5550 Bernkastel, Germany
Tel: (06531) 2022
39 Rooms - Double DM 65-130
Open: All year
Credit cards: All major
Lovely River Moselle town
Located 75 km SW of Koblenz

The little town of Braubach lies on the Rhine almost opposite Koblenz. In amongst a mixture of modern and old houses you find the Zum Weissen Schwanen leaning against the old city wall where the large tower extends into the street. Step behind the half-timbered facade and you enter a gem of a country rustic tavern: warm pine paneling, bottle-glass dimpled windows hung with hand-crocheted curtains, and simple pine tables and carved chairs. Your genial hosts, Erich and Gerhilde Kunz, will probably be there to welcome you. Although they speak but a few words of English, their warm smiles and exuberant gestures overcome any language barrier. A few bedrooms are found in the converted stables behind the tavern. While these are charming, the inn's choice rooms lie in a nearby watermill where a huge wooden waterwheel slowly turns at the building's center. Around the waterwheel passages and staircases lead to the bedchambers. The bedrooms are a country delight - rustic handicrafts surround old pine beds topped with plump gingham pillows and comforters. The Kunz family has a restaurant at the heart of the mill. The hotel gives you a wonderful feel of days gone by. There is nothing pretentious about the Zum Weissen Schwanen: it is just an old-fashioned inn in a picturesque, but non-touristy, town run with great pride by very nice people.

HOTEL ZUM WEISSEN SCHWANEN
Owner: Erich Kunz
Brunnenstr 4
5423 Braubach, Germany
Tel: (02627) 559
14 Rooms - Double DM 75-95
Open: All year
Lovely old watermill
Located 130 km NW of Frankfurt

The Alte Rheinmuhle is in a little niche of Germany, practically surrounded by Switzerland, only 2 1/2 miles east of Schaffhausen. The distance between the countries is so short and the town so Swiss that customs are friendly and casual although you do need your passport to cross the border. The Alte Rheinmuhle is truly a wonderful transformation of an old mill to functioning inn and accomplished with delightful taste. The building dates from 1674 and sits right on the edge of the Rhine. On the first floor is a beautiful dining room whose large windows overlook the river. The hotel has earned an outstanding reputation for its cuisine and extensive wine cellar. Some of the restaurant's specialties include superb venison and wild rabbit, and the highlight for dessert is the most scrumptious cassis sherbet to be found anywhere. I discussed the rooms with the management and was told that all rooms are decorated in a country style and furnished with antiques - some even have four-poster beds. Our room, number fourteen, with twin beds, is set under old heavy beams. However, other rooms seen in passing were more modern in decor and style. Do request a room facing the river - it would be a shame not to take advantage of the mill's serene setting. While the rooms are relatively inexpensive in price the restaurant is expensive.

ALTE RHEINMUHLE
Owner: Othmar Ernst
Junkerstrasse 93
7701 Busingen, Germany
Tel: (07734) 6076 Telex: 793788
16 Rooms - Double DM 95
Open: All year
Credit cards: AX DC
Old mill on the Rhine
Located on the Swiss border

Dinkelsbuhl is a medieval walled town, just as picturesque as, but less crowded than, its more famous neighbor, Rothenburg ob der Tauber. Found on a quiet side street, the Gasthof Zum Goldenen Anker offers outstanding hospitality and dining. Frau and Herr Scharff are the generous hosts who have owned the Gasthof for 20 years. Their son, a well-known chef, has created the gourmet menu served in the three intimate dining rooms. Fine food and wine are served in rustically elegant surroundings of carved pine, lace tablecloths and fresh flowers. Romantic alcoves are perfect for a special occasion, or simply a meal with friends. The low, beamed ceilings are from the original house which was built in 1687. We can attest to the quality and selection of wines, as we were lucky enough to be escorted on a tour of the Goldenen Anker's well-stocked wine cellar, followed by, of course, a winetasting. A restaurant with rooms more than a hotel, the Gasthof Zum Goldenen Anker offers 15 very comfortable guest bedrooms. They are recently refurbished and very fresh, featuring contemporary pine furniture, pretty coverlets and lace curtains. All have a private bath, phone and television with cable channels in English, French and German. Some antique pieces and old paintings add character to the narrow hallways and stairwells.

GASTHOF ZUM GOLDENEN ANKER
Owner: Elfriede Scharff
8804 Dinkelsbuhl, Germany
Tel: (09851) 822
15 Rooms - Double DM 80-85
Open: All year
Credit cards: All major
Walled town on the Romantic Road
Located 120 km NE of Stuttgart

There is something very endearing about the simplicity of the Schloss Fursteneck. One would never just happen upon this hotel. It is set in the Bavarian Hills in a village that is mostly comprised of a castle and a church. By no means luxurious, this hotel, however, sparkles under the management of Erika Vilhelm. She bustles about with a warm smile and pride that keep the twelve rooms under her care spotless. Erika sees that the menu highlights the regional specialties and that her garden and windowboxes are full of blooms and color. Under arched ceilings, the restaurant is very cozy; tables are decked with either blue or red checked cloths. There are actually three adjoining dining rooms to choose from: the Gaststube, the Jagerzimmer (a round room with a hunting motif that overlooks a steep drop to the River Ohr), and the Kaminzimmer (named for the fireplace that warms it). The hotel has only two rooms with full bath and private toilet. Again, I stress the rooms are simple but sweet with matching prints used for the comforter covers and the curtains. In this region one can hike between hotels. Set out with only a luncheon pack and have your bags delivered to your next hotel. Contact Erika for specific details and arrangements.

SCHLOSS FURSTENECK
Owner: Adrian Forster
Manager: Erika Vilhelm
8397 Fursteneck, Germany
Tel: (08505) 1473
12 Rooms - DM 25 per person per night
Open: All year
Credit cards: All major
Located 195 km NE of Munich

Located in the historic section of Partenkirchen, the Gasthof Fraundorfer has been in the Fraundorfer family for 80 years and is still very much a homey, family-run inn. Its facade is decorated with murals and windowboxes of healthy red geraniums, while inside a marvelously atmospheric restaurant awaits. Walls and ceilings entirely in mellow knotty pine foster a warm, rustic feeling here, where tradition is taken seriously. Frau Fraundorfer explained that one of the wooden tables in the room is what is called in German a "stammtisch". This table is the exclusive territory of a specific group of regulars, and each person in the group has his own place at which he always sits. In fact, some of the chairs have brass plaques engraved with the occupant's name. Photos of "stammtisch" regulars adorn the wall above the table, some dating back 50 years. Home-cooked meals accompanied by German beers and wines are served in this charming dining room. A worn staircase leads to the guest bedrooms which vary in size and furnishings, although most are in a reproduction Bavarian style. Do not expect elegance, but homey comfort. Most rooms have private bath, and some have phones, televisions, and balconies. This inn is truly a friendly place, where family photographs of the healthy, blond Fraundorfers decorate the upstairs hallway and Bavarian music is performed every week.

GASTHOF FRAUNDORFER
Owner: Family Fraundorfer
8100 Garmisch-Partenkirchen, Germany
Tel: (08821) 2176
24 Rooms - Double DM 70-130
Closed: Nov 15 to Dec 15 & 3 weeks in Apr
Credit cards: AX VS
Restaurant
Located 89 km S of Munich

The old saying, "don't judge a book by its cover", certainly applies to the Hotel-Restaurant Adler. This recently built hotel-restaurant is set back from the road and partly hidden by trees, thus not too much character is evident from the exterior. However, the moment one enters the foyer with its old baby carriage filled with plants and flowers, it is obvious that a treat is in store. The warm open lobby area has a dark tiled floor, comfortable couches, and dried flower arrangements which all combine for a real feeling of old Germany. The Boddicker family has owned and managed the Hotel-Restaurant Adler since 1971 with obvious care and pride. They have decorated the restaurant and breakfast room with cherished family antiques and achieved the ideal balance of country elegance and "gemutlichkeit". The focal point of the charming breakfast room is a large, 100-year-old organ, now converted to a player piano which plays traditional "oom-pah-pah" tunes. The main restaurant offers a delicious menu including tempting pastries and desserts which are a house specialty. Each table is a cozy corner unto itself, adorned with white tablecloths, fresh flowers, china and glassware. The 15 bedrooms are all very comfortable and tastefully decorated; most with some antique accents. All have private bath. The Hotel-Restaurant Adler promises a gourmet meal and a good night's rest; German country inn style.

HOTEL-RESTAURANT ADLER
Owner: Family R. Boddicker
7809 Gutach/Breisgau, Germany
Tel: (07681) 7022
15 Rooms - Double DM 78-100
Closed: January
Credit cards: AX DC MC
Located 20 km NE of Freiberg

One fortunate day while exploring the Black Forest region, we stumbled across the picturesque village of Haslach. This little town is centrally located in the middle of the Black Forest area, and as we searched for an atmospheric restaurant for lunch, we happily spotted the Hotel Gasthof Zum Raben. Its pretty half-timbered facade features a small turret flanked by balconies, and windowboxes overflowing with pretty red geraniums. The Zum Raben is located just off Haslach's historic market square, and is the town's oldest inn. Only German is spoken here, but the welcome is warm and genuine. Enter through the cozy restaurant, where a reasonably priced, traditional menu is served. The dark wood paneled room with its old parquet floor is brightened by fresh wild flower bouquets. An old green tile fireplace, old paintings and pretty cushions on the wooden chairs complete this historic and homey picture, a true "Schwarzwald slice of life". A back staircase leads to the small bedrooms, most of which share a bath. Some have antique painted furniture, but, in general, the rooms and hallways are very modest. The Hotel Gasthof Zum Raben is a bargain for those travellers who seek "local color" and do not mind simple accommodation.

GASTHOF ZUM RABEN
Owner: Gunter Fackler
Kinzigtal
7612 Haslach, Germany
Tel: (07832) 2270
10 Rooms - Double DM 52
Closed: first 2 weeks in November
Credit cards: None accepted
Black Forest village
Located 35 km NE of Freiburg

The 300-year-old Zur Backmulde enjoys a quiet location off the pedestrian street of Heidelberg's picturesque "old town". It is a very small and atmospheric establishment which offers an intimate restaurant of twelve tables, and seven bedrooms for guests. Pass under the old stone arched doorway to enter the softly lit restaurant filled with fresh flowers, antique pieces, knickknacks, and even a "kitchen witch". An old cradle holds a display of dried flowers, harvest breads, and regional wines. One is tempted to hide away and spend the entire afternoon in this cozy nook, the only reminder of the world outside coming from the stained lead glass windows letting in the sun's rays. There is no lack of good food, as the menu here is extensive and changes daily. Frau Klose provides a solicitous welcome to guests staying overnight in her homey bedrooms, all of which have a shower and w.c. Lovely antiques dress up the hallways and several of the bedrooms, while fresh and dried flower bouquets brighten the atmosphere throughout. The breakfast room is very unusual and features a small fountain under a central skylight, surrounded by an abundance of green plants. The room is decorated in forest green tones and gives the feeling of an oasis. Certainly a tranquil way to begin the day, with the soothing background noise of the fountain's running water.

ZUR BACKMULDE
Owner: Family Klose
Schiffgasse 11
6900 Heidelberg, Germany
Tel: (06221) 22551
7 Rooms - Double DM 95-105
Closed: January 15 to February 15
Credit cards: None accepted
Located in the old town of Heidelberg

The Hotel Garni am Kornmarkt is located in Old Heidelberg near the Tourist Office and beginning of the pedestrian section of the Hauptstrasse. It is tranquilly located on a pretty little square which is very near the Heidelberg Castle tram station. This informal little bed and breakfast hotel offers the best of homey hospitality, location, and price. The pretty facade is painted a dusky red with white trim. A former private home, the house is 250 years old. Walk past bikes propped up in the hall to the tiny reception area where Ingeborg Wachter will extend her warm welcome. She offers 16 guest bedrooms, half of which have private bath. Clean, modern furnishings make for comfortable, if unimaginative, accommodation. Room size varies, and some have views of the famous Heidelberg Castle on the hill above. Breakfast is served in a very inviting room furnished in old tapestry chairs and tables and a large antique sideboard. Bright yellow daisies adorn the tables as Frau Wachter serves a satisfying Continental breakfast. Her parakeets chirp in the next room as guests chat and make sightseeing plans for the day. This is an easy task from the Hotel Garni am Kornmarkt, as the atmospheric old section of Heidelberg is literally at the front door, and most sights are within easy walking distance.

HOTEL GARNI AM KORNMARKT
Owner: Frau Ingeborg Wachter
Kornmarkt 7
6900 Heidelberg, Germany
Tel: (06221) 24325
16 Rooms - Double DM 80-120
Closed: December 24 to January 15
Credit cards: AX
Parking garage nearby
Located centrally in the old town of Heidelberg

A warm and gracious welcome is assured at the charming Hotel Reichspost in Heidelberg. The hotel is quiet, located on a peaceful residential street slightly removed from the historic section of town. The pretty yellow facade and white shutters are freshly painted, and complemented by geraniums in the ground floor windowboxes. Inside the small entryhall guests are greeted by hosts Herr and Frau Obrecht. The hotel business is in the Obrechts' blood, for they have been hoteliers all their lives, as was Herr Obrecht's father before him. A large oil painting of "Grandfather Obrecht" hangs in the front hall, as well as an engraving of the grand Hotel Strand which he built. Other prints and paintings in the hallways and up the winding staircase depict all kinds of sailboats, since the Obrecht family's second passion after hotelkeeping is sailing. It seems they take a month off every year and disappear for an extended cruise on their own sailboat. Of the 30 guest bedrooms, half have private baths. Character is added to the bedrooms and hallways by family antiques and Oriental rugs. The breakfast room and lounge is decorated in yellow and white with lace tablecloths and fresh flowers on small round tables. The effect is cheerful and pretty, a welcoming place to begin the day.

HOTEL REICHSPOST
Owner: Family Obrecht
Gaisbergstrasse 38
6900 Heidelberg, Germany
Tel: (06221) 22252
30 Rooms - Double DM 80-110
Closed: January and February
Credit cards: None accepted
Elevator
Located six blocks west of the train station in Heidelberg

The Hotel Gasthof Zum Engel, located high on a hill, is a good sized, typically German country hotel and restaurant. The large building is built in farmhouse style, with a pleasant tree-shaded terrace in front, providing a perfect spot for an open air lunch. The Zum Engel is capably run by the Hagenmeier family and very good English is spoken. The feeling is very welcoming as one enters the long, tiled entry hall with its gilt mirror and fresh flower arrangement in a large copper pitcher. The large, friendly restaurant is located just off this entryhall. It is an airy room with many windows, ladder backed wooden chairs, warm light wood walls, brass chandeliers and fresh flower arrangements. The extensive menu offers a wide variety of choices including game dishes such as pheasant, duck, rabbit and venison. Oriental carpeted stairs lead up to the 28 guestrooms, 21 of which have private bath. The highlight of these rooms is their pretty views of the surrounding rolling green and forested hills of the Black Forest countryside. Guests will find tasteful contemporary furnishings in their spotlessly clean rooms. The Hotel Gasthof Zum Engel is a restful spot to eat a delicious meal and spend a comfortable night while exploring this popular vacation region.

HOTEL GASTHOF ZUM ENGEL
Owner: Family Bertolk Hagenmeier
7801 Horben-Langackern
bei Freiberg im Breisgau, Germany
Tel: (0761) 29111 and 29112
28 Rooms - Double DM 78-120
Open: March to November
Credit cards: All major
Black Forest village
Located 5 km S of Freiburg

The introduction to this marvelous castle hotel is first an expanse of lawn, intricate turrets and then an old timbered courtyard. Up a flight of stairs, the hotel entrance is a majestic banquet hall. The dining room is very regal. Take notice of a handsome, intricately inlaid door, lovely flower arrangements and the crest of the family above both entrances. The present family has lived in the castle as far back as 927. Herr Bircks, both manager and chef, is a charming man, exuding pride in the castle and offering a warm welcome for each guest. The breakfast room looks out through large windows onto the lush surrounding countryside. Climb a steep staircase in the direction of the bedchambers onto a terrace that also enjoys an expansive view and is used in warmer months for dining. Down a timbered hallway, the bedrooms are all named for renowned actors and many overlook either the valley or the weathered tiles of another castle wing. The highlight of the adjoining armaments museum is an iron hand, unique because of its moveable parts. In summer months the courtyard becomes a stage for afternoon and evening plays. Also, to the delight of children and adults, a steam train provides scenic rides through the valley.

BURGHOTEL GOTZENBURG
Owner: Family Von Berlichingen
Manager: J. Bircks
7109 Jagsthausen, Germany
Tel: (07943) 2222
15 Rooms - Double DM 85-100
Closed: November to mid-March
Credit cards: AX DC VS
Located 82 km N of Stuttgart

Sylt is beautiful; a narrow island of sand dunes jutting into the North Sea atop Germany's far northern border. Sheltered behind the dunes, the village of Kampen flies the British and German flags in the garden of Hinchley Wood, the home of Sam and Anne Smith. More than 25 years ago, Anne brought her husband and three young children from England to her island home and they turned their house into an English bed and breakfast. Sam's oil paintings crowd the walls around the chintz sofa and chairs which look just as "at home" here as their counterparts do in proper English parlors. The bedrooms are tiny and neat, about half of them having private bathrooms. When I visited, the house was crowded with German holidaymakers and Anne happily had her guests underfoot as she bustled around making breakfast. Sam entered the dining room to a chorus of "Good Morning", a greeting from his guests. His enquiries as to the weather, their breakfast, and their plans for the day were all in English - for Sam speaks only a few words of German. While Anne cares for their guests, Sam entertains them with his reminiscences of his career in the Royal Air Force and laments the island's lack of interest in his favorite game - cricket. Anne and Sam's special brand of sincere warmth and hospitality attracts visitors from all over the world and from all walks of life.

HINCHLEY WOOD
Owner: Anne & Sam Smith
2285 Kampen-Sylt, Germany
Tel: (04651) 41546
12 Rooms - Double DM 130
Open: All year
English style Bed & Breakfast
Located 230 km NW of Hamburg

Almost touching the Belgian border, the little town of Monschau hides in a deep ravine. Hugging the banks of the tumbling River Rur, the town is a jumble of tiny picture-perfect houses. Located on the marketplace, the small Muhlen Berg Hotel Weinstube is just as toy-like as the surrounding houses. Downstairs is the wine bar where the owner Herbert Lehnen is the friendly waiter, barman and hotel receptionist. His wife remains behind the scenes producing simple yet well-cooked German food. A steep, narrow staircase winds upstairs to the bedrooms. The higher you climb, the narrower and creakier the stairs. One tiny, less desirable room faces the back of the house. The others face the market place with two on each floor, their low ceilings held up by rough hewn beams. Pretty sprigged papers give a country feel though the furnishings are simple. An added bonus is a gleaming pine whirlpool and solarium tucked into the back of the house on the second floor. A delightful museum to visit while in the town is the Rotes Haus, whose interior remains just the way it was when it was the home of a prosperous 18th-century wool merchant.

MUHLEN BERG HOTEL WEINSTUBE
Owner: Herbert Lehnen
Markt 6
5108 Monschau, Germany
Tel: (02472) 2737 Telex: 8329423
7 Rooms - Double DM 94-99
Open: All year
Credit cards: All major
Exceptionally beautiful town
Whirlpool, solarium
Near the Belgian border
Located 170 km SW of Cologne

The Gasthof Zum Baren is a wonderfully atmospheric and friendly old inn located in historic Meersburg, arguably the most picturesque town on Lake Constance. In the Gilowsky family for five generations, the Zum Baren is now smoothly run by young Michael Gilowsky and his attractive wife. Upstairs, a treasure chest of unique bedrooms awaits. Our room had a beautifully carved wooden ceiling, country pine furniture, dainty print wallpaper and lace curtains. Some rooms have old painted furniture and all have antique touches and pretty wallpapers. It is important to note that the Zum Baren is a "gasthof" not a hotel: thus bedrooms are not equipped with telephones or televisions, although all have private bath or shower. Downstairs, the two cozy dining rooms are decorated with pewter plates and typical blue stoneware filling shelves above carved wooden furniture and comfy window benches with pretty print cushions and pillows. A wood parquet floor, low, beamed ceiling and white tile stove add to the pervading feeling of "gemutlichkeit". Both dining rooms contain only large tables for six to eight persons. This is purposely done to encourage guests to share a table, perhaps some wine, and certainly some good conversation. A very warm and charming inn, the Gasthof Zum Baren holds a special place in our hearts.

GASTHOF ZUM BAREN
Owner: Family Gilowsky
Marktplatz 11
7758 Meersburg, Germany
Tel: (07532) 6044
16 Rooms - Double DM 88-100
Closed: November 15 to March 15
Credit cards: None
Picturesque old town
Located 170 km SE of Stuttgart

The Hotel Blauer Bock dates from 1297 when the original structure was built as a Benedictine chapel. It has been a gasthof since the early 1800s, and today offers up-to-date accommodation and the refreshing Seasons restaurant. The 75 guestrooms vary in furnishings and bath facilities, and about half have recently been refurbished in a very comfortable and tasteful style. Soft colors, paintings, and reproduction antique furniture are combined to create a refined atmosphere. Unrefurbished rooms are likely to be brightly modern and not as comfortable, but the price will be a bargain. The Seasons restaurant welcomes guests through an archway festooned with garlands of dried flowers. The smaller dining room is for lighter meals, a light and airy room with white tile floors, wrought iron chairs, and marble-topped tables. A salad bar with a cornucopia of appetizing selections as well as imaginative sandwiches are offered here. The adjacent room is very attractively decorated with wood paneling, moss green upholstery, fresh flowers and ficus trees. It is a vegetarian's paradise whose menu offers healthy ingredients in a wide variety of unusual, nutritious dishes. A happy discovery, the Hotel Blauer Bock offers a fresh, country hotel atmosphere in the bustling city of Munich.

HOTEL BLAUER BOCK
Owner: Frau Ruhland
Sebastiansplatz 9
8000 Munich, Germany
Tel: (089) 2608043
75 Rooms - Double DM 80-130
Open: All year
Credit cards: None accepted
Restaurant, parking garage
Located on the Sebastiansplatz, near the old section of Munich

Frau Furholzner solicitously takes guests under her wing at the Pension Schubert, and she spoils them with generous breakfasts and comfortable, spotless rooms. Located on a quiet side street, the atmosphere at the Pension Schubert is not at all hotel-like. There is no lobby or public area to speak of, but if you are looking for homey comfort and a place to rest your head at night, this is a reasonably priced alternative. The pension is found on the second floor of a former villa, thus the rooms are all high-ceilinged and vary in size. Furnishings are a mixture of antiques and contemporary pieces, complemented by pretty drapes and Oriental rugs. Only three of the six rooms have private bath. The foyer displays many family knickknacks and mementos and creates a cheerful, informal atmosphere. The tiny breakfast room has lace covered tables and antique furnishings and is an agreeable place to meet other guests and plan sightseeing excursions for the day. For joggers and travellers who enjoy walking in Europe's city parks, the Theresienwiese park is easily found just a block to the west. The Pension Schubert is a good choice for travellers who prefer to spend their time and money outside of their hotel, appreciate a home-like ambiance, and do not require all the services offered in a hotel. However, Frau Furholzner seems to be constantly booked, so early reservations are advised.

PENSION SCHUBERT
Owner: Frau Furholzner
1 Schubertstrasse
8000 Munich, Germany
Tel: (089) 535087
6 Rooms - Double DM 65-78
Open: All year
Credit cards: None accepted
Located 5 blocks S of main train station

A hallway full of family antiques leads to a reception desk brightened by a bouquet of fresh flowers at the charming Gasthof Zur Rose in Oberammergau. The gasthof is well located on a quiet street one block from the central square. The friendly and gracious Frau Stuckl welcomes guests to her establishment where she encourages visitors to get to know one another. All her family members are experts on local sights and history, and in fact her talented son is currently the director of the famous Passion Play which takes place every 10 years in Oberammergau. Frau Stuckl's artistic touches are found throughout the Zur Rose, from colorful dried flower arrangements and strategically placed paintings, to pleasing combinations of fabrics. Formerly a farmer's stable, the gasthof is almost 200 years old, and has been in Frau Stuckl's family for 37 years. The two dining rooms are bright and airy, filled with pretty fabrics, rustic furniture, and green plants. The kitchen is much appreciated by guests as it offers Bavarian specialties as well as dishes more familiar to travellers. The 29 bedrooms are simple and pretty, and 10 have private bath. A visit to this antique-filled inn is a delight, enhanced by Frau Stuckl's helpful hospitality.

GASTHOF ZUR ROSE
Owner: Family Stuckl
Dedlerstrasse 9
8103 Oberammergau, Germany
Tel: (08822) 4706 or 4772
29 Rooms - Double DM 54-58
Closed: November
Credit cards: All major
Beautiful Bavarian village
Located approximately 80 km SW of Munich

The Adam Hotel's character and charm are representative of its owner, Herr Adam. He advertises the hotel as "fur Menschen mit Herz", "for people with heart". This little inn is located at the far end of town on a quaint side street just before the Burg Gasse, an easy walk from the center of the village. The Adam Das Kleine Hotel is favored by many who have come to know, understand and love the temperament of its owner. Herr Adam, your host and also your chef, will prepare his version of a gastronomic meal and then offer you the secret of his recipes in the form of cookbooks (for sale, of course). The restaurant is only for hotel guests and the evening meal is at the selection of Herr Adam. The bedrooms, a mix of cherished tidbits and lovely furnishings, are found up a steep, narrow, winding stairway. We were pampered with the large "honeymoon" suite, an especially appealing room with a wall of lead-paned windows looking out onto the castle gardens - a romantic view in one of the most romantic towns in Germany. Herr Adam is a personable man, particularly if you praise his cuisine. For breakfast you can order anything you want as long as you are willing to pay for the extras a la carte.

ADAM DAS KLEINE HOTEL
Owner: H.V. Adam
Burggasse 29
8803 Rothenburg, Germany
Tel: (09861) 2364
20 Rooms - Double DM 120-130
Open: Easter to October
Delightful town on the Romantic Road
Located 140 km SE of Frankfurt

The Gasthof Hotel Kloster-Stuble is a perfect little inn, combining reasonable prices with history, charm, and a good location. Just two blocks from the central market square of Rothenburg ob der Tauber, the Kloster-Stuble is tucked away on a side street behind an old church. This tranquil location affords a restful night's sleep and pretty views of the surrounding countryside from most bedroom windows. Twelve comfortable bedrooms are offered here, all with private shower and w.c. and furnished in beautiful country pine reproductions. Downstairs, the dining room and "stube" are cozily rustic. Murals depicting life in days gone by decorate the stube walls, while in the adjoining dining room pretty rose colored walls and tablecloths set a romantic tone. Tables are dressed with gleaming silver, china and glassware, topped off with pink candles and fresh flowers. French doors lead out onto two lovely terraces which enjoy a scenic view of church spires and distant hills. A sense of history prevails in this inn dating from 1300. Old duck decoys are displayed in a pretty pine hutch in the entryway, and country antique touches add atmosphere throughout. Rudolf Hammel is the young, energetic host at the Kloster-Stuble who does an admirable job attending to guests' needs as well as chef's duties.

GASTHOF HOTEL KLOSTER-STUBLE
Owner: Rudolf Hammel
Heringsbronnengassechen 5
8803 Rothenburg, Germany
Tel: (09861) 6774
12 Rooms - Double DM 80-90
Closed: January and February
Credit cards: All major
Delightful town on the Romantic Road
Located 140 km SE of Frankfurt

The Hotel Goldener Adler is managed by the Rapp family. This very ancient building, in bygone days a postal stop, has a mix of modern and traditionally furnished rooms, some of which also enjoy a bird's eye view of the square. (Note that this can be a disadvantage on a noisy weekend night.) You can order light meals on the terrace of the outdoor cafe or enjoy a more formal presentation of lunch or dinner in the hotel's fine restaurant. The entrance to the hotel is through gigantic doors, reminders of the era when horse-drawn coaches would come clomping through the portals. Inside, the hotel is quite simple. Most of the bedrooms are very basic but a few are especially large and have some antique furnishings which, although rather fussy, have character. Schwabisch Hall is an outstanding medieval town - comparable in many ways to the much better known walled town of Rothenburg which is on every tourist route. The central plaza is one of the prettiest in Germany and always teeming with activity - a "real town" with women carefully selecting their produce for the evening meal from small stalls in the square and children neatly dressed in uniforms gaily chatting on their way to school. The prime objective in coming to Schwabisch Hall should be to soak in the wonderful ambiance of this lovely old city - and for this, the Hotel Goldener Adler could not be more ideally located.

HOTEL GOLDENER ADLER
Owner: Marion & Peter Rapp
Am Marktplatz 11
7170 Schwabisch Hall, Germany
Tel: (0791) 6168
20 Rooms - Double DM 110-130
Colorful medieval town
Located 68 km NE of Stuttgart

The friendly Heim family has been welcoming guests into their home since 1959 and Herr Heim still keeps the old guest books filled with entries and artwork by former guests. Believe it or not, some of the original guests still visit the Pension Heim, but now they are accompanied by children and even grandchildren. Herr Heim was originally a cheesemaker by trade, and in fact he is featured in the local cheese museum. However, he had to choose another profession, and so opened this pension which gradually grew year by year due to demand. It is easy to see why guest numbers continued to increase, as the entire family is warm and genuine and the house spotless and homey. Cheerful houseplants brighten all the rooms and hallways and a rustic feeling pervades the dining rooms and "stube". Home-cooked meals are offered if guests so desire, and the ambiance is very convivial, fostering many new friendships. Upstairs, most of the comfortable bedrooms have balconies which overlook spectacularly unspoilt mountain scenery, even offering a glimpse of the famous Zugspitze on a clear day. The rolling hills and pastures of this region make it ideal for relaxed hiking in the summer and cross country skiing in the winter. Pension Heim offers comforts such as private bath or shower in each room, direct dial phones, and even a sauna. Just the right ending to a day of enjoying all the activities that this scenic area has to offer.

PENSION HEIM
Owner: Family Heim
Aufmberg/Ostallgau
8959 Seeg, Germany
Tel: (08364) 258
18 Rooms - Double DM 90-98
Closed: November to December 20
Credit cards: None accepted
Located 120 km SW of Munich, just N of Fussen

It is difficult to pinpoint the best feature of the Gasthof Hecht because one must choose between its abundant country charm, wonderfully warm and friendly hosts, and extremely reasonable rates. The 300-year-old gasthof is located on the picturesque main street and square of Wolfach where its half-timbered facade overflowing with vari-colored geraniums has long been a welcome sight for travellers. The ground floor contains two atmospheric dining rooms with pewter and pottery collections, beamed ceilings, wood paneled walls and fresh flower bouquets. A friendly neighborhood gathering was in progress when we arrived, adding to the convivial ambiance. Leave your diet at home, as traditional, home-style meals are served here including pork and veal dishes, plenty of vegetables and mouthwatering tortes for dessert. We were ushered to our contemporarily furnished and very clean bedroom by one of the Sattlers' three personable sons. Of the 17 guest bedrooms, all have private bath or shower. The homey upstairs hallways are rich with family antique pieces and Oriental rugs, reflecting the good taste of the Sattler family who also live here. A guest at the Gasthof Hecht truly has the feeling of visiting a private home rather than a hotel.

GASTHOF HECHT
Owner: Klaus Sattler
7620 Wolfach
Schwarzwald, Germany
Tel: (07834) 538
17 Rooms - Double DM 70-74
Closed: January 8 to February 8
Credit cards: None accepted
Restaurant, television room
Located 40 km NE of Freiburg

A picturesque drive past green meadows and flower bedecked chalets leads to the lovely Gasthof Hirschen in the tiny hamlet of Oberwolfach-Walke. Healthy geraniums adorn the Hirschen's many windowboxes, and a small stream flows by across the street. Full of country charm, the Hirschen dates from 1609 and is one of the oldest inns in the Black Forest. Its picturesque dining room is filled with antique items, fresh flowers and waitresses wearing the traditional dirndl. The menu is enticing, offering a delicious variety of local dishes. Follow the Oriental rug runners up the old staircase to the first floor lobby area which displays an antique clock, sitting area with a huge vase of purple daisies, and a doll cabinet filled with antique dolls. There are 17 guestrooms, all of which have private bath. The rooms are not overly large, but are charmingly furnished and very clean. Apartments are also available in a nearby annex. Sunny days are enjoyed on the flower filled terrace or in the tranquil garden, the only audible sound the birds in surrounding trees. In winter cross country skiing is a popular sport in this region of forests and rolling hills. From its quiet rural location to the warm welcome of the Junghanns family, it is easy to see why the Gasthof Hirschen is a popular country inn for travellers "in the know".

GASTHOF HIRSCHEN
Owner: Family Junghanns
7620 Oberwolfach-Walke, Germany
Tel: (07834) 366
17 Rooms - Double DM 76-88
Closed: three weeks in November
Credit cards: All major
Sauna, solarium, indoor bowling
Located 5 km N of Wolfach which is 40 km NE of Freiburg

Ireland

The first impression of Ballycormac House is delightful: a sparkling white, 300-year-old cottage beyond green lawns bordered by flower-filled gardens. The interior is just as attractive - snug cottage rooms with pretty wallpapers and restful color schemes complemented by comfortable country antiques. Several bedrooms are at the top of narrow staircases, tucked under the beamed roof, so it's as well not to bring too much luggage. Rosetta is a cordon-bleu cook offering delicious dinners around the large antique pine refectory table. Every other week during the summer week-long trail rides are offered and from November to March you can enjoy foxhunting holidays - please call or write for brochures outlining these programs. If you do not ride or hunt you can venture out each day to such places as Bunratty Castle and Folk Park, Clonmacnois Abbey and Lough Derg, returning each night to your cozy country cottage. To find Ballycormac House follow the N52 northeast from Nenagh through Borrisokane to Ballingarry (15 miles) where you turn left for a 2-mile drive to Aglish.

BALLYCORMAC HOUSE
Owner: John & Rosetta Paxman
Aglish near Borrisokane
Nenagh
Co Tipperary, Ireland
Tel: (067) 21129
5 Rooms with private bathrooms
£12 per person B & B
Open: All year
Credit cards: None accepted
Farmhouse
Located 50 miles NE of Limerick

Just as you arrive in Bantry town you see the entrance gate to Bantry House on your right. Dating from 1750, this stately home has fine views of the bay and, like so many grand Irish houses, is struggling to keep up its elegant buildings. The current descendant of the Earls of Bantry, Egerton Shellswell-White has restored a wing of the house in a more modern vein, offering bright airy rooms on a bed and breakfast basis. At the time of my visit, overnight guests took breakfast and dinner at a large pine refectory table set before the blackened kitchen range. In the daytime, this room doubles as a tea shop but construction is under way to add a more formal dining room in a remodeled wing. The main house is open to visitors who tour the baronial rooms with the aid of a typed sheet which explains the house's treasures on a room-by-room basis. In contrast to the grand formality of the house, the guestrooms are country cozy: large pastel decorated rooms where brass and iron bedsteads are topped by sprigged comforters. Bantry is on the N71 between Skibbereen and Kenmare.

BANTRY HOUSE
Owner: Egerton Shellswell-White
Bantry
Co Cork, Ireland
Tel: (027) 50047
10 Rooms, 6 with private bathrooms
£15 per person B & B
Open: All year
Credit cards: None accepted
Stately home
Located in the center of Bantry

The Gables was built by the owner of nearby Blarney Castle for the parish priest and it served as a rectory until the Lynches purchased it as their family home in 1971. Berna Lynch offers guests a friendly welcome to her home and provides lots of information on Blarney. The Gables is most attractively decorated: lovely antique furniture graces the large dining room, the welcoming lounge and several of the bedrooms. Accommodation is offered in two large family rooms with private bathrooms and showers and two smaller bedrooms which share a large old-fashioned bathroom with a huge tub. There are many activities to occupy you in Blarney besides the obligatory visit to the castle to kiss the Blarney stone: an excellent riding school is five minutes way, golf fifteen minutes and the shopping in Blarney is excellent, with the stores staying open till dusk during the summer months. There are several places to eat in town but if you make arrangements in advance Berna is happy to offer you a traditional Irish dinner. The Gables is 5 miles from Cork and well signposted on the outskirts of the village. If you are arriving from Killarney drive through the village onto the Cork road and take the second turning to the left signposted for the Gables.

THE GABLES
Owner: Berna Lynch
Stoneview
Blarney
Co Cork, Ireland
Tel: (021) 385330
4 Rooms, 2 with private bathrooms
From £11.50 to £13.50 per person B & B
Open: March to October
Credit cards: None accepted
Country home
Located 5 miles NW of Cork

Bobbie Smith is a caring hostess carrying on the tradition of warm farmhouse hospitality started by her mother over 20 years ago. The house is the home of the Smiths and their three young daughters - books, games and family mementos are scattered all over the place and you soon feel at home. Children have an informal library/playroom to entertain themselves in if the weather is inclement and on fine days the outdoors offers lots to keep them busy - two playful dogs, (Mildred) the pet sheep, outdoor toys and a croquet lawn - and there are always the cows to watch as they come home every morning and evening to be milked. Bobbie learnt her cooking skills in the Australian outback catering to camping groups. The nearest she comes to a campfire meal these days is a summer barbecue in the garden - our supper was fresh grilled trout and salads, followed by coffee and conversation before the blazing fire in the lovely, old-fashioned drawing room. Ask for the bedroom with the large feather mattress: its comfort will surprise you. All rooms are attractively decorated with family antiques and furniture that Bobbie has bought at local auctions. Take the N9 from Dublin to Royal Oak (south of Carlow), turn left into Bagenalstown (Muine Bheag) and right in the village for the 4-mile drive to Lorum Old Rectory.

LORUM OLD RECTORY
Owner: Bobbie Smith
Kilgreaney, Bagenalstown
near Borris, Co Carlow, Ireland
Tel: (0503) 75282
5 Rooms sharing 2 bathrooms
£12 per person B & B
Open: All year
Credit cards: DC VS
Farmhouse
Located 17 miles E of Borris

Bruckless House was built in the late 18th century by the Cassidy brothers, traders and merchants who took pickled herring from Donegal town, traded them for arms and ammunition in Sligo, then went on down to Portugal where they sold the guns to Napoleon and pickled herrings to Wellington. Later the house was owned by a passionate communist, Commander Fjorde, who is remembered for his many good works in the area. Both he and his wife are buried in the garden. Continuing the tradition of owners with an unusual or colorful past Clive and Joan Evans and their family moved here from Hong Kong where Clive had been for many years a senior superintendent in the Hong Kong police. They have opened their home to guests, offering five comfortable bedrooms that share a large upstairs bathroom and a downstairs toilet. Joan is kept busy running the house and offering her guests, not only delicious breakfasts and dinners (using fresh vegetables picked from the garden), but seafood lunches served farmhouse-style round the kitchen table. The Evans have several horses and, if you book in advance, arrangements can be made to go riding. Bruckless House is an ideal place to stay for visiting Glencolumbkille Folk Museum, a collection of thatched Donegal farmhouses where you learn an appreciation for the hardy lives that the local people led. From Donegal take the N56 towards Killybegs. Bruckless House is on the right in the village of Bruckless.

BRUCKLESS HOUSE
Owner: Clive & Joan Evans
Bruckless, Co Donegal, Ireland
Tel: (073) 37071
5 Rooms sharing 1 1/2 bathrooms
£13 per person B & B
Open: April to September
Credit cards: None accepted
Farmhouse
Located 13 miles W of Donegal

A hundred years ago there were many grand Victorian homes in Cahersiveen, on the Kerry peninsula, but today Mount Rivers is the only one remaining. Derrick McKenna's grandfather built the house and furnished it in the grand Victorian style as befitted his status as the area's doctor. The years have been kind to Derrick's family home - the gracious furniture, elegant silver and grand crystal remain as do the original fireplaces and light fixtures. The addition of modern bathrooms tucked into the corners of most of the bedrooms is the only obvious 20th-century modification. Like the sitting and the dining room, the bedrooms are filled with lovely old Victorian furniture. Everywhere I looked, displays of Victoriana cluttered the sideboards and mantleshelves. Mount Rivers is a perfect place to stay to soak up the beauties of the Ring of Kerry. An especially exciting trip is to visit the island of Skellig Michael, a craggy rock topped by an ancient monastery reached by climbing a winding stone staircase - arrangements can be made on arrival in Cahersiveen. The day trip operates only in clear, calm weather. Cahersiveen is 40 miles from Kenmare and 30 miles from Tralee on the Ring of Kerry.

MOUNT RIVERS
Owner: Derrick & Noreen McKenna
Cahersiveen
Ring of Kerry
Co Kerry, Ireland
Tel: (0667) 2509
6 Rooms, 4 with private bathrooms
From £11 to £13 per person B & B
Open: Easter to October
Credit cards: None accepted
Country home on the Ring of Kerry
Located 40 miles W of Kenmare

The Londonderry Arms was built in 1848 as a coaching inn by the Marchioness of Londonderry. Her great-grandson, Sir Winston Churchill, inherited it in 1921. Frank and Moira O'Neill bought the hotel in 1947 and more recently their son Frank Junior has taken over the operation of this delightful seaside hostelry. Frank takes great care to keep an olde worlde atmosphere in all the public rooms - bottle glass windows and dark carved furniture offer a club-like feel to the dining room. Guests gather in the back lounge for tea and scones or retire to the front sitting room to read. Upstairs the bedrooms are attractively, though plainly, decorated - those at the front have a more spacious feel to them with views of the town and the sea. One of the back bedrooms has Oriental-style antique furniture. Around you the scenic Antrim coast is full of cliffs, headlands and a succession of stunning views. You can detour into one of the Glens of Antrim where the mountains run inland parallel to each other and the world-famous Giant's Causeway is an hour's drive away. Carnlough is 35 miles north of Belfast. If you are arriving from County Donegal take the A2 to Coleraine, the A26 to Ballymena and the A42 to Carnlough.

LONDONDERRY ARMS
Owner: Frank O'Neill
Carnlough
Co Antrim BT44 0EU, Northern Ireland
Tel: (0574) 85255
15 Rooms with private bathrooms
From £19.00 to £21.50 per person B&B
Open: All year
Credit cards: All major
Small seaside hotel
Located 18 miles NW of Larne

This is one of those welcoming places that guests return to time and time again - one couple is scheduled for their nineteenth visit to this lovely home. A profusion of wildflower arrangements graces the hall, dining and sitting rooms and their smell blends with that of the furniture polish used to keep the lovely old furniture gleaming bright. A hearty farmhouse dinner is served round the large dining room table - the vegetables, fruits, lamb and beef are fresh from the farm and carefully cooked by Agnes Harrington. Upstairs three of the bedrooms have en-suite bathrooms - one, a family room, has two lovely old brass and iron beds. The other three bedrooms share two bathrooms upstairs and a third downstairs. There are lots of places to go and things to see in the area - in Carrick on Shannon you can rent a cabin cruiser and meander along the River Shannon and her lakes, stopping off to visit the villages and their pubs along the way. Glencarne House is on the N4, Dublin to Sligo road, betweeen Carrick on Shannon and Boyle.

GLENCARNE HOUSE
Owner: Agnes Harrington
Carrick on Shannon
Co Roscommon, Ireland
Tel: (097) 67031
6 Rooms, 3 with private bath
£12 per person B & B
Open: March to October
Credit cards: None accepted
Farmhouse
Located 34 miles SE of Sligo

Parkstown House is 7 miles north of Cashel at Horse and Jockey - a pub and a cluster of houses on the Cork to Dublin road. This elegant old home is full of grand antiques and everything is in tiptop condition. There is no air of faded glory to Parkstown House - the wooden floors gleam and the furniture is so highly polished it reflects the lovely displays of Waterford crystal and family silver. A large master bedroom interconnects with a smaller twin bedded room that has a large bathroom. The remaining three bedrooms share the facilites of a large bathroom. Ena Maher finds that once guests have discovered her home they often go no farther, making it their base for explorations down to Waterford and the Knockmealdown mountains and up to Loch Derg. The nearby Horse and Jockey restaurant is a very pleasant place to dine but if you want to splurge you will do no better than the Four Seasons Restaurant in the Cashel Palace Hotel. The gentle lowing of the cows ambling up to the dairy every morning and evening are the only sounds that punctuate the pastoral tranquility of Parkstown House.

PARKSTOWN HOUSE
Owner: Joe & Ena Maher
Horse & Jockey
near Cashel
Co Tipperary, Ireland
Tel: (0504) 44315
5 Rooms, 1 with private bathroom
From £12.50 to £14.50 per person B & B
Open: April to September
Credit cards: None accepted
Country house
Located 7 miles NE of Cashel

It is worth visiting Northern Ireland just to stay here. The house is lovingly decorated, with gracious antiques and bouquets of fresh garden flowers adding the finishing touches. Our bedroom (overlooking an immaculate garden) had more comforts than many four star hotels: sightseeing information; a tray set with teapot, kettle, teabags, coffee and chocolate and even a little box of After Eight Mints by the bedside. Plump comforters top the beds, fluffy towels hang on the old-fashioned towel rail - all coordinating in shades of pink with the curtains and the carpet. In addition two bedrooms have small bathrooms with showers neatly built into the rooms. All this and wonderful farmhouse food as well - five courses of it beautifully cooked, served and presented. Be warned: do not overindulge in the first four courses as the dessert trolley offers tempting desserts. The end of the day is celebrated with a cup of tea and cakes with Elizabeth and James around the drawing room fire. It goes without saying that you should plan on staying here for several days. If you are arriving from County Donegal take the N13 to Derry. Cross the Foyle Bridge and at Limavady, take the A37 towards Coleraine and turn right on the A29 (Garvagh and Cookstown) for 7 miles turning left on the B66 towards Ballymoney - the house is on the right.

GREENHILL HOUSE
Owner: James & Elizabeth Hegarty
24 Greenhill Road, Aghadowey nr Coleraine
Co Londonderry, BT51 4EU, Northern Ireland
Tel: (026 585) 241
7 Rooms, 2 with private bathrooms
From £11.50 to £12.50 per person B & B
Open: March to October
Credit cards: None accepted
Farmhouse
Located 9 miles S of Coleraine

Cleevaun has the advantage of being purpose-built as a bed and breakfast so each of the bedrooms has a modern en-suite bathroom. The weather was blustery and cool when we stayed, but inside efficient central heating kept the house toasty and we appreciated the abundance of hot water in the shower and the luxury of warm towels hot from the heated towel rail. The furniture in all the bedrooms is light modern pine, the decor tasteful and uncluttered, and several rooms have lovely views over the fields to the mouth of Dingle Bay. The very nicest touch is the note that Ursula Sheehy leaves in each of her guestrooms inviting guests to the lounge for a cup of tea or coffee and to browse through books "which will help you appreciate the beauty and folklore of the area. It would be a pity to have come so far and not experience the peace and tranquility which the unspoiled scenery of this area has to offer". Tommy and Ursula provide their guests with lots of information on where to dine in nearby Dingle and in the morning offer the choice of a traditional Irish breakfast, cheese and fresh fruit or hot crumpets and syrup with bran muffins. Children are very welcome and there is a large garden with play equipment. Cleevaun is 1 mile out of Dingle on the road to Slea Head.

CLEEVAUN
Owner: Tommy & Ursula Sheehy
Lady's Cross
Dingle
Co Kerry, Ireland
Tel: (066) 51108
5 Rooms with private bathrooms
£12 per person B & B
Open: March to October
Credit cards: None accepted
Bed & breakfast on the Dingle Peninsula
Located 1 mile W of Dingle

Helen Kirrane works very hard to ensure that her house is picture-perfect: guests praise its pretty decor and return here to make it their home away from home in Dublin. The sitting room was the most elegant I saw in a guesthouse, with its soft pastel Chinese silk carpet and exquisite antique furniture. The adjacent dining room table was set for what Helen terms her breakfast celebration when she serves home-baked cakes and pies, yogurt and fish as well as the traditional Irish breakfast. Upstairs the bedrooms are individually decorated in soft pastels. Those at the front are soundproofed to ensure a quiet night's sleep while those at the back have delightful views across the garden and cricket ground to the river bank. All rooms have direct dial phones, color televisions and bathrooms with showers. There is parking for cars in front and the 63 and 84 buses leave nearby for the 2-mile ride into the city. Anglesea Townhouse is located in the Ballsbridge suburb of Dublin near the American Embassy.

ANGLESEA TOWNHOUSE
Owner: Sean & Helen Kirrane
63 Anglesea Road
Ballsbridge
Dublin 4, Ireland
Tel: (01) 683877 Telex: 91475
7 Rooms with private bathrooms
£18 per person, breakfast £6.50
Open: All year
Credit cards: VS
Guesthouse
Located 10 minutes from the center of Dublin

The location is absolutely perfect - just off St Stephen's Green in the heart of Georgian Dublin. As its name suggests, the house stands as a tall narrow, four-story, Georgian townhouse. While the house is over 200 years old, everything has been restored and renovated adding light and freshness. Up the tall narrow staircase the 10 bedrooms each have small bathrooms with showers neatly tucked into the corner. All are decorated in soft pastels accented with pretty patterned drapes, furnished with light pine furniture and equipped with television and radio. If you have difficulty with stairs, or large unwieldy suitcases, you may want to request one of the bedrooms on the lower floors. A snug lounge occupies the front room of the house on the ground floor. Accessed by a narrow flight of winding stairs, the old basement is now a small comfortable restaurant, The Ante Room, where guests are served their breakfast. The lunch and dinner menus offer Irish ingredients cooked in the popular French style. The garden is now a secure car park where guests can store their cars for the duration of their stay and set out to explore this interesting city on foot, returning home to rest and recuperate whenever they are tired.

GEORGIAN HOUSE GUEST HOUSE
Owner: Annette O'Sullivan
20 Lower Baggot Street
Dublin 2, Ireland
Tel: (01) 604300
10 Rooms with private bathrooms
From £27 to £32 per person B & B
Open: All year
Credit cards: All major
Guesthouse
Located in the center of Dublin

I sought out Smyth's Village Hotel because I had received such a nice letter of recommendation from Elizabeth and Charlie Sweeney. I arrived at Smyth's, letter in hand, to find that the Sweeneys were in residence - back again for their eighth visit, for they - like many others - make this their home when they arrive from Shannon, rest up for a few days and return here at the end of their holiday to spend time with their friends the Smyth family. The hotel was built in 1974 and designed as three interconnecting Irish cottages. The Smyth family pride themselves on reflecting the simple culture and traditions of Irish village life. Everything is simple and functional Irish country style - the Liscannor flag floors, Donegal tweed curtains (lined in the bright red woolen fabric from which Connemara girls used to make their petticoats), homespun tablemats, sugan (rope and wood) chairs, latch-key doors, blackened beam ceilings, and the roaring turf fire hung with blackened pots. Upstairs bedrooms are more spacious than those on the ground floor, but all have private bathrooms and central heating. From Shannon go to Sixmilebridge where you turn towards Tulla, drive through Kilmurry and Kilkishen and turn right for Feakle - the hotel is on the outskirts of the village. The roads are small and narrow and it's easy to get lost so ask for a map when you make your reservation.

SMYTH'S VILLAGE HOTEL
Owner: The Smyth Family
Feakle
Co Clare, Ireland
Tel: (0609) 24002
12 Rooms with private bathrooms
£12.65 single, £22.50 double
Open: April to October
Credit cards: None accepted
Countryside hotel
Located 20 miles NE of Shannon Airport

Betty Breen offers a most congenial place to stay for visitors to this, the sunniest and driest part of Ireland. Betty takes great pride in her home and the flower filled garden that surrounds it. Guests meet each other around the dining room table in the evening when Betty serves a four course dinner - on the occasion of my last visit, fresh grilled trout and mouthwatering strawberry pie with an abundance of cream from the farm's cows were the order of the day. Betty and Tom find that many of their guests stay several days, so she can consult them about just what they would like for dinner. Upstairs the bedrooms are prettily decorated and in immaculate order: several are large family rooms and all have beautiful views of the lovely garden. In the field facing the farmhouse are the ruins of a 13th-century church and some old stones. Tom is happy to draw maps for hikers showing them where to go and what to see. Fishermen can try their luck in the River Bann that flows through the 285-acre farm. Clone House lies 2 miles southwest of the village of Ferns. From the N11 coming south take the first left after passing the church, turn first right and follow signs for the farm down the country lanes.

CLONE HOUSE
Owner: Betty & Tom Breen
Ferns
Co Wexford, Ireland
Tel: (054) 66113
5 Rooms sharing 2 bathrooms
£12 per person B & B
Open: All year
Credit cards: None accepted
Farmhouse
Located 70 miles S of Dublin

This welcoming farmhouse is an ideal place to stay if you intend to make a daytrip to the Aran Islands. Mary will make your ferry reservations, ensure that you receive an early breakfast and that a hot dinner awaits you on your return. Run by a mother and daughter team, both called Mary, Corrib View Farm has such good food that they often find that guests who intend to stay for only one or two nights extend their visits. Daughter Mary does the cooking and very nicely so - just as you think your meal is over she presents cakes "to nibble" with your coffee. All the fruits and vegetables are fresh from the garden. The bedrooms are small and snug - one larger family room has a private bathroom while the other four rooms share two bathrooms. A fire burns brightly in the sitting room and the house is warmed by central heating. Old family furniture decorates the rooms and an atmosphere of homely friendliness prevails. Corrib View Farm is located in a peaceful country setting yet near enough to main roads to make it ideal for exploring Connemara. From Galway take the N84 (Castlebar road) for 6 miles to Clonboo Cross where the 2-mile drive to Corrib View Farm and Annaghdown are signposted to your left.

CORRIB VIEW FARM
Owner: The Scott Family
Annaghdown
Galway
Co Galway, Ireland
Tel: (091) 91114
5 Rooms, 1 with private bathroom
£12 per person B & B
Open: May to September
Credit cards: None accepted
Farmhouse
Located 8 miles N of Galway

Dinner at Lennoxbrook is usually trout fresh from the stream, and, if you care to, you can catch it yourself (or Paul will gladly catch it for you if you arrive early in an afternoon). A choice of a red or white wine is offered with dinner and, while trout is always available, Pauline also offers pork and lamb fresh from the farm. There are lots of activities besides fishing, which are especially appealing to children: large grounds where they can romp and play, a swing on the oak tree, a dinghy to row in the stream, the donkey Mrs, a large old haybarn, hens to feed and children to play with (Paul and Pauline have three young children). Ancient monuments abound in the surrounding area, with Newgrange, Knowth and Dowth being the primary attractions. Besides having lots to see and do, the farmhouse is quite lovely. Beautiful family antique furniture, mementos and pictures decorate every room for Paul is the fifth generation of his family to call Lennoxbrook home. The front bedrooms are particularly prettily decorated, their small print papers complementing the lovely old furniture. Lennoxbrook is about an hour and a half's drive from Dublin Airport, making it an ideal place to stay if your destination is Donegal. The house is on the N3, Dublin to Cavan road, 3 miles beyond Kells (often labelled Ceanannas Mor on maps).

LENNOXBROOK
Owner: Paul & Pauline Mullan
Kells (Ceanannas Mor)
Co Meath, Ireland
Tel: (046) 45902
5 Rooms sharing 2 bathrooms
£12 per person B & B
Open: March to November
Credit cards: None accepted
Farmhouse
Located 10 miles NW of Navan

Just down the road from the Park Hotel, Hawthorne House offers visitors an immaculate guesthouse within steps of Kenmare's busy streets, yet far enough away to ensure a peaceful night's sleep. A large car park provides safe off-road parking. Inside, the old house has received a complete facelift with light pine replacing all the old woodwork and doors, and pastel paints and soft pastel carpets giving a light, airy feel. The bedrooms, all named after disticts around Kenmare, are very nicely decorated in a bright modern style. Derrynid and Neidin are superior rooms, having the additional facilities of a spacious sitting area, color television, hairdryer and electric blanket. The restaurant has a very feminine flavor, with pine chairs and tables covered with pink and white tablecloths, pink carpet and pink velvet drapes. Ann Browne cooks a very nice four course dinner and guests select wine from a list compiled by her husband Jerry who is head waiter at the adjacent Park Hotel. There are lots to see and do in the area - Ann gives advice and even has printed sheets outlining six daytrips from Kenmare. Kenmare is about a three-hour drive from Shannon, a perfect spot for touring the Ring of Kerry.

HAWTHORNE HOUSE
Owner: Ann Browne
Shelbourne Street
Kenmare
Co Kerry, Ireland
Tel: (064) 41035
8 Rooms with private bathrooms
From £12 to £14 per person B & B
Closed: February
Credit cards: None accepted
Guesthouse near the Ring of Kerry
Located in the center of Kenmare

Carriglea House is an immaculate farmhouse with a breathtaking location overlooking the Lower Killarney Lake and the distant Torc and Mangerton Mountains, and adjacent to Muckross House and Killarney National Park. The rooms are well furnished and lots of well-placed family antiques add a great deal of charm. Five bedrooms are in the main house and four, even lovelier rooms, in an adjacent cottage. Marie Beazley is happy to cook dinner for her guests (all the fruits and vegetables come from the garden) or give them information on where to eat in town. The advantage of staying here is that you can appreciate the extraordinary beauties that surround Killarney without getting involved in the congestion of the town. Carriglea House is 2 miles from the centre of Killarney on the road to Kenmare, the N71. To avoid disappointment advance reservations are recommended.

CARRIGLEA HOUSE
Owner: Michael & Marie Beazley
Muckross Road
Killarney
Co Kerry, Ireland
Tel: (064) 31116
9 Rooms, 6 with private bathrooms
From £12 to £14.50 per person B & B
Open: Easter to October
Credit cards: None accepted
Farmhouse
Located 2 miles S of Killarney

Bill and Bobbe Gilmore did not feel that retirement in their native America was for them, so they came to Kinsale and converted Ardcarrig into the lovely country house they had always dreamed of owning. And they run their small establishment just as a country house should be, with every attention given to the care and well-being of their guests. Sherry, port and brandy are on the library table for guests to serve themselves, bathrooms are stocked with "goodies", breakfast is served with the morning paper - the list could run on and on. The layout of the house and grounds makes it unsuitable for children but perfect for those in search of a romantic hideaway - there is even a large outdoor pool (unheated) where you can bask on sunny days. The large green bedroom has stunning views across the rooftops to the harbor below, the pink room is romantic with a flowery print and an impressive four-poster, while the blue room offers woodland views and has its bathroom down the hall. Breakfast is a grand gourmet feast with such delights as cream cheese and dill omelette with smoked salmon making regular appearances. Kinsale has a vast array of restaurants offering every conceivable variety of dinner fare in all price ranges. Ardcarrig is on Compass Hill overlooking Kinsale Harbor directly above the Trident Hotel.

ARDCARRIG
Owner: Bill & Bobbe Gilmore
Compass Hill, Kinsale
Co Cork, Ireland
Tel: (021) 772217
3 Rooms with private bathrooms
From £27 single to £44 double
Open: April to December
Credit cards: None accepted
Country house
Located 18 miles S of Cork

Kinsale is full of historic interest, a town of narrow streets with slate-hung houses surrounding a picturesque harbor. For a small town Kinsale boasts a remarkable number of gourmet restaurants and you can do no better than to stay at one of them, the Blue Haven. Sitting at a crossroads in the center of the town, this pretty white building with blue awnings and trim has tremendous character. The bar bustles with activity, a sunny conservatory overlooking the flower-filled, walled patio offers excellent bar food and a most reasonably priced tourist menu. The dining room serves splendid dinners accompanied by fine wine from a list with over 70 selections. Every bedroom is decorated in soft colors with well-chosen fabrics and thick sand colored carpets. Several of the larger rooms have sitting areas - all have immaculate modern bathrooms. Bath towels are artistically arranged atop the beds, each arrangement topped by a fresh flower - the same kind of care and attention to detail is found in everything associated with this small hotel run with great style by Brian and Anne Cronin. The Blue Haven is in the center of Kinsale - 18 miles south of Cork.

BLUE HAVEN HOTEL
Owner: Brian & Anne Cronin
Kinsale
Co Cork, Ireland
Tel: (021) 772209
9 Rooms, 7 with private bathrooms
From £30 single to £50 double
Open: March to December
Credit cards: All major
Small seaside hotel
Located 18 miles S of Cork

Glebe House is located deep in the countryside, a 15-minute drive from Kinsale. Guy and Kathy are American and Glebe House and Ireland are their home. A house party atmosphere prevails and they do everything themselves from gardening to cleaning and cooking. The cooking really merits a special mention, for besides splendid dinners Kathy offers enough creative breakfast menus that you can stay for a week and never have the same thing twice. Belgian waffles heaped high with fresh garden fruits and thick cream, herbed scrambled eggs with kippers and sausage, French toast with homemade preserves - all beautifully presented. The upstairs bedroom is large and has a huge bathroom. The three smaller downstairs bedrooms share a bathroom. To find Glebe House take the N71 from Cork through Innishannon, turn left after the bridge and Glebe House is the first house on the right before entering the village of Ballinadee.

GLEBE HOUSE
Owner: Guy & Kathy Velardi
Ballinadee, Bandon, near Kinsale
Co Cork, Ireland
Tel: (021) 778294
4 Rooms, 1 with private bathroom
From £13 to £16 per person B & B
Open: May to October
Credit cards: None accepted
Country house
Located 8 miles SW of Kinsale

CLOSED

The Lighthouse is my very favorite type of bed & breakfast: tiny snug rooms in an adorable little house on a quiet street, yet within easy strolling distance to everything that a picturesque town has to offer. Art and Ruthann are American-born Irish who returned to Ireland after their children were grown to make Kinsale their home. They bought a small, almost derelict, house and over a period of years added to and restored its small rooms, placing antiques and country-style treasures in every nook and cranny. The finishing touch was a captain's walk atop the house, which offers stunning views across rooftops to Kinsale Harbor. I questioned Ruthann about the advisability of children in a house that is brimming with valuable antique toys - "Absolutely no problem, I love children, I let them admire our things and promptly supply them with dolls and animals, games and toys." I saw evidence of this as I visited the rooms - two beds were piled with stuffed toys on the pillows and games stacked by the side for the little girls who were staying there with their parents. Kinsale is 18 miles south of Cork - stop by The Blue Haven for a map directing you to The Lighthouse.

THE LIGHTHOUSE
Owner: Art & Ruthann Moran-Salinger
The Rock
Kinsale
Co Cork, Ireland
Tel: (201) 772734
6 Rooms, 3 with private bathrooms
From £12 to £14 per person B & B
Open: February to November
Credit cards: None accepted
Bed & breakfast
Located 18 miles S of Cork

The hill behind Coolatore House is at the very center of Ireland: from its top you can see six counties - as far as the Wicklow Mountains (all I saw was blustery rain but despite inclement weather it was fun to stand in the middle of Ireland). Ann Galvin chatted to me as I sampled the cheesecake she had prepared for the evening meal. As we visited her six children came repeatedly in and out and I wondered how she could happily hold a conversation, cook dinner and deal with her family all at the same time. Needless to say, children are very welcome and babysitters readily available. The farmhouse is spotless and a cheery fire always burns in the drawing room grate. Up the grand staircase are five nicely decorated bedrooms, two with private bathrooms, the other three sharing two bathrooms. The Clonmacnois monastic ruins and round tower overlooking the River Shannon are a half hour's drive away and should not be missed. Coolatore House is midway between Dublin and Galway (N6), 4 miles off the N6, between Horseleap and Moate - the house is very well signposted.

COOLATORE HOUSE
Owner: Ann Galvin
Rosemount
Moate
Co Westmeath, Ireland
Tel: (0902) 36102
5 Rooms, 2 with private bathrooms
£12 per person B & B
Open: May to September
Credit cards: None accepted
Farmhouse
Located midway between Dublin & Galway

Roundwood House is situated near Mountrath, in a scenic spot at the foot of the Slieve Bloom Mountains. The house was built in the 1740s for Anthony Sharp upon his return from America - he attached this elegant Palladian home to his grandfather's simple Quaker cottage which still remains at the back of the house. Roundwood House had pretty much fallen into disrepair by the time it was purchased by the Georgian Society in the 1970s - their careful restoration is being continued by Frank and Rosemarie Kennan who forsook the corporate life of IBM. The gray appearance of the outside of the house belies its colorful interior - bright white and blue for the hall and bold yellows, blues and reds for the bedrooms - all done in true Georgian style to give a dramatic impact to the lovely high-ceilinged rooms. Modern bathrooms and central heating are the only visible 20th-century modifications. Collections of books and paintings and beautiful antique furniture combine with the friendliness of your hosts Frank and Rosemarie to make this a most inviting place to stay. There is no need to worry about bringing children along because a portion of the top floor of the house is a nursery with plenty of toys and games to keep children amused for hours. To find Roundwood House take the N7 from Dublin to Mountrath and follow signs for the Slieve Bloom Mountains which will bring you to the house 3 miles out of town.

ROUNDWOOD HOUSE
Owner: Frank & Rosemarie Kennan
Mountrath, Co Laois, Ireland
Tel: (0502) 32120
6 Rooms with private bathrooms
£16 per person B & B
Closed: January
Credit cards: AX MC VS
Country house
Located 10 miles W of Portlaoise

Mornington House is a most delightful manor house, offering you a glimpse of what it was like to live the life of the landed gentry of Ireland - at a very reasonable price. Warrick O'Hara is the fifth generation of his family to call this home - and you are encouraged to make it yours. Family portraits and pictures gaze down upon you as you dine around the enormous dining room table. Anne has such a reputation for her food that she offers cookery classes locally. As an accompaniment to your meal you can choose from a red or white house wine. The two front bedrooms are enormous in size: one has a large brass bed sitting center stage and requires a climb to get into it. The other front bedroom has twin brass beds and shares the view across the peaceful grounds. The third bedroom is small only by comparison with the front rooms, and looks out to the side garden and the woods. The O'Haras are very involved in foxhunting and while they do not have horses available for guests' use, good horses are available in the area. Mornington House is a difficult place to find - take the N4 from either Sligo or Dublin to Mullingar, then the Castlepollard road north to Crookedwood where you turn left, then take the first right and the entrance to the house is on your right after a mile.

MORNINGTON HOUSE
Owner: Warrick & Anne O'Hara
Mornington
Multyfarnham near Mullingar
Co Westmeath, Ireland
Tel: (044) 72191
3 Rooms with private bathrooms
£12 per person B & B
Open: May to September
Credit cards: None accepted
Country house
Located 53 miles NW of Dublin

Ardeen was an especially welcome haven after exploring the Donegal coast on a particularly gloomy wet summer's day. This attractive Victorian house was once the town doctor's home and Anne Campbell and her husband, who owns the local hardware store, had always admired Ardeen's airy rooms and large riverside garden, so, when it came up for sale, they jumped at the opportunity to call it home. Breakfast around the large dining room table is the only meal that Anne prepares, though she is happy to offer advice on where to eat in Ramelton. The bedrooms are decorated to a high standard and guests can plan their sightseeing from the warmth of the sitting room. Ardeen is an ideal base for exploring the Donegal coastline, visiting Glenveagh National Park and the Glebe Art Gallery with its fine collection of Irish paintings. If you are arriving from Donegal take the N56 to Letterkenny and on the outskirts of the town look for the T72, signposted for Rathmullen. It's a 7-mile drive to Ramelton: when you reach the river turn right, following the bank, and Ardeen is on your right.

ARDEEN
Owner: Anne Campbell
Ramelton
Co Donegal, Ireland
Tel: (074) 51243
4 Rooms sharing 1 bathroom
£12 per person B & B
Open: Easter to September
Credit cards: None accepted
Country home
Located 10 miles NE of Letterkenny

Charles Waterhouse spent several years of the Second World War around the Khyber Pass pursuing a colorful career as the aide-de-camp to the Governor of the Northwest Territories of India. Subsequently he settled at Tahilla Cove and built this delightful resort overlooking a most picturesque bay. The furnishings and decor throughout are very plain, the atmosphere most inviting and the company of your hosts, fellow guests and the locals just what you come to Ireland to experience. In the evening guests gather with locals in the bar to chat with Charles and Molly, while son Jamie tends the bar. Dinner and breakfast are served in the dining room whose large windows frame a magnificent view of the cove and its little harbor. The bedrooms share the same bucolic view: four are in the main house and an additional five across the garden in a separate building. The bedrooms are plainly furnished and have a pleasant old-fashioned air to them. An especially memorable daytrip can be arranged to Skellig Michael, a small rocky island topped by an ancient monastery reached by climbing hundreds of winding stairs from the landing cove - Jamie can make your reservation and supply you with a packed lunch. Tahilla lies 12 miles west of Kenmare on the Ring of Kerry.

TAHILLA COVE GUESTHOUSE
Owner: The Waterhouse Family
Tahilla
Ring of Kerry
Co Kerry, Ireland
Tel: (064) 45104
9 Rooms with private bathrooms
£20 per person B & B
Open: Easter to October
Credit cards: All major
Seaside guesthouse
Located 12 miles W of Kenmare

Fanad Head is a lovely peninsula jutting out into the Atlantic Ocean at the far north of Ireland. If you are looking for a place to stay that has that end-of-the-earth feel about it, a place where you will see few visitors and be surrounded by beautiful countryside, then you can do no better than to stay with Sadie Sweeney at her farmhouse. This 100-year-old creeper-covered house, its windowboxes laden with colorful flowers, presents a welcoming picture to visitors - the interior does not disappoint for Sadie has taken great care to decorate the bedrooms prettily with matching curtains and wallpaper. Three are roomy doubles and twins and two are cozy singles. All five share two nicely appointed bathrooms. Wholesome farmhouse food is served in the dining room - the meats and vegetables fresh from the farm. Guests are welcome to visit the farmyard and watch, or participate in, the cow milking. From Letterkenny take the R245 through Ramelton and follow signs for Kerrykeel where you turn sharp left in the center of the village and follow the ocean to the tiny village of Rosnakill. The farmhouse is on your left just as you enter Tamney.

SWEENEY'S FARMHOUSE
Owner: Sadie Sweeney
Tamney near Kerrykeel
Fanad Head
Co Donegal, Ireland
Tel: (074) 59011
5 Rooms sharing 2 bathrooms
£11.50 per person B & B
Open: April to September
Credit cards: None accepted
Farmhouse
Located 25 miles NE of Letterkenny

This working farm with 100 acres laid down to grain production and cattle is a delight for adults and children alike: as well as farm activities there are pony rides (on a leading rein), tennis courts and a childrens' game room. Whenever David Kent is not occupied with farm matters, he loves to talk to visitors and discuss the farm and what to do and see in the area. (The Waterford crystal factory is a big draw and Margaret is happy to make an appointment to tour.) Margaret is one of those people who shows her appreciation of her guests by feeding them lavishly. She delights in the preparation of dishes made from beef from the farm, homegrown fruits (strawberries, raspberries, gooseberries, apples and rhubarb, to name but a few) and vegetables - her specialty is her homemade ice cream. Guests are served after-dinner coffee in the lounge and often linger for discussions around the fireside. Upstairs several of the simply decorated bedrooms are large enough to accommodate an extra child or children. To find the house take the road from Waterford toward Dunmore East. After about 4 miles, at the Maxol garage, take the left fork toward Passage East. Foxmount Farm is signposted on the right about 2 miles before Passage East.

FOXMOUNT FARM
Owner: Margaret Kent
Dunmore East Road
Waterford
Co Waterford, Ireland
Tel: (051) 74308
6 Rooms sharing 2 bathrooms
£12 per person B & B
Open: April to mid-October
Credit cards: None accepted
Farmhouse
Located 5 miles E of Waterford

The Old Coach House is a favorite because the house is especially lovely and because Liz and Michael Purnell make you feel at home. The Purnells have a very caring, casual, fuss-free manner that makes a stay here particularly pleasant. The Old Coach House was once a huge barn on the grounds of their home. Michael's conversion has been done with great style: lattice windows have been inset in the thick walls and the rooms have been designed to give a spacious, country-cozy feel. The large sitting room is the center of the house where guests gather to relax and chat. In the dining room the well polished table is laid with china, glass and silver. Liz enjoys cooking a wide repertoire of dishes. Above, the bedrooms are particularly spacious and beautifully furnished: smart Sanderson wallpapers grace the walls and match the drapes and bedspreads. This is a perfect place to stay to enjoy a visit to the nearby Waterford crystal factory and the John F. Kennedy Memorial Park. From Waterford turn toward Dunmore East (by the Tower Hotel). After about 4 miles (at the Maxol garage) take the left fork toward Passage East, take the first left, pass the modern houses and The Old Coach House is on your right.

THE OLD COACH HOUSE
Owner: Michael & Liz Purnell
Blenheim Heights
Waterford
Co Waterford, Ireland
Tel: (051) 74471
4 Rooms with private bathroom
£15 per person B & B
Closed: for Christmas
Credit cards: None accepted
Country home
Located 4 miles E of Waterford

CLOSED

Westport is one of the few architecturally pre-designed towns in Ireland. Its architect, James Wyatt, made the most of the site: the river is walled in and treelined, and he designed an attractive octagonal town center. The waterfront lies away from the town, many of its old buildings transformed into pubs and restaurants. Just a short drive beyond the waterfront lies Rosbeg House with Clew Bay dotted with little green islands at its front and Croagh Patrick (the cone shaped holy mountain of Ireland) at its rear. Brian and Kay O'Brien came here several years ago and have turned this 250-year-old house into a comfortable place to stay. The two larger front bedrooms have private bathrooms and four smaller bedrooooms share two bathrooms. A television room is there for guests to use and breakfast is taken in an attractively decorated room just off the large family kitchen. Brian and Kay recommend places nearby for dinner. Westport is 65 miles northwest of Galway. Rosbeg House is 2 miles to the west of the town on the road to Croagh Patrick.

ROSBEG HOUSE
Owner: Brian & Kay O'Brien
Westport
Co Mayo, Ireland
Tel: (098) 25879
5 Rooms, 2 with private bathrooms
From £12 to £14 per person B & B
Open: March to October
Credit cards: None accepted
Farmhouse
Located 2 miles W of Westport

When Otto and Patricia built their home they used a traditional Georgian design and gave it an old-fashioned feel with ceiling moldings and traditional doors and decor. Friends suggested they open as a farm guesthouse so, taking the plunge, they added extra bathrooms and opened their doors. How fortunate they did, for now visitors can enjoy this welcoming home and the flower-filled garden that surrounds it. Patricia prepares good homely meals, with homemade soup, wiener schnitzel accompanied by farm fresh vegetabes and followed by plum pie being the order of the day for our meal. (Otto came to Ireland from East Germany so Patricia enjoys serving a mixture of Irish and German dishes.) Proportions are large enough to satisfy even the heartiest of eaters. The bedrooms are decorated in soft pastels, the orthopedic beds topped by soft woolen bedspreads. One guestroom has the advantage of a king-size bed and a private bathroom. Wicklow is a pleasant small town round a harbor just an hour's drive south of Dublin and the Dun Laoghaire ferry and north of the Rosslare ferry. The Wicklow Mountains, Powerscourt Gardens, Glendalough and the Vale of Avoca are close at hand. As you enter Wicklow town turn right at the Grand Hotel, towards the top of the hill take the first right on Ashtown Lane and Lissadell House is on your right.

LISSADELL HOUSE
Owner: Otto and Patricia Klaue
Ashtown Lane off Marlton Road
Wicklow, Co Wicklow, Ireland
Tel: (0404) 67458
4 Rooms, 2 with private bathrooms
£12 to £14 per person B & B
Open: March to November
Credit cards: None accepted
Farmhouse
Located 33 miles S of Dublin

Italy

One of the joys of researching a guidebook is to discover a "jewel" of an inn - it is rather like a treasure hunt. Rarely though do we find an excellent hotel which we have not heard of previously. However, the Country House, located on a small lane less than half a mile from the lower gates into Assisi, is just such a find. The inn is actually an ancient peasant's cottage which Silvana Ciammarvghi, the owner, has lovingly restored and transformed into a small pension. It is not surprising that the hotel is so loaded with charm, for Silvana loves antiques and has an eye for beautiful wooden chests, tables, chairs, mirrors and beds. In fact, the first floor of this inn is an antique shop. Most of the furniture in the house is for sale but, no problem: when a piece is sold, another takes its place from the shop downstairs. All of the rooms have style and taste and are decorated with an antique "country" ambiance. When we first visited the Antichita "Three Esse" Country House it had only recently opened. On our last visit many improvements had been made making this small inn even more attractive. Silvana was there to greet us again and was as charming as ever. She speaks excellent English and will be glad to welcome you to her "home" which would make an excellent location for exploring Umbria.

ANTICHITA "THREE ESSE" COUNTRY HOUSE
Owner: Silvana Ciammarvghi
S. Pietro
06081 Assisi, Italy
Tel: (075) 816 363
12 Rooms - Double Lire 56,000
Breakfast only served
Open: All year
Inn combined with antique shop
Countryside location near Assisi
Located 177 km N of Rome

For a splendid, moderately priced little inn just off the Piazza del Commune in the heart of Assisi, the Hotel Umbra is a wonderful choice. If you are expecting a luxury hotel with fancy décor, this will not be the hotel for you. Although the public rooms have accents of antiques and a cozy ambiance, they are "homey" rather than grand. The bedrooms, which are clean and fresh, are simple rather than deluxe. Nevertheless, because of the absolutely delightful small terrace at the entrance which is oozing with charm, the Umbra would have won my heart even if the inside had been a disaster. You reach the Umbra by way of a narrow little alley leading off from the Piazza del Commune. The entrance is through wrought iron gates which open to a tiny patio - a green oasis of peace and quiet where tables are set under a trellis covered with vines whose leaves provide shade and paint a lacy pattern of shadows. From this intimate terrace there is a lovely view. Some of the bedrooms, too, have a panoramic vista of the Umbrian hills and valley. There is a cute little dining room and several small drawing rooms. This small, family owned and managed hotel is a real asset to the wonderful medieval city of Assisi.

HOTEL UMBRA
Owner: Alberto Laudenzi family
Via degli Archi
06081 Assisi, Italy
Tel: (075) 812 240 Telex: 66122
27 Rooms - Double Lire 60,000
Closed: mid-January to mid-March
Credit cards: All major
Central location off main square
Located about 177 km N of Rome

The Hotel Florence is a moderately priced hotel in the charming ancient port of Bellagio. The location is prime - right on the main square. Across the street by the lake is a little tea terrace where you can have a snack while watching the boat traffic. If you are lucky enough to snare a front room with a balcony, you can step out through your French doors and be treated to a splendid view of Lake Como. There is a small reception area and, down a few steps, an intimate lounge with a fireplace, beamed ceiling and chairs set around tiny tables. A staircase leads to a guest dining room with a fireplace and ladderback chairs and to the guestrooms. On our last visit we were pleased to find many of the guestrooms have been redone - many with antique furnishings. Ours was a very cheerful, bright corner room with French doors opening onto a terrace where lounge chairs were invitingly set for viewing the lake. The hotel is owned by the Ketzlar family, who are real pros: the inn has been in their family for 150 years and is now managed by Mrs Freidl Ketzlar and her daughter, Roberta. They both speak excellent English and are extremely gracious. Bellagio is such an atmospheric little town that we are happy to be able to recommend a pleasant, well-run, moderately priced hotel.

HOTEL FLORENCE
Owner: Ketzlar family
22021 Bellagio (Lake Como)
Italy
Tel: (031) 950 342
48 Rooms - Double Lire 84,000-98,000
Open: April 25 to October 10
Credit cards: All major
Village center, near ferry
Lakefront location
Located 78 km N of Milan

How lucky to find a "picture perfect" inn in the splendid ancient upper town of Bergamo (Citta Alta). And what a picture. The Hotel Agnello d'Oro sits just off the main Piazza Viejo, smugly facing its own tiny, intimate square, complete with tinkling fountain. The hotel, an olive drab with brown shutters and an awning in front, is tall and skinny - only two rooms wide but rising six stories high. An area of potted row-hedge defines the outdoor terrace. Inside, too, this old hotel is great. An ancient desk sits in the tiny lobby and to the right is a wonderful restaurant with crowds of copper, plenty of colorful old plates on the walls, cozy chairs and wooden tables covered with bright red and white checked tablecloths. The effect is cluttered but, oh, so gay. Upstairs the rooms are not for the fussy. They are very basic, but they are perfect for those on a budget whose love of romantic ambiance surpasses their desire for perfection in sleeping quarters. Even the fussy among you might adore waking up in the morning, opening the French doors, and stepping out onto your tiny balcony to greet the day. The front rooms are prime, with flowerboxes on the iron railings. Another plus - although the government gives the Hotel Agnello d'Oro a third class rating, Michelin gives a two fork approval to the restaurant.

AGNELLO D'ORO
Via Gombito, 22
24100 Bergamo (Citta Alta)
Italy
Tel: (035) 249 883
25 Rooms - Double Lire 52,500
Credit cards: AX VS
Very basic small budget hotel
Marvelous walled medieval city
Located 47 km NE of Milan

The Peralta is special - very special - not really a hotel at all, but rather a miniature medieval village tucked high in the coastal hills northeast of Pisa. This cluster of buildings had fallen into ruin when the famous Italian sculptress, Fiore de Henriquez, discovered the village, fell in love, and decided to bring the hamlet back to life. Fifteen years of reconstruction has resulted in a dream of a retreat. Fiore de Henriquez has her home and studio in one of the buildings - the others now house the few lucky guests who find their way to this secluded paradise. This hotel is definitely not for everyone. Those who like a slick hotel with the assurance that everything will always work perfectly had best find other accommodation. There are no promises here that there will never be a shortage of water or problems with the electrical power. But this is a small price to pay for those of you who love to walk through groves of chestnut trees, pick wildflowers along secluded paths, read a favorite book while soaking in the sunshine or, best yet, do absolutely nothing at all except enjoy the breathtaking view out over the valley to the sea. There is no planned activity at the hotel except for the camaraderie of fellow guests. However, if you want to do a little sightseeing, the Peralta is well located. Florence is only about 90 minutes away, Lucca (one of my favorite of Italy's walled cities) is about a half an hour's drive, Carrara (where Michelangelo came to hand-pick marble for his masterpieces) just a short excursion to the north and the seaside town of Viareggio close by. Although the concept of the Peralta is rustic, it far surpassed what I had expected. Although the rooms are simple, there is an elegance to their simplicity. Obviously the talents of Fiore de Henriquez were called upon in the design and decor - each room abounds with rustic charm, with extensive use of handmade tiles, what appear to be hand-loomed fabrics and attractive wooden beds and chests. Especially appealing is the tiny lounge where comfy sofas are grouped around a cozy fireplace. You will also be delighted to discover, tucked high on a tiny plateau above the hotel, a delightful pool with a terrace where guests can enjoy a splendid view to the sea.

Many of the guests are British - probably because all the space at the hotel is controlled by a travel agency in London. Most of the staff are also from Britain, and, I might add, those I met were exceptionally friendly and fun. The restaurant is closed on Thursdays so, except for breakfast, guests need to drive to one of the nearby towns for meals. Since it is also the staff's day off on Thursday, there are no arrivals scheduled for that day. Whatever day you do arrive, be sure you have a reservation. The hotel is really secluded and you will certainly not want to take a long drive only to discover the hotel is full - which it usually is. When you make your reservation, you will receive a map with directions on how to get to the Peralta. However, should you be arriving prior to receiving a map, this will help: drive to Camaiore (just north of Lucca) then watch for a sign to Pieve di Camaiore. You will wind up in the trees where occasionally you will spot, if you look carefully, a few handwritten signs to the Peralta, giving encouragement that you are not lost. Don't give up. Just keep driving as the road twists and becomes narrow and steep and then ends... at which point you park your car and continue on foot for the last quarter mile. (Leave you luggage in the car and someone will retrieve it for you later). I assure you the journey is worthwhile.

PERALTA
Manager: Philip Harrison Stanton
Pieve Di Camaiore, Lucca, Italy
Tel: (0584) 951230
14 Rooms - Double Lire 83,000
Open: Easter to October
Credit cards: None accepted
Res: Harrison Stanton & Haslam Ltd
25 Studdridge St, London SW6 3SL
Tel: London (01) 736-5094
No children under 16
Swimming pool
Located 35 km NE of Pisa

If you are looking for a budget hotel to use as a base for exploring the hill towns of Tuscany you can do no better than to stay at the Pensione Salivolpi. Although the address is Castellina in Chianti (in the heart of the famous Chianti wine region), you will actually find the hotel on the outskirts of town, on the left-hand side of the road leading from Castellina to the small town of Sant Donato. The old, weathered stone farmhouse sits almost on the road. It is only when you pull into the parking area that the lovely position of the inn is revealed - behind the main building there is a beautiful view terrace featuring a lovely large swimming pool. What a surprise to find such a wonderful addition to an inexpensive accommodation. The bedrooms are pleasant, reflecting the nice taste of the Salivolpi family who personally oversee the operation of their small hotel and will assist you with ideas for sightseeing excursions while exploring Tuscany. With Florence only 30 minutes north and Siena 15 minutes to the south, the Pensione Salivolpi provides a simple, but very pleasant, base of operation.

PENSIONE SALIVOLPI
Owner: Etrusca Salivolpi
Via Fiorentina - Loc. Salivolpi
53011 Castellina in Chianti, Italy
Tel: (0577) 740 484
19 Rooms - Double Lire 55,000
Open: All year
Credit cards: None accepted
No restaurant
Swimming pool
Located 20 km N of Siena

The Anna Maria is located in Champoluc which is a small town almost at the end of the beautiful Ayas Valley which stretches north into the Alps almost to the Swiss border in northwest Italy. As you drive through the town of Champoluc you will see a small sign for the Anna Maria on the right side of the road just before you leave town. Turn right on this little lane which winds up the hill and you will see the Anna Maria on your right set in a serene pine grove. The Anna Maria is not a luxury hotel, but rather an old mountain chalet which is now a simple, but very charming, inn. There is a large deck for sunning which stretches across the entrance. Inside there is a lovely dining room - my favorite room - which exudes warmth and coziness with its wooden Alpine-style country chairs, wooden tables, and gay red checked curtains at the windows. Upstairs the bedrooms are not luxurious but most inviting, with wooden paneling on the walls and a rustic ambiance, and best of all - every bedroom has a private bathroom. Perhaps the most winning feature is Anna Maria, the owner, who is your hostess and oversees her little inn with a gracious charm. The atmosphere is "homey" - not for the fussy but wonderful for those who love the friendliness of a country inn in a mountain village.

ANNA MARIA
Owner: Anna Maria
11020 Champoluc, Italy
Tel: (0125) 307 128
25 Rooms - Double Lire 75,000-107,000
Excellent value
Open: Jul through Aug & Dec through mid-Apr
Chalet style - lovely setting
Mountain location - NW Italy
Located 175 km NW of Milan

I was puzzled to receive a hotel questionnaire response postmarked St Simon's Island, Georgia. But quickly all was explained. It was from James Adams who had been living in Europe, perfecting his Italian cooking skills at one of the finest restaurant-hotels in Italy, the Locanda del Sant'Uffizio - Ristorante da Beppe. The owner, Giuseppe Firato ("Beppe"), speaks no English so when our request for information arrived, he asked his American protege to respond. After visiting the hotel, I can only say that it was more perfect than anticipated. Below is Jamie's wonderful letter describing so superbly his "home away from home".

"Originally in the 1500s the Locanda del Sant'Uffizio was a Benedictine monastery and served as such up until the mid 1800s after which time it passed into private hands serving as a farm. In 1972, Signore Giuseppe Firato (Beppe), a man from the village, bought the farm and slowly began converting it into its present form. Naturally at first there were only several rooms while the rest of the buildings were used for farming and wine growing. Through the years rooms have been added very carefully, with great respect for the traditional aesthetics, and now there are 35 guestrooms. All furnishings are antique and every detail of the decor has been rigorously overseen personally by Signore Beppe and his wife, Carla, with the result being a very tasteful, elegant, yet relaxed hotel cozily nestled amongst the vineyards in the hills of Monferrato. Other features include a tennis court, a swimming pool (in front of which one can have breakfast and lunch in the warm months) and, last but not least, there is the Ristorante da Beppe, an exquisite restaurant serving the finest of Piemontese cuisine. It is of course owned and operated by the Firato family, and, in fact, the restaurant preceded the hotel. It has earned one Michelin star and has been rated highly in notable Italian guides such as Espresso and Veronelli. When one combines the charm and relaxation of this elegant hotel with the pleasures of such a refined table, one is left with a very memorable experience."

I cannot resist adding a few more words - there are so many features that make the Locanda del Sant'Uffizio very special. Without a doubt, the Firato family is responsible for the ambiance of warmth and hospitality which radiates throughout the hotel. Signore Beppe was born in the tiny village (population 50) where the hotel is located. When his father who owned a small bar died, Signore Beppe took over - although he was only a boy at the time. The rest is history: the bar grew into a restaurant, the restaurant into a tiny hotel, the small hotel into a delightful resort. Such a success story is not surprising when you meet Signore Beppe. He speaks no English. He does not need to. His charismatic charm transcends all language barriers. It is no wonder his restaurant - isolated in the countryside - is filled each night with chicly dressed Italian clientele: Beppe greets each of them with an exuberant warmth, and the food is outstanding, truly a gourmet delight. Also, excellent wines are served, most of which are produced from grapes grown on the property and matured in large oak vats in the winery adjacent to the hotel. The price of the dinner is expensive (but for a six course meal with wines included - a bargain). You will not find the town of Cioccaro di Penango on your map so pinpoint instead the town of Moncalvo - the hotel is 5 kilometers south. Note: This hotel is definitely not cheap, but one of the best values we found in Italy. Comparable hotels in resort areas would cost twice as much - and not be so special.

LOCANDA DEL SANT'UFFIZIO
RISTORANTE DA BEPPE
Owner: Giuseppe Firato
14030 Cioccaro di Penango, Italy
Tel: (041) 91 271
35 Rooms - Double Lire 125,000
Closed: January and August 10 to 20
Credit cards: All major
Swimming pool, tennis
Located 90 km E of Turin, N of Asti

On our last research trip to Italy we stayed at the Loggiato dei Serviti in Florence. What a refreshingly pleasant experience. Many of the hotels in Florence are lovely, but fabulously expensive: others are reasonably priced but shabby and dark. So it was an exceedingly happy surprise to find a light, airy, antique-filled small hotel - at an extremely reasonable rate. The Loggiato dei Serviti has only recently opened, so perhaps that is why the prices are so excellent for the value received - there are plans to add another 11 rooms soon, and also to add more amenities such as direct dial phones, piped music, hair dryers, TVs and mini-bars. I am afraid that the prices might mushroom with the improvements - I hope not. In the meantime, although this is not a deluxe hotel, I think you will be very pleased. There is a small reception area as you enter, beyond which is an intimate little bar where snacks are served (there is no restaurant at the hotel). A miniature elevator - just large enough for two people to squeeze into - takes you upstairs to the spacious bedrooms, each with private bath and each decorated individually with antiques. If friends or family are travelling, there are two suites, one of which even has two bedrooms and two bathrooms. Again, these suites are excellent values - and most attractive.

LOGGIATO DEI SERVITI
Owner: Budini Tattai sons
Piazza S.S. Annunziata, 3
50122 Florence, Italy
Tel: (055) 263592 or 219165
19 Rooms - Double Lire 130,500
Open: All year
Credit cards: All major
Antique-filled small hotel
Located in the heart of Florence

The Bencista is a gem. A real "find" for the traveller who wants a congenial, appealing, family run hotel near Florence which has charm and yet is reasonably priced. This delightful old villa, romantically nestled in the foothills overlooking Florence, is owned and managed by the Simoni family who are always about, personally seeing to every need of their guests. Simone Simoni speaks excellent English, and on the day of my arrival he was patiently engrossed in conversation with one of the guests, giving him tips for sightseeing. Downstairs there are a jumble of rooms, each nicely decorated with rather dark, Victorian furniture. Upstairs are the bedrooms which vary in size, location, and furnishings. Some are far superior to others; however, they are all divided into only two price categories: with or without private bathroom. Many people return year after year to "their own" favorite room. During the season, reservations are usually given only to guests who plan to spend several days at the hotel - this is an easy requirement because the hotel is beautifully located for sightseeing in both Florence and Tuscany. (If you do not have a car, there is a bus at the top of the road which runs regularly into Florence.) Two meals (breakfast and lunch or dinner) are included in the price and there is an excellent kitchen serving simple, good Italian cooking. One of the outstanding features of the pensione is its view - there is a splendid terrace where guests can enjoy a sweeping panorama of Florence.

PENSION BENCISTA
Owner: Simone Simoni
50014 Fiesole (Florence), Italy
Tel: (055) 59 163
*35 Rooms - Double Lire 140,000 **
** Rate includes 2 meals*
Credit cards: None accepted
Lovely old villa - overlooking Florence
Located 8 km NE of Florence

When we first saw the Pensione Giulia it was rated by the government as a third class pensione. However, the hotel is no longer a simple pensione. On our last visit we were pleased to note that all the rooms now have a private bathroom and even a swimming pool has been built into the garden. The inn is a superb old Victorian-style villa in a large park which extends down to Lake Garda. A dramatic staircase at the end of the hallway leads to the simple bedrooms. In addition to the rooms in the main villa, guest rooms are available in a modern annex. On the same level as the entrance hall is a dining room which is quite appealing with enormous chandeliers and antique-style chairs. On a lower level, opening out onto the garden, is another dining room which is quite modern and lacking in charm. When the weather is warm, the favorite place to dine is on the terrace where tables are set to enjoy the sun and a view of the lake. Wherever you choose to dine, you will enjoy good home-style Italian cooking - it is not surprising that the food is well prepared since Signora Bombardelli, the owner, is usually bustling about in the kitchen personally overseeing the preparation of the next meal. She does not speak much English, but is extremely gracious and is always about seeing that her guests are happy. Not fancy, the Pensione Giulia offers a very pleasant stay at reasonable prices with a superb lakefront location.

PENSIONE GIULIA
Owner: Bombardelli family
25084 Gargnano, Lake Garda, Italy
Tel: (0365) 71022
16 Rooms - Double Lire 82,000-87,000
Open: April to October
Credit cards: MC
Swimming pool - all rooms now with private bath
On the western shore of Lake Garda
Located 141 km E of Milan

If you love picturesque chalet-style hotels in quiet, isolated surroundings, then the Hotel Vigiljoch will definitely be your cup of tea. There is absolutely no highway noise: there are no cars. The only way to reach the hotel is by cable car which you take from the town of Lana which is near Merano in the mountains of northeastern Italy. The cable car rises quickly from the floor of the valley and has a breathtaking view of the vineyards and apple orchards. When the cable car reaches the tip and slowly joggles into the terminal you will see the Hotel Vigiljoch just to the left of the station. In summer, flowers will be bursting from every window and umbrellas will be gaily decorating the front terrace. Inside you will find quite simple bedrooms, but many of which have balconies with a sweeping view of valley and mountain. The bedrooms are small but pleasantly furnished with furniture painted in an Alpine motif. A sprinkling of antiques highlights the lounges. My very favorite room is an intimate, wood-paneled dining room whose wonderful country prints of blue and red mingle with delightful, light wooden furniture.

HOTEL VIGILJOCH
1-39011 Vigiljoch
Lana bei Merano, Italy
Tel: (0473) 512 36
41 Rooms - Double Lire 80,000
Open: Jun to Oct and Dec 20 to Apr 20
Credit cards: None accepted
Pool, mountaintop setting
Accessible only by cable car
Near Merano in Northern Italy
Located 24 km W of Bolzano

The Antica Locanda Solferino, once an old tavern, is an excellent choice if you are looking for a simple, small hotel that is moderately priced. Here you will receive great value, for this is a very pleasant, tiny hotel charging rates that are most reasonable in the very expensive city of Milan. The location is good too - on a tiny street near the Piazza della Republica, within walking distance of most of Milan's attractions. The hotel's main claim to fame is its restaurant of the same name which serves delicious food in a delightful, cozy dining room. (Even if you do not stay at the hotel, you might want to stop by for a meal.) A small desk in the lobby serves both the dinner clientele and also the hotel guests. From the reception area stairs lead to the upper level where 11 rooms are tucked away. Each room, although small, reflects excellent taste. The room I saw had a wonderful antique wooden bed and was appealingly furnished in an olde worlde style. Because all of the rooms were occupied, I was able to see only one room, but the manager told me that although all are individually decorated, they are very similar in ambiance. On my last visit to Milan I had hoped to stay at the Antica Locanda Solferino, but, although I called several months prior to my arrival, the hotel was fully occupied. This was actually no surprise since the hotel is very popular. But be forewarned: if you want accommodation, plan far in advance.

ANTICA LOCANDA SOLFERINO
Manager: Curzio Castelli
Via Castelfidardo, 2
20121 Milan, Italy
Tel: (02) 659 9886
11 Rooms - Double Lire 112,600
Open: All year
Credit cards: None accepted
Located near center of Milan

The Castello di Gargonza is not a traditional hotel at all, but rather a romantic walled, storybook village, surrounded by forests and perched at the crest of a hill. The 900-year-old complex of stone buildings now receives guests. Nineteen of the picturesque farmhouses are available by the week. Most have one or two bedrooms plus a kitchenette and many also have a fireplace - perfect for chilly evenings. Each small cottage is named and when you make a reservation, the hotel will send you a map of the town and a description and a sketch of each of the houses so that you can choose what most appeals to your needs. In addition to the "housekeeping" houses, there are also seven regular guestrooms. The village oozes with charm: staying here is like stepping back to medieval times. However, the decor leaves something to be desired, with an extensive use of plastic furniture interspersed with more traditional pieces. However, the overall ambiance is terrific and the hotel is a fabulous bargain, especially for two couples travelling together or families with children who want a homebase for exploring Tuscany. Note: Although the address is the town of Monte San Savino, the hotel is actually located about 8 kilometers west, on road 73 to Siena.

CASTELLO DI GARGONZA
Owner: Count Roberto Guicciardini
Azienda Castello di Gargonza
52048 Monte San Savino Arezzo, Italy
Tel: (0575) 847021 Telex: 571466 Redco I
*7 Rooms - Double Lire 135,000 **
** 3 night minimum*
19 Houses - from Lire 650,000 weekly
Open: Easter through December
Credit Cards: AX
Walled hilltop castle
Located 35 km E of Siena

Lo Spedalicchio is an old medieval fortress which has been restored and brought back to its original role of sheltering travellers. It is located only about a 10-minute drive from Assisi, in the center of Ospedalicchio di Bastia. The town itself holds no charm, but the hotel is attractive and shows taste throughout in its decor. There is convenient parking in front of the hotel from which it is only a few steps into a very large reception area. A lounge opens off to the left with sofas and chairs upholstered in a deep-blue fabric which contrasts nicely with the old stone walls and the high vaulted ceilings. The dining room is spacious with many tables and moderns chairs, giving the impression that the hotel perhaps is used for groups or large functions. Upstairs the bedrooms are quite attractive - all reflecting the mood of the old castle with tiled floors, heavy off-white drapes hanging from wooden rods, antique (or reproduction of antique) furniture, and bedspreads which appear to be made from hand-loomed fabric. The castle is just off the main highway between Florence and Assisi so is conveniently located for an overnight stop.

LO SPEDALICCHIO
Manager: Mrs Giancarla Costarelli
Piazza Bruno Buozzi, 3
06080 Ospedalicchio di Bastia, Italy
Tel: (075) 809323
25 Rooms - Double Lire 80,000
Open: All year
Credit Cards: VS DC AX
Ten-minute drive from Assisi
14th-century castle
Located 170 km N of Rome

Our first introduction to La Scuderia was one idyllic evening when we sat outside in the garden with friends enjoying an absolutely simple, yet superb dinner. Perhaps the magic was the balmy air, the delicate wine or just the delicious homecooked meal - but it was truly a memorable event. The little restaurant is owned and operated by Stella Casolato and her beautiful daughter, Monica. Stella stays busy in the kitchen while Monica serves the tables with a gracious, gentle efficiency. It was not until I revisited the restaurant the following day that I realized that a few rooms are also available. I had expected to find spotlessly clean, nice rooms - but what a surprise to discover that, although extremely reasonable, the rooms are charming with accents of antiques. There are only three guestrooms which share a very large, beautifully kept bathroom down the hall. In addition there is a suite with its own private bath - a wonderful bargain for families or friends travelling together. Although this is a simple inn, it is extremely appealing and the warmth of Stella and Monica should make this a wonderful choice for those looking for an inexpensive base for exploring the Chianti wine region.

LA SCUDERIA
Owner: Stella & Monica Casolato
Badia a Passignagno
50020 Sambuca Val di Pesa, Italy
Tel: (055) 807 1623
3 rooms sharing one bathroom - Lire 45,000
1 suite with private bath - Lire 350,000 week
Open: All year
Restaurant closed Wednesdays
Credit cards: None accepted
Beautiful little restaurant with rooms
Located 32 km S of Florence

How smug I felt at "discovering" the Castel Pergine, for here is a picturebook castle perfect for the budget minded tourist. No need to forfeit romance and glamor for even though the Castel Pergine is inexpensive, it has a fabulous location dominating a hilltop above the town of Pergine. Luckily, this castle has been delightfully transformed into a small hotel with incredible views out over the valleys and wooded hills. From the tower you can even see two small lakes in the distance inviting a picnic. The Castel Pergine is far more famous as a restaurant than a hotel (Michelin gives the kitchen a two fork rating.) The dining room has a wonderful medieval decor, gorgeous views, and delicious food. There are, however, a few simple bedrooms. The ones I saw were somewhat camp-like with basic beds, a wash basin, and a chest of drawers. None of the rooms had private bathrooms, although there are, of course, facilities on each floor. But for the price conscious the total ambiance of this castle in the sky is worthy of any budget itinerary - especially if you are with children who will love their personal Disneyland-like castle.

CASTEL PERGINE
Owner: Fontanari family
38057 Pergine, Italy
Tel: (461) 531 158
12 Rooms - Double Lire 60,000-80,000
Open: May through October
Ancient castle - lovely views
Excellent for children
Hilltop castle - 2.5 km E of Pergine
Located 152 km NW of Venice

I am such a romantic that, as the boat chugged across the lake from Stresa to the medieval fishing village of Isola dei Pescatori and I saw the Hotel Verbano with its reddish-brown walls, dark green shutters, and tables set on the terrace overlooking the lake, my heart was won - completely. The lobby is a bit shabby with its rather lumpy and worn furniture; however, the room then opens onto a very nice dining room whose arched windows overlook Lake Maggiore. A second dining area is set up on the terrace with romantic views of the lake. Upstairs the twelve bedrooms vary considerably. One I saw was quite drab but another was very charming with hand painted furniture. The views from some of the bedrooms are very nice. The Hotel Verbano has a marvelous restaurant. When we first visited, the same cook had been creating meals for 28 years. Unfortunately, she is now gone, but the owners wrote that they still have an excellent kitchen featuring wonderful home-style Italian cuisine and freshly caught fish from the lake. This is not a hotel for those who want everything "perfect", but for those who love a romantic setting at a reasonable price, this special small hotel has great appeal.

HOTEL VERBANO
Owner: Zacchera family
28049 Isola dei Pescatori, Stresa
Borromee Isole, Lake Maggiore, Italy
Tel: (0323) 30408 Telex: 200269
12 Rooms - Double Lire 96,000
Open: mid-April through October
Credit cards: VS AX DC
Lovely lakefront restaurant
Island in Lake Maggiore
Located 80 km NW of Milan

Many years ago I stayed at the Piccolo Hotel - and liked it very much even though it is quite basic and on the busy road that leads into town. On my last trip to Italy I revisited the Piccolo and decided to include it in this book because hotel prices are astronomic in Portofino and it is the best choice for anyone who wants to stay here without spending a fortune. The Piccolo sits just above the road, on the right-hand side, as you drive into the village. The appearance is of a small villa, which indeed I am sure it used to be. The reception area used to be the entrance hall beyond which is a lounge area and then the dining room. Stretching across the front is a balcony where tables are set for snacks and lounging, a favorite spot for guests, especially on warm days. Downstairs there are accents of antiques which give a homey ambiance to an otherwise modern feel. The bedrooms are upstairs and are basic in decor although some have French doors opening out to pretty little wrought iron balconies. A flight of steps up from the hotel leads to a pleasant path which winds through the trees to the center of Portofino, surely one of the most colorful fishing villages in Italy.

PICCOLO HOTEL
Owner: Bezzi family
Via Duca degli Abruzzi, 31
16034 Portofino, Italy
Tel: (185) 69015
26 Rooms - Double Lire 100,000-114,000
Open: March through November
Credit cards: None accepted
Located 22 km E of Genoa

The Pensione Villa Maria is perhaps best known for its absolutely delightful terrace restaurant which has a bird's eye view of the magnificent coast. Whereas most of the hotels capture the southern view, the Villa Maria features the equally lovely vista to the north. Although it is a tiny inn, the Pensione Villa Maria is easy to find because it is on the same path which winds its way from the main square to the Villa Cimbrone. After parking your car in the main square of Ravello, look for the signs toward the Villa Cimbrone. If you follow the signs along a path through the village you will find, after about a five-minute walk, the Pensione Villa Maria to the right of the path, perched on the cliffs. The building itself is a romantic old villa with a garden stretching to the side where tables and chairs are set - a favorite place to dine while enjoying the superb view. Inside, there is a cozy dining room and upstairs bedrooms which, although simple, all have a private bathroom. The hotel is owned by the gracious Vincenzo and Carla Palumbo who speak excellent English should you call for a reservation. (They also own the more modern, but very pleasant, Hotel Giordano in Ravello.) How lucky to be able to have the best of all worlds should you be on a budget - a wonderful view, location, plus a charming villa.

PENSIONE VILLA MARIA
Owner: Carla & Vincenzo Palumbo
Sulla Strada per Villa Cimbrone
84010 Ravello, Italy
Tel: (089) 857 170 or 857 255
7 Rooms - Double Lire 70,000-82,000
Wonderful view garden terrace
Hilltop town above Amalfi coast
Located 66 km S of Naples

For those of you who love the enchantment of roaming the lakes by boat and getting the first glimpse of your hotel as the boat glides into port, the Hotel Sole is definitely for you. The Hotel Sole is located on the northern end of Lake Garda in the ancient port of Riva del Garda. Although the city of Riva has mushroomed to accommodate the influx of tourists, the old section which surrounds the harbor has retained a great deal of medieval charm with colorful old buildings, towers, etc. The hotel is located next to the pier where the ferries dock. At the rear of the hotel an excellent outdoor terrace looks out over the lake and all its activity. The hotel is extremely simple, but there is a very lovely atmosphere to the hotel and the location is perfect for those who want to stay in the medieval town of Riva and explore Lake Garda by boat. Its terraces are set with umbrella-canopied tables where one can dine or just enjoy a hot cup of coffee. Who cares if the interior is not a decorator's dream? You will love sitting all day, watching the show as boats of all shapes, sizes, and colors move in and out of this tiny harbor.

HOTEL SOLE
Owner: Antonio Zampiccoli
Manager: Aldo Calderan
38066 Riva del Garda, Italy
Tel: (0464) 55 26 86
25 Rooms - Double Lire 75,000-104,000
Open: April 11 to October
Credit cards: All major
Next to the ferry landing
N shore of Lake Garda
Located 170 km E of Milan

The Hotel Condotti is located on a tranquil side street near the bottom of the famous Spanish Steps in Rome. One has the feeling of being in a quiet refuge, away from the hustle and bustle - yet just a block away the neighborhood is a fascinating melange of luxurious shops, restaurants and artists' workshops. The Hotel Condotti's interior is pretty and fresh, cleverly furnished with a tasteful mixture of old and new. The lobby features contemporary overstuffed couches topped with colorful pillows, and antique accent pieces such as the inlaid wood reception desk. A tray with an aperitif selection sits temptingly near the sitting area on a beautiful old escritoire. This is an intimate city hotel, offering a small number of rooms and personalized service from a staff that is very helpful and speaks very good English. All the bedrooms are charmingly decorated with white wooden furniture complemented by attractive, vividly colored curtains, bedspreads and upholstery. A minority of the bedrooms contain bath or shower, thus it is wise to reserve well in advance to receive the desired type of accommodation. A Continental breakfast is the only meal offered at the Condotti, and it is served in the cheerful breakfast room where bright yellow tablecloths, freshly painted white walls, and original oil paintings create a sunny atmosphere that is a pleasure to wake up to.

HOTEL CONDOTTI
Owner: Ottaviani Hotels
Via Mario de'Fiori, 37
00187 Rome, Italy
Tel: (06) 6794661 Telex: 611217
20 Rooms - Double Lire 146,000
Open: All year
Credit cards: All major
Located near the bottom of the Spanish Steps

The very dapper concierge of the Hotel Sistina greeted us in his morning suit of grey striped pants, pearl grey vest, striped tie and black tailcoat. We found him to be an extremely accommodating fellow, as indeed is the entire staff at the charming Hotel Sistina. One enters into a tasteful lobby area decorated with greenery in two very large urns, a maroon and gold carpet, and a mix of antique and reproduction furniture. A very pleasant sitting room adjoins the lobby and guests are invited to relax here at their leisure. Here comfy couches in colorful floral prints and pretty oil paintings in gilt frames are lit by the soft Venetian glass lamps, and it is a tempting spot to linger. A new breakfast room was not yet completed at the time of our visit, but it is sure to be as fresh and bright as the rest of the Sistina. In warm weather guests may also enjoy breakfast on the pretty upstairs terrace at umbrella-shaded tables. Bedrooms, all with modern private baths, are spotless and comfortable although the decor (featuring white walls and contemporary white furniture) is not inspired. However, some of the rooms are more appealing with very pretty fabrics used for curtains, coverlets and upholstery. The Hotel Sistina is located on a relatively busy street, and some of the front rooms may suffer from traffic noise; however, the location is very convenient for sightseers and businessmen alike, near the top of the Spanish Steps.

HOTEL SISTINA
Owner: Ottaviani Hotels
Via Sistina, 136
00187 Rome, Italy
Tel: (06) 475 8804 Telex: 611217
27 Rooms - Double Lire 147,000
Open: All year
Credit cards: All major
Located near the top of the Spanish Steps

The gracious Hotel Siviglia enjoys a quiet location three blocks from the central railroad station and across the street from the Russian Embassy in Rome. In fact, we felt very secure during our stay here, as an armed Italian guard surveys this embassy 24 hours a day. Built in 1880 as a private residence, the stately, mustard colored facade, pretty lobby and friendly staff provide a warm welcome. Venetian glass chandeliers, gilt mirrors and oil paintings dress the lobby and reception areas where armchairs offer a comfortable spot to wait, or simply to recuperate after a day's sightseeing. Coffees or cocktails can be ordered from the tiny, wood paneled bar area which is part of the main lobby. On a warm Roman evening, it is a treat to enjoy an aperitif at a table in the adjoining outdoor courtyard filled with flowering plants and statuary. An elevator or small, sweeping staircase lead to the upstairs rooms, all of which have private bath or shower. Our room was spacious and lovely with old inlaid wood furniture and a delicate Venetian glass chandelier. Not all the rooms have antiques, but all are tasteful and comfortable with spotless housekeeping evident throughout. Tall old windows in many of the rooms open onto the central courtyard, while others give views over the rooftops of Rome.

HOTEL SIVIGLIA
Owner: Signora Mongelli Grazia
Via Gaeta, 12
00185 Rome
Italy
Tel: (06) 404 1195 Telex: 612225
41 Rooms - Double Lire 110,000
Open: All year
Credit cards: AX VS DC
Garden courtyard, bar, elevator
Located about 3 blocks N of the railroad station

San Gimignano is one of the most fascinating of the medieval Tuscany hill towns. Most tourists come just for the day to visit this small town. As you approach, this looks like a city of skyscrapers: come even closer and the "skyscrapers" emerge as 14 soaring towers - dramatic reminders of what San Gimignano must have looked like in all her glory when this wealthy town sported 72 giant towers. If you are lucky enough to be able to spend the night, San Gimignano has a simple but very charming hotel, La Cisterna. The hotel is located on the main square of town and it fits right into the ancient character of the square with its somber stone walls softened by ivy, arched shuttered doors, and red tiled roof. Inside the medieval feeling continues with lots of stone, vaulted ceilings, leather chairs, and dark woods. The bedrooms are not fancy, but pleasant, and some have balconies with lovely views of the valley. La Cisterna is probably more famous as a restaurant than as a hotel. People come from miles around because not only is the food delicious, but the dining rooms are delightful. Especially charming is the dining room with the brick wall, sloping ceiling supported by giant beams, and picture windows framing the gorgeous Tuscany hills.

LA CISTERNA
Piazza della Cisterna
53037 San Gimignano, Italy
Tel: (577) 940 328
46 Rooms - Double Lire 58,000 - 87,000
Credit cards: All major
Excellent restaurant
Hilltown famous for its towers
Located 54 km SW of Florence

The Castel San Gregorio is a sensational, small 12th-century stone castle just a short drive from Assisi, reached after following a winding road through a forest which emerges at the top of a hill to a truly romantic, secluded hideaway. There is a terrace to the side where tables and chairs are strategically placed to capture a splendid view of the valley far below. The castle, dating from 1140, has been meticulously reconstructed preserving its original appearance without, and maintaining a castle-like ambiance within. The hotel is quite dark due both to the character of the building and coverings on many of the walls. The olde worlde ambiance is further enhanced by the bountiful use of excellent antiques. The reception desk is in the front lobby: to the left as you enter is an ornate living room; to the right is a dining room where one large table is set each night for the guests to eat together "family style". A restaurant is located on a lower level, open to the general public, where elegant dining is offered in a beautifully decorated room. The bedrooms I saw, although somewhat dark, were all quite outstandingly decorated with a collection of fine antiques. Surrounding the hotel are many walking paths leading through the quiet wooded hills. You will probably not be able to find San Gregorio on any of your maps - the best bet is to find the tiny town of Pianello - San Gregorio is only a few kilometers to the south.

CASTEL SAN GREGORIO
Owner: Bianchi Claudio
Via San Gregorio, 16
06081 San Gregorio, Italy
Tel: (075) 803 80 09
12 Rooms - Double Lire 81,000
Closed: January
Credit cards: AX DC
Wonderful hilltop castle
Located 16 km NW of Assisi

The Residence San Sano is a small hotel which recently opened in San Sano - a hamlet in the center of the Chianti wine-growing region. Although the finishing touches had not all been completed when we visited, we were charmed by the hotel which is incorporated into a 16th-century stone building. The gracious young owners, Giancarlo Matarazzo and his German wife, Heidi, were both school teachers in Germany prior to returning to Italy to open a small hotel. They have done a beautiful job in the renovation and in the decor. A cozy dining room serves guests excellent meals - featuring typically Tuscan-style cooking. Each of 11 bedrooms is delightfully furnished in antiques and each has a name incorporating some unique feature of the hotel - the name evolving from the time during reconstruction when Heidi and Giancarlo remembered each room by its special feature. My favorite room was the "Bird Room": here birds had claimed the room for many years and had nested in holes which went completely through the wall. With great imagination, the holes were left open to the outside, but on the inside were covered with glass. Now the birds can still nest while guests have the fun of watching the babies. Another room is named for a beautiful, long-hidden Romanesque window which was discovered and incorporated into the decor, another room is named for its very special view, another for an antique urn uncovered - each room displaying great imagination.

HOTEL RESIDENCE SAN SANO
Owner: Heidi & Giancarlo Matarazzo
Loc. San Sano
53010 Lecchi in Chianti, Italy
Tel: (0577) 746 130
11 Rooms - Double Lire 100,000 - 115,000
Open: All year
Credit cards: None accepted
Building dates from the 16th century

I know frustratingly little about the Locanda San Vigilio, yet I can hardly wait to return. The day I visited, the owner was away and the man at the front desk insisted that he had strict instructions that no one was to see the hotel. The need for privacy is apparent because its sensational parklike grounds are open to the public and, without protection, the quiet of this small hotel would be invaded by curious tourists. However, my heart was won completely by the charming dining room, elegantly decorated with country antiques and superbly positioned with large windows overlooking the lake. I cannot tell you anything about the seven bedrooms until I pay another visit to the hotel (hopefully the next time with confirmed reservations). The hotel is part of a gorgeous estate situated on a small peninsula which juts into Lake Garda. You can glimpse the magnificent, private family villa from the path which leads through towering cypress trees to a tiny yacht harbor, next to which is a wonderful, old, two-story building with a red tiled roof and rows of large arched windows capturing views of the lake. I am not sure what the original use this annex served, but now it houses the small hotel, Locanda San Vigilio. I received a letter from the owner which closed with "Our hotel is one of the most beautiful places in Europe, one of the best places for relaxing" - I can certainly believe it.

LOCANDA SAN VIGILIO
Manager: Agostino Guarlenti
37016 San Vigilio, Garda, Italy
Tel: (045) 7255 089 Telex: 481874
7 Rooms - Double Lire 107,000
Open: Easter to October
Credit Cards: AX
Not suitable for children
16th-century lakefront hotel
154 km W of Venice, 3 km N of Garda

Having heard about à lovely little chalet tucked amidst the pines high in the mountains near the French border, I was beginning to wonder what awaited me as the road wound through the ski town of Sauze d'Oulx with its unattractive jumble of modern concrete ski hotels. However, the road soon left the resort town and continued twisting higher and higher into the mountains until suddenly Il Capricorno came into view nestled in the forest to the left of the road. Just as you enter there is a tiny bar, and, beyond, a cozy dining room enhanced by dark wooden chalet-style chairs, rustic wooden tables, and a stone fireplace whose wood is stacked neatly by its side. There is not a hint of elaborate elegance - just a simple cozy country charm. The perfect kind of inn to come "home" to after a day of skiing or walking the beautiful mountain trails. The bedrooms, too, are simple but most pleasant with dark pine handmade furniture, neat little bathrooms, and, for a lucky few, balconies with splendid mountain views. However, the greatest assets of this tiny inn are the owners, Mariarosa and Carlo Sacchi. Carlo personally made most of the furniture and will frequently join the guests for skiing. Mariarosa is the chef, and a fabulous, gourmet cook. This is a very special little hideaway for very special people.

IL CAPRICORNO
Owner: Mariarosa & Carlo Sacchi
10050 Sauze d'Oulx, Italy
Tel: (122) 852 73
8 Rooms - Double Lire 107,000
Open: Jul to Sep 15 and Dec to May
Credit cards: None accepted
Tiny inn - very personalized
Mountain setting near France
Located 218 km SW of Milan

Although the Berghotel Tirol is a new hotel, it happily copies the typical chalet style of the Dolomites. Inside, too, the tasteful decor follows the delightful Alpine motif with light pine furniture, baskets of flowers, and a few antiques for accent pieces. However, what is so very special about the Berghotel Tirol is its marvelous location on a hillside looking over the lovely village of Sexten and to the fabulous mountains beyond. Many of the rooms have large balconies which capture the view and the warmth of the mountain sun. The Berghotel Tirol is not actually in the town of Sexten (sometimes called Sesto on the maps), but in a suburb called Moos. This is one of the most scenic areas of the Dolomites and the town of Sexten one of the most attractive of the mountain towns. In addition to the natural beauty, there is a wonderful network of trails leading in every direction to tempt all into the crisp mountain air. When you return at night to the hotel it is rather like a house party. Most of the guests come for at least a week and table hopping is prevalent as the knicker-clad guests share their day's adventures. Acting as hosts to the "house party" are the extremely gracious, cordial owners, the Holzer family, who seem to be dedicated to seeing that everyone has a good time.

BERGHOTEL TIROL
Owner: Kurt Holzer family
39030 Sexten (Sesto), Italy
Tel: (0474) 70386
*30 Rooms - * Double Lire 84,000-118,000*
** Rate includes 2 meals*
Open: Dec 20 to Apr 26 and May 20 to Oct
Credit cards: None accepted
Beautiful mountain valley
Dolomites - near Austria
2 km SE of Sexten toward Moos
Located 44 km E of Cortina

A pensione usually means a compromise in accommodations, so what a delightful surprise the Palazzo Ravizza provides. Even though the government has categorized this hotel as a pensione it is, without a doubt, my choice of where to stay in Siena. A 17th-century mansion, the Palazzo Ravizza has belonged to the same family for nearly 200 years. There are only 28 bedrooms, which definitely vary in quality of decor and location. This is certainly one of the occasions when you will want to request the most deluxe room possible, for, although all rooms are adequate, the ones in the top category are real gems, containing some antique furnishings and possessing lovely panoramic views of the Tuscany hills. The more expensive rooms are also more tranquil since they overlook the garden rather than the street which can be noisy. The Palazzo Ravizza is only a short walk from one of the most gorgeous cathedrals in Italy. It is also only a stroll from the enormous plaza where the running of horses takes place. The furniture in the small lounge is comfortable and cozy and the dining room is charming. The total effect is one of excellent taste and marvelous value. One of the joys of Siena is wandering the intriguing little twisting streets so, although there are several deluxe villa-style hotels in the immediate vicinity, I would stay right in Siena itself since it has such a lovely small hotel.

PENSIONE PALAZZO RAVIZZA
Owner: S. Iannone
Plan dei Mantellini, 34
53100 Siena, Italy
Tel: (0577) 280 462
28 Rooms - Double Lire 91,000
Open: All year
Credit cards: None accepted
Located in heart of Siena
Located 68 km S of Florence

As soon as you cross the moat and enter the wonderful medieval village of Sirmione, look to your right. At the end of the street is a sign to the Grifone, a weathered old stone cottage with brown shutters, red-tiled roof, roses creeping up the walls, and a terrace overlooking the lake and castle. Within this quaint building are two separate operations: the simple Hotel Grifone and a small restaurant abounding with antiques and charm. The hotel portion of the house, with an entrance to the rear, has 17 bedrooms on the upper floor. In contrast to the marvelous decor of the restaurant, the hotel is quite drab. The very basic rooms show no warmth or style; however, they each have the luxury of a private bathroom. Also, although this is a budget hotel, it has a prime Sirmione location. What is more, if you are lucky enough to get one of the rooms in the front, you will have the added bonus of a little balcony overlooking one of the finest views in town. Note: we are including this small hotel although we have heard complaints that the hotel never answers letters - this is a problem since, when we call, no one ever seems to speak English. Please let us know your comments.

HOTEL GRIFONE
Owner: Luciano Maracolini
25019 Sirmione
Lake Garda, Italy
Tel: (30) 916 014
17 Rooms - Double Lire 95,000
Open: April 20 to October
Credit cards: None accepted
Excellent restaurant in building
Waterfront location on Lake Garda
Located 127 km E of Milan

The road to the Pensione Stefaner winds up a tiny mountain valley in the heart of the Dolomites. The road is gorgeous, but extremely narrow, and twists like a snake around blind curves whose roadside mirrors are a necessity, not an optional precaution. As we rounded the last curve before Tiers the valley opened up and there spread before us a sweeping vista of majestically soaring mountains. Across soft green meadows painted with wildflowers and dotted with tiny farm chalets rose an incredible saw-toothed range of gigantic peaks. Suddenly the journey seemed worth the effort for the scenery alone even if the Pensione Stefaner proved to be a disaster. Luckily, though, the Pensione Stefaner is very nice. The outside is especially attractive - a chalet with flower-laden balconies. Inside, the inn is a bit too "fussy" for my taste, but the valley is so spectacular that I am sure you will be spending most of your time on the beautiful walking trails which lace the valley. The Pensione Stefaner has some antiques scattered throughout for accents, but the furniture is new. The bedrooms are light and airy and many have balconies. Although there was no one who spoke English when I was there, friendliness prevailed. In fact, there was even a gentle, lazy German Shepherd lounging in the lobby offering a friendly welcome.

PENSIONE STEFANER
Owner: Stefaner family
39050 Tiers, Italy
Tel: (0471) 642 175
*16 Rooms - * Double Lire 64,000-80,000*
** Rate includes 2 meals*
Closed: November
New chalet-style inn
Lovely mountain setting
NE Italy in Dolomites
Located 17 km E of Bolzano

In the dramatically beautiful Dolomites of northeastern Italy there are many picturesque villages nestled in the mountains. Most are filled with attractive, but newly built, houses. There is one exception. In the tiny hamlet of Eggen is the Gasserhof Eggen, an old farmhouse (which has been converted into a restaurant) hugging the side of the main road. Although the building traces its heritage to the 12th century, the interior is plain - a most ordinary looking small restaurant. However, there is a very old, pub-like room whose walls have been blackened from the open fire which extends along one wall which you may see on request. Rafters overhead, bottle-glass windows, heavy copper pots and rustic wooden country tables and chairs complete the picture of what was at one time the core of the home. On the outside wall there are remains of very old paintings which at one time probably covered much of the buildings. Besides the restaurant, there are three rooms sharing one bath, each extremely simple although clean and suitable for travellers on a tight budget. A nice bonus is the owner's daughter, Inge Weissensteiner, a very pleasant young woman who speaks English. Note: Eggen is just a few kilometers from Obereggen (see driving instructions under the Hotel Bewallerhof on page 242).

GASSERHOF EGGEN
Owner: Weissensteiner family
39050 Eggen
Val d'Ega, Italy
Tel: (0471) 615 742
3 Rooms: Double Lire 30,000
Credit cards: None accepted
Restaurant with a few rooms
Located 23 km SE of Bolzano

The Bewallerhof is not a luxury hotel, but an exceptionally appealing small hotel tucked into a remote mountain valley. The Bewallerhof has it all: a meadow of green velvet stretching out in front to a far vista of beautiful mountains peaks, spectacular giant walls of granite forming the backdrop, wild flowers in the fields, cows munching grass in the distance, birds singing, walking trails spider-webbing out in every direction, pleasant decor, good food, and a large, sunny terrace. Even with excellent maps, the inn is extremely tricky to find. Although finding it is half the fun, I will give you a few hints. The Bewallerhof is located in the Val d'Ega (the Ega Valley) between the towns of Eggen (also called Ega) and Obereggen (also called San Floriano). If you are driving from Bolzano head southeast through the Val d'Ega for approximately 10 miles watching for the turn to the right for Obereggen. If you arrive at Nova Levante you have gone too far, so turn back and ask directions. Should you be coming from Cortina, follow the "Old Dolomite Road" west from Cortina watching carefully for the turnoff toward Nova Levante. When you reach Nova Levante it is only about 3 miles until you reach the road to the left for Obereggen. These general instructions should help you in pinpointing the town on your own detailed map.

HOTEL BEWALLERHOF
Owner: Eisath family
39050 Obereggen (San Floriano)
Val d'Ega, Italy
Tel: (0471) 615 729
*21 Rooms - * Double Lire 98,000*
** Rate includes 2 meals*
Open: Jul to Oct 15 and Dec 20 to Apr 10
Old farmhouse in fabulous setting
Surrounded by the Dolomites
Located about 25 km SE of Bolzano

The Gasthof Obereggen, located in the Val d'Ega (Ega Valley) is very simple, but quite wonderful. The inn is situated on the side of a hill overlooking a gorgeous mountain valley in one of the most beautiful mountain regions of northeastern Italy. The town of Obereggen is a ski resort and the lift is just a few minutes' walk away. From the sun-drenched deck which extends generously out from the hotel, there is an absolutely glorious vista across the green meadows to the mountains. Behind the hotel even more majestic mountains poke their jagged peaks into the sky. Inside there is a cozy dining room. Mr Pichler must be a hunter, for trophies line the walls and there is a typical tiled stove against one wall to keep the room toasty on a cold day. The inn has 12 bedrooms - those on the second floor open out onto lovely view-balconies. The greatest asset of this inn, and the real reason for its inclusion, is Mrs Pichler: she is very special - running her little inn with such a warmth and gaiety that just being in the same room with her is fun. Mrs Pichler speaks no English, but her hospitality crosses all language barriers, and her abundant and delicious "home style" cooking speaks to all who love to eat. Note: Obereggen is almost impossible to find on any map, although the Val d'Ega is usually indicated - please see general driving instructions given under the Hotel Bewallerhof (page 242).

GASTHOF OBEREGGEN
Owner: Pichler family
39050 Obereggen (San Floriano)
Val d'Ega, Italy
Tel: (0471) 615 722
*12 Rooms - * Double Lire 75,000*
** Rate includes 2 meals*
Credit cards: None accepted
Simple inn, wonderful hospitality
Located 25 km SE of Bolzano

The Stella d'Italia is located in San Mamete, a tiny, picturesque village nestled along the northern shore of Lake Lugano, just a few minutes' drive from the Swiss border. The hotel (which has been in the Ortelli family for three generations) makes an excellent choice for a moderately priced lakefront hotel. Mario Ortelli, an extremely cordial host, showed us throughout the hotel which has two adjoining wings, one quite old and the other a new addition. My choice for accommodation would be in the original part which has more olde worlde ambiance - the rooms I saw here were very pleasant with large French windows opening onto miniature balconies capturing views of the lake. The lounges and dining room have a few antique accents, but basically have a modern ambiance. The nicest feature of the hotel is the superb little lakefront garden - in summer this is where all the guests "live". Green lawn, fragrant flowers, lacy trees, and a romantic vine-covered trellised dining area make this an ideal spot for whiling away the hours. Steps lead down to a small pier from which guests can swim. The ferry dock for picking up and dropping off passengers is adjacent to the hotel. Another interesting feature for golf enthusiasts is that there are several courses within an easy drive from the hotel - one of these near the town of Grandola is one of the oldest in Italy.

STELLA D'ITALIA
Owner: Mario Ortelli
San Mamete
22020 Valsoldo
Lake Lugano, Italy
Tel: (0344) 68139 or 61703
36 Rooms - Double Lire 77,000
Open: April through September
Credit cards: All major
Lakefront hotel, swimming pier
8 km E of Lugano, 100 km N of Milan

The Pensione Accademia is enchanting - a fairytale villa with delightful gardens, romantic canal-side location, cozy antique-filled interior and professional, caring owners. The hotel has a fabulous setting on an oasis of land almost looped by canals. In front is a beautiful, completely enclosed, "secret" garden whose walls are so heavily draped with vines that it is not until you discover black iron gates that you see steps leading down to the villa's own gondola landing. As you leave the garden and enter the wisteria-covered palazzo, the magic continues with family heirlooms adorning the spacious rooms where sunlight filters through large windows. A staircase leads upstairs where some of the guestrooms are located in the original villa and others, connected by a hallway, in a portion of the hotel borrowed from an adjacent building. No two of the guestrooms are alike, none are "decorator perfect" - they are like guestrooms in a private home. Some of those in the front have canal views but are noisier than those looking over the garden. The only hitch to this picture of perfection is that your chances are slim of snaring a room in this romantic hideaway - the hotel is so special that loyal guests reserve "their" own favorite room for the following year as they leave. Spring and fall are most heavily booked - your chances are better in July and August and the prices are even a little lower.

PENSIONE ACCADEMIA
Manager: Franco Marzollo
Dorsoduro 1058
3123 Venice, Italy
Tel: (041) 52 10188
26 Rooms - Double Lire 100,000-144,000
Open: All year
Credit cards: All major
Beautiful 17th-century palazzo
Located near Accademia landing

The Agli Alboretti Hotel is conveniently located just steps from the Accademia boat landing. Although only a two star hotel, it has much more charm than many others charging much higher prices. But it is not price alone that makes the hotel appealing: there is a cozy ambiance from the moment you step into the intimate lobby, paneled with dark mellowed wood and decorated with some attractive prints on the walls and a perky ship model in the window. At the front desk will be either Dina Linguerri or her daughter Anna. I did not meet Anna, but her mother is most gracious and speaks excellent English. Beyond the reception area is a small lounge and then one of the very nicest features of the hotel - a tranquil garden sheltered by an overhanging trellis which in summer is completely covered by vines - a welcome, cool oasis after a day of sightseeing. In the garden, white wrought iron tables and chairs are set for morning breakfast or afternoon tea. The guestrooms vary in size, but all have a private bath or shower. My preference would be one with the small tub, since the shower is the type which does not have a separate enclosure. Whichever room you have, however, it should be quiet since the hotel is tucked onto a peaceful square.

AGLI ALBORETTI HOTEL
Owner: Dina & Anna Linguerri
Accademia 882-884
30123 Venice, Italy
Tel: (041) 523 0058
19 Rooms - Double Lire 95,000
Closed: 2 weeks in November
Credit cards: None accepted
Simple hotel with nice courtyard
Located near the Accademia boat stop

Although La Residenza, with its arched windows, lacy detailing, and columned balcony, is a brilliant example of the finest 15th-century Venetian architecture, I was at first a bit half-hearted in my enthusiasm due to the somewhat dilapidated condition of the small plaza it faces. When I visited the hotel, the massive door was locked and I started to turn away until I discovered a discreetly camouflaged small button incorporated into a brass lion ornament to the left of the door. This I rang and the owner, Franco Tagliapietra, leaned out the window and instructed me in Italian to push open the door when he released the lock. How glad I was that I had persevered. After entering the door and climbing up a flight of stairs, I was magically surrounded by a beautiful, museum-quality room with walls and ceiling adorned with intricate plaster designs. The softly toned walls and the marble floor were enhanced by dark wooden furniture. All of the bedrooms have a private bath and are accented with fine antiques. You might have a problem booking this small hotel, since no one seems to speak English. However, perhaps get an Italian speaking friend to call for you. This is definitely an excellent value. As a final note, it is no wonder the palace is so splendid - it was the residence of the Gritti family, a most prestigious name in Venice.

LA RESIDENZA
Owner: Franco Tagliapietra
Campo Bandiera e Moro
30122 Venice, Italy
Tel: (041) 528 5315
15 Rooms - Double Lire 94,000
Closed: Nov to Dec 15 and Jan
Credit cards: None accepted
Beautiful 15th-century palace
A few minutes from St Mark's Square

At first glance the Pensione Seguso appears quite simple: a rather boxy affair without much of the elaborate architectural enhancements so frequently evident in Venice. However, the inside of the pensione radiates warmth and charm and elegant taste. The hotel is located on the "left bank" of Venice - across the Grand Canal from the heart of the tourist area, about a 15-minute walk to St Mark's Square (or only a few minutes by ferry from the Accademia boat stop). For several generations the hotel has been in the Seguso family who do a marvelous job in providing a homelike ambiance for the guest who does not demand luxury, but appreciates quality. One delightful surprise is that this hotel has so much to offer. In front there is a miniature terrace harboring a few tables set under umbrellas. Several of the bedrooms have wonderful views of the canal (although these rooms are the noisiest due to the canal traffic). The most pleasant surprise is that the value-conscious tourist can stay at the Pensione Seguso with breakfast and dinner included for what the price of a room alone would cost for most hotels in Venice. I recently revisited the Pensione Seguso and was delighted to find it even prettier than I had remembered. Although mellowed with age, this hotel gleams with the refinement of a beautiful family home, with Oriental rugs setting off dark wooden antique furniture and excellent heirloom silver services.

PENSIONE SEGUSO
Owner: Seguso family
Grand Canal Zattere, 779
30123 Venice, Italy
Tel: (041) 52 22 340 or 52 86 858
*36 Rooms - * Double Lire 134,000-151,500*
** Rate includes 2 meals*
Credit cards: None accepted
Easy walk from the Accademia boat stop

The Casa Frollo, located on Giudecca Island across from St Mark's Square, is a real gem: a moderately-priced oasis just minutes from the heart of Venice. Once you arrive at Giudecca Island (getting off at the Riva degli Schiavoni dock), walk to your right and you will see the Casa Frollo. You enter through huge doors and then climb the stairs to your right to bring you into an enormous reception-all-purpose room. The owner, Flora Soldan, is frequently at the desk as you enter. She can understand a little English, but if you have a problem communicating, her son Pablo who understands better is usually close at hand. My heart was won the moment I stepped into the room which is brimming with priceless antiques and was enveloped by its awesome size. The room runs the length of the building and the front windows (where tables are set for breakfast and drinks) open onto a sensational view of Venice. The rear windows open onto a lazy, lush garden. For those on a tight budget, there are some rooms without baths. For budget splurgers, request a bath and a view of Venice.

CASA FROLLO
Manager: Soldan family
Fondamenta Zitelle, 50
Giudecca, 50
30123 Venice, Italy
Tel: (041) 2 22723
26 Rooms - Double Lire 75,000-92,000
Open: March 18 to November 21
Credit cards: None accepted
17th-century palace
Splendid view of St Mark's Square
Located on Giudecca Island

The Hotel Turm belongs to the Romantik Hotel Chain. Just being a member of this exclusive "club" indicates the hotel is pretty special because to belong the inn must have the owner personally involved in the management and the interior must have an antique ambiance. The Hotel Turm is no exception. There is an especially attractive little dining room with vaulted whitewashed ceilings and chalet-style rustic wooden furniture. There are a few antiques in the hallways and lounges. The bedrooms are simple, but very pleasant, with light pine furniture and fluffy down comforters on the beds. There is a swimming pool on the terrace where one can swim or lounge while gazing out to the little town and the mountains beyond. There is even a small indoor pool. The Hotel Turm dates back to the 13th century and Mr. Pramstrahler takes great care to maintain touches of the olde worlde charm by interspersing antique chests, cradles, chairs and ancient artifacts.

ROMANTIK HOTEL TURM
Owner: Pramstrahler family
1-39050 Vols am Schlern
Sudtirol, Italy
Tel: (0471) 72 014
24 Rooms - Double Lire 86,000-123,000
Closed: November to end of December
Credit cards: VS
Indoor and outdoor pools
Mountain setting NE of Bolzano

Portugal

The Paloma Blanca (White Dove), originally a beautiful private home built in the early 1930s, was in the process of more than doubling its size when we visited Aveiro. The manager proudly showed us the new construction, while explaining the painstaking measures being taken to remain faithful to the original structure. By the time of your visit, the new and the old should be a harmonious whole of pale yellow stucco with red tile roof and wooden balconies - all surrounded by garden which should soon feature a swimming pool. Inside, the hotel is unpretentious and comfortable. The high-ceilinged, smallish bedrooms are found off rambling hallways. They are simply decorated with attractive, regional-style wood furniture, and pretty woven throw-rugs that pick up the earthtones in the cloth-like wallpaper. The bathrooms are small and modern. All the rooms have televisions - an unusual feature in Portugal. There are a few larger rooms (for four people) which, if available, will be let as doubles. It is worth requesting a room away from the noise of Aveiro's streets. There are plans to build a restaurant, but when we were there only breakfast was served in a cozy and charming second-floor room overlooking the garden. The handsome ceilings here and in the tiny bar on the ground floor are original and lovingly preserved. The Paloma Blanca offers an intimate atmosphere for a city hotel.

PALOMA BLANCA
Rua Luis Gomes de Carvalho, 23
3800 Aveiro, Portugal
Tel: 34 26039 Telex: 37353
22 Rooms - Double ESC 3,100-4,200
Credit cards: None accepted
Friendly staff, swimming pool
Nearest airport: Porto (70 km)
Nearest train station: Aveiro

On N10, just outside of Azeitao (home of Lancers wine), is the enchanting and peaceful Quinta das Torres inn, surrounded by 34 acres of farmland. Sculpted gardens and a large stone pond complete with pavillion and swan add to the idyllic scene. A private manor house for centuries, Quinta das Torres was built in 1580 as a palace for the Count of Aveiro. The family of the proprietors have called this home for over a hundred years, offering guests accommodation since 1931. The ivy-covered, low stone structure surrounds a central patio with fountain. The main house contains splendid, if not perfectly preserved, public rooms, a good restaurant, the private rooms of the residing family members and a tiny chapel where mass is said on Sundays. A suite occupies a corner of the main house, and comprises an enormous sitting room with fireplace, a large colorfully tiled bedroom with brass, white-canopied beds and a stone terrace overlooking the orange groves which provide fresh juice for breakfast - and all for just a few additional dollars. Across the patio are the remaining bedrooms, each different in size and decoration, and all furnished with antiques; electric blankets and modern plumbing being among the few concessions to progress. A sampling: room 6, our favorite, has a fireplace and canopy beds; room 10 has wonderful trundle-type beds and a huge bath; and room 2 has a private balcony.

QUINTA DAS TORRES
Estrada Nacional
2925 Azeitao, Portugal
Tel: 20 80001
*12 Rooms - Double ESC 5,016-8,520 **
** 8,250 is the price of a 4-person bungalow*
Credit cards: None accepted
Extensive grounds
Nearest airport: Lisbon (23 km)
Nearest train station: Setubal (12 km)

Historic Braga is a must-see city. Although, on its own merit the Hotel do Elevador would not normally be included, in our opinion it is the best choice for accommodation in the vicinity of Braga. Just a few kilometers from Braga, atop the Bom Jesus do Monte - a major sight in its own right - you find the Hotel do Elevador named for its proximity to the funicular which transports sightseers up and down the mountain. Around 100 years old, the two-story hotel is built down the mountainside facing Braga. Renovated in 1967, it provides contemporary, if a tad dowdy, comfort to travellers who want a touring base in this area. Apart from the reception (very friendly) and a few bedrooms, the main level is devoted to a lounge/bar with comfortable, well-worn furniture and the glassed-in restaurant which juts out over the hillside and the sculpted rear garden. The food is only adequate, but the view is outstanding. The majority of the bedrooms are downstairs - all have panoramic views of the city below. Bedrooms come in two sizes: spacious and twice as spacious (for a well-spent $8 more). The larger rooms have a foyer entrance, bigger bathroom, and an extra table and chairs. The decor is a curious blend of comfy armchairs, Oriental rugs, pseudo-antique beds and colorfully flowered drapes at wood-framed windows - an eclectic mixture that provides a pleasant ambiance.

HOTEL DO ELEVADOR
Bom Jesus do Monte
4700 Braga, Portugal
Tel: 53 25011
25 Rooms - Double ESC 7,500-9,000
Credit cards: All major
Lovely views, quiet
Nearest airport: Porto (60 km)
Nearest train station: Braga (6 km)

Just a few kilometers northeast of the lively and lovely seaside town of Aveiro, this square, red roadside inn is an interesting melange of modern comfort and pseudo-antique-style decor. Lots of wood and leather accent the lounge, bar and the attractive blue-and-white restaurant, which offers above-average fare and excels at enormous seafood specialty dishes. The bedrooms are upstairs off long hallways with arched, brick ceilings. All are carpeted with an unusual royal blue carpet patterned with gold escutcheons. The antique-reproduction furnishings are quite handsome, particularly in the doubles and suites, whose dark-wood "bilros" beds are more elaborately carved and ornate than those in the twins. All the bedrooms have high, white, wood-plank ceilings, white bedspreads and tiled bathrooms. Curiously, bright flowered wallpaper provides a colorfully disharmonious note to the otherwise appealing bedrooms. The suites, for an additional $5, are extremely spacious and feature a larger bathroom, and small sitting rooms with television. The Albergaria's location, on the main road into Aveiro, makes it very convenient and easy to find. But, this also means that the front rooms are noisy, so request a room overlooking the fields at the back of the hotel. The friendly staff will strive to make your stay pleasant in every way.

ALBERGARIA DE JOAO PADEIRO
Cacia
3800 Aveiro, Portugal
Tel: 34 91326
27 Rooms - Double ESC 3,500-4,800
Credit cards: All major
Convenient location
Nearest airport: Porto (55 km)
Nearest train station: Aveiro (6 km)

Over 100 years ago, a Portuguese sardine magnate constructed an elegant family townhome on a quiet square in the peaceful fishing village of Faro. Today that house is a small pension on a busy square in the capital city of the Algarve, owned and run by an English family. The square, two-story granite and whitewashed building fronts the square directly and has iron grilles and balconies. The main floor contains two bedrooms, an attractive and good dining room and a small bar. In the summertime, a popular outdoor bar is set up under the grape arbors in the courtyard. From here, stairs lead up to a small, brick, rooftop terrace, used for sunning during the day and barbecues and entertainment on summer evenings. Most of the bedrooms are around a gallery hallway reached up a stone staircase off the entryway. They vary in size and, accordingly, price. All are modestly decorated with regional wood furniture, but they manage to preserve some original 19th-century charm due to the unusually high, molded ceilings, hardwood floors and tall windows. Our particular favorite is room 11, an airy, green and white corner room. The double room reached through the restaurant downstairs is probably the best of them all - it's extra-large, quaintly decorated and has a spacious bath - but remember its location is a noisy one.

CASA DE LUMENA
Praca Alexandre Herculano, 27
8000 Faro, Portugal
Tel: 89 22028
*12 Rooms - Double ESC 3,000-9,000 **
** Price range reflects low to high season*
Credit cards: All major
Nearest airport: Faro (8 km)
Nearest train station: Faro (1 km)

This little gem, in the colorful fishing town of Lagos, is an excellent budget choice on the often expensive Algarve. Its location in the heart of town makes it ideal for exploring Lagos on foot - it's just a few blocks from the main network of restaurants, bars and boutiques - but also makes it a trial to find and park nearby (we stopped in front just long enough to unload our luggage before going in search of parking). The rose-colored manor dates back to the 18th century, and was converted to an albergaria in 1966. Winding tile-and-stone stairways access the rambling hallways of the multi-leveled house, off which are found intriguingly decorated bedrooms - no two remotely alike. They have names instead of numbers and crowd a smattering of antiques into their diminutive dimensions. (There is one suite, most often used for four people.) Spaciousness they cannot claim, but for color they are hard to beat. For example, we had the blue-and-white "Romantico", the topmost room with steeply slanted ceiling, painted-iron twin beds, marble-topped dressing and side tables and an L-shaped three-level bathroom. A special and welcome feature is the sunny, interior stone patio, sporting bougainvillea and a fountain, just outside the cozy lounge with its fireplace and tiny, gleaming bar.

CAZA DE SAO GONCALO
Rua Candido dos Reis, 73
8600 Lagos, Portugal
Tel: 08 62171 Telex: 57411
13 Rooms - Double ESC 4,200-6,000
Credit cards: All major
Open: April to October
18th-century manor house
Nearest airport: Faro (80 km)
Nearest train station: Lagos

The dramatically terraced, wine-producing region flanking the Douro River is famous for its scenery, but not well-known for inviting accommodation. The tiny Lamego Inn, situated on a lush green hillside overlooking the pretty little town of the same name, has recently undergone interior renovation (when we were there it was awaiting only exterior paint), and offers plain, pleasant lodging in an area of the country that should not be missed. Once a private villa, the small, cream-colored stucco building has a flat rooftop - ideal for sunning - and bright red shutters. The surrounding countryside is carpeted with vineyards and dotted with pine trees, and the tranquil back garden, highlighted with a central, square fountain and umbrella tables, commands a beautiful view of Lamego. The inn is located near the lovely Nossa Senhora de Remedios nature park and right next door to the Raposeira champagne adega, both of which should be visited while you are there. The interior consists of a small sitting room with stone hearth, a tiny corner bar, a spacious, attractive and reasonable dining room with a panoramic view, and seven high-ceilinged bedrooms with tiled baths. The rooms vary in price according to size (though all are within budget range), and are simply and comfortably furnished in dark wood, the beds topped with earth-tone chenille spreads.

ESTALAGEM DE LAMEGO
Estrada N2
5100 Lamego, Portugal
Tel: 54 62162
7 Rooms - Double ESC 2,580-3,756
Credit cards: MC VS
Nearest airport: Porto (155 km)
Nearest train station: Peso da Regua (15 km)

This roadside inn is appropriately called "Mountain Shelter", since it is tucked against a mountainside, shaded by trees, and overlooks the breathtaking sierra of Monchique and, on a clear day, beyond to the sea. It is located just a few kilometers from the quaint mountain village of Monchique, known for its brass and woven wool handicrafts, and only 25 kilometers from the beach and bustling Algarve, making it an ideal spot for those travellers seeking tranquility without sacrificing convenience. Broad stone stairs lead up to a wide terrace which runs the length of this modern building. Here you can enjoy lunch and the panoramic view of the valley below. Inside, the dining room has picture windows, a sunken fireplace and excellent regional cuisine (try the "asadura", a delectable specialty consisting of grilled pork, chopped and mixed with oil, garlic, lemon and cilantro, served over rice). The bedrooms upstairs are cozy, simply decorated with painted iron beds and flowery bedspreads. They all have spotless wood floors, cork ceilings and colorfully tiled bathrooms. For a surprisingly small additional sum you can occupy a suite that includes a small sitting room and fireplace. All the bedrooms share the unforgettable view.

ESTALAGEM ABRIGO DA MONTANHA
Estrada da Foia
8550 Monchique, Portugal
Tel: 82 92131
8 Rooms - Double ESC 8,000
Credit cards: All major
Mountain setting
Nearest airport: Faro (81 km)
Nearest train station: Portimao (25 km)

Mons Cicus, the Latin derivate for Monchique, is a tranquil, luxurious hideaway on the road between the market town of Monchique and Foia peak. Tourists flock to Foia for the same view available from the hotel's terrace: over the green hills of the Serra de Monchique to the town of Portimao and beyond to the Atlantic. Built as a private home about 25 years ago, it is currently under meticulous French ownership. The dazzling-white structure is tucked against a forested hillside, has royal-blue shutters, terracotta-tiled roof and is fronted by an expanse of green lawn which has two pools, a tennis court and a sauna. The wood-beamed restaurant and bar on the main floor are charming, with marble floors and open fireplaces. Upstairs, there are three bedrooms in the original house and five in a newer addition, all of which are spacious and simply elegant. They are carpeted in soft colors, decorated in beige, blue or yellow and white, have high ceilings and handsome wood furniture. The high wood beds with their tapestry-like spreads are striking. The older rooms all have terraces and cavernous marble baths. Blue-and-white room 3 has the largest terrace (even the bathroom has one), and is our favorite. The few rooms without terrace are more economical, but none is expensive, and a view is worth every additional escudo. Mons Cicus offers a wonderful retreat into self-indulgence.

HOTEL MONS CICUS
Estrada da Foia
8550 Monchique, Portugal
Tel: 82 92650 Telex: 58362
8 Rooms - Double ESC 6,600-7,000
Credit cards: All major
Swimming pools, tennis
Nearest airport: Faro (81 km)
Nearest train station: Portimao (25 km)

In the 14th century, King Dom Dinis had massive fortifications built around the tiny towns on the border with Spain to protect Portugal from that country's aggression. The hilltop town of Monsaraz was one of these, and its walls still stand as testimony to the King's successful strategy. But the heyday of threatened conflict is past, and Monsaraz is now just a picturesque, sleepy, cobblestoned village. But if tranquility, dramatic setting and traditional atmosphere are your cup of tea, this estalagem in the heart of town off a peaceful stone-paved square offers an ideal overnight stop for a bargain-basement price. Though constructed in 1970, the whitewashed inn, with its bright-blue-painted cornerstones, green door, red terracotta roof and stone-framed windows, looks outside and in like a century-old house. All is dark and cozy within; low stone doorways lead to the red-tiled, wood-beamed lounge and spotless restaurant, both with whitewashed, open stone fireplaces. The bedrooms are up the back stairs through heavy wooden doors and overlook the surrounding countryside. They are furnished in plain, carved regional wood, the beds topped with rough woven spreads. In back is a garden terrace with tables and chairs, and a pool.

ESTALAGEM DE MONSARAZ
Largo de Sao Bartolomeu
7200 Monsaraz
Portugal
Tel: 66 55112
7 Rooms - Double ESC 3,200
Credit cards: All major
Swimming pool, medieval atmosphere
Nearest airport: Lisbon (200 km)
Nearest train station: Reguengos de Monsaraz (17 km)

Our favorite hotel in medieval Obidos, this inn was originally an early 19th-century convent, converted in the 20th century to a modest hostelry, then carefully refurbished by its current owner in 1978. It enjoys a relatively peaceful street-front location slightly removed from, but within easy walking distance of, the center of town. It also boasts the only really good restaurant in Obidos, whose charming decor - heavy wood-beamed ceiling, red-tile floor and open stone fireplace - promises a pleasurable dining experience whether or not you are a guest in the hotel. Ten bedrooms are being added to the existing thirteen, and should be completed soon. Several of these new rooms will have fabulous views of the city and castle. Although every room guarantees traditional flavor, only five are found in the original convent building; their beautifully preserved wood ceilings and unusual dimensions making them the most appealing. All of the bedrooms have high ceilings, textured whitewashed walls, tile floors, painted wrought-iron beds and traditional dark-wood furniture. There is a sitting room upstairs with fireplace, two cozy bars (one open to the public, one for hotel guests only), and an interior garden patio where guests can dine in fine weather. For simple, old-fashioned comfort, this inn offers an exceptional value.

ESTALAGEM DO CONVENTO
Rua Dom Joao de Ornelas
2510 Obidos
Portugal
Tel: 62 95217 Telex: 44906
13 Rooms - Double ESC 5,500-6,000
Credit cards: MC VS
Nearest airport: Lisbon (80 km)
Nearest train station: Obidos

This roadside inn (built in 1950) occupies the former site of a "quinta", or farm, within sight of the enchanting hilltop town of Obidos. The large whitewashed and red-roofed building is set back from the main road (N8) just north of town, and is flanked on one side by a circular stone tower which houses a bar/lounge on its upper two levels and a tiny stone-walled discotheque in the basement. The accommodations here are simple, but not ordinary. The larger-than-average bedrooms - each slightly different - have high ceilings, regional-style wood furniture and colorful bedspreads, offering noteworthy comfort (and an occasional crack in their whitewashed walls) for their modest price. Pretty, hand-painted wood ceilings grace the big, sunny breakfast room (there is no restaurant) and the spacious lounge. There is also a homey little sitting/television room off which extends a nice esplanade where you can relax on a hot afternoon or warm evening. Thanks to its countrified setting, the Mansao da Torre is able to offer such attractive features as two swimming pools, tennis court and a garden with children's playground, yet you're still within walking distance of medieval Obidos, and a short drive from Caldas da Rainha.

MANSAO DA TORRE
Casal do Zambujeiro
2510 Obidos
Portugal
Tel: 62 95247
12 Rooms - Double ESC 5,160
Credit cards: All major
Swimming pools, rural setting
Nearest airport: Lisbon (75 km)
Nearest train station: Caldas da Rainha (3 km)

This is a spanking-new (1985) whitewashed and iron-balconied inn in the heart of medieval Obidos. It fronts the stone-paved Rua Direita, the main street in town, which is lined with art galleries and souvenir shops, and leads up to the castle. Along with the obvious advantages of its central location comes the inconvenience of parking. (You'll need to stop just long enough to unload your luggage before going in search of a parking place on a side street.) The hotel occupies the site of a former private residence which had fallen into disrepair. The owner rebuilt from the ground up, creating modern comfort while recreating a traditional ambiance throughout. The handsome public rooms are furnished in wood and leather and plentifully accented with colorful painted tiles. There are two attractive bars - one for the general public and the other for hotel guests only. Breakfast is the only meal served. The bedrooms vary in price according to location, decor and plumbing (bathtub or shower), but all are approximately the same size, have whitewashed walls, regional-style wood furniture, flowery spreads and drapes and brightly tiled baths. To us, bedroom location seemed inconsequential - overlooking old stone ramparts in back, narrow side streets, or the Rua Direita seemed equally appealing - but the corner doubles (at double the price) with wood-beamed ceilings are definitely more charming.

ALBERGARIA RAINHA SANTA ISABEL
Rua Direita
2510 Obidos, Portugal
Tel: 62 95115
20 Rooms - Double ESC 4,200-7,000
Credit cards: All major
Central location
Nearest airport: Lisbon (80 km)
Nearest train station: Obidos

This handsome estate dates back to the 17th century, when its history was entwined through a scandalous marriage with that of the nearby Paco de Calheiros, also a guesthouse. Since then, the property has changed hands several times, currently being owned and occupied by three elderly sisters of the Pimenta Lopes family, whose uncle acquired it in 1917. A tiny sign about a kilometer outside Ponte de Lima on the way to Ponte da Barca points across the road to the stone and whitewashed farmhouse - recently and faithfully restored. There are four bedrooms with bath on the main floor - two large (ask for the big one at the back, it's worth the few dollars more), and two somewhat smaller, but each charming in its simplicity. The walls and threshholds are thick stone, the wood floors creaky, the ceilings high and the furnishings a variety of plain, handsome antiques. A beautiful wood staircase, under a cathedral-ceiling skylight, leads upstairs to a gallery and six additional bedrooms under the eaves. These are quaint and offer an interesting budget option, but they are also tiny and share a hallway bath. The dining room (which will prepare dinner if there's a full house) has one long table, a fireplace at one end, and a marvelous old kitchen with a stone oven and open hearth at the other. The setting is bucolic, but just moments from historic Ponte de Lima.

CASA DE CRASTO
4990 Ponte de Lima, Portugal
Tel: 58 961156
10 Rooms - Double ESC 6,720
Credit cards: None accepted
Private manor house
Nearest airport: Porto (93 km)
Nearest train station: Viana do Castelo (23 km)

Just south of Portimao is Praia da Rocha, an expanse of broad beach flanked by the rocky cliffs so ubiquitous in the Algarve. At the east end of the beach, opposite a stone fortress and across the street from the sea, is the Vila Lido. Jacqueline Kennedy was a guest here before the private villa was converted into an inn 15 years ago. Like so many structures in the south, the turquoise-shuttered house is whitewashed, with the carved chimneys, so characteristic of the region, jutting from its red-tile roof. A low stone- and-plaster wall surrounds the property and broad stone steps lead to the arched entryway where a tiny plaque gives the only indication that this is other than a private residence. Inside, the albergaria is meticulously cared for, the public rooms a delight. A sunny sitting room with polished parquet floors gives onto a verandah at the front of the house, both ideal for coffee or cocktails while sea-gazing. French doors lead from there into a charming breakfast room with hand-painted walls, carved ceiling, massive fireplace and delicate furniture. A few of the bedrooms have decorative fireplaces, and all retain a genuine olde worlde flavor with their sculpted ceilings, tall windows, spacious dimensions and solid chestnut doors, but the furnishings are relatively modern and uninspired. Rooms 21, 22 and 25 have terraces, the latter room being the largest and slightly more expensive.

ALBERGARIA VILA LIDO
Av. Tomos Cabreira
Praia da Rocha
8500 Portimao, Portugal
Tel: 82 24127
10 Rooms - Double ESC 5,750-6,000
Credit cards: All major
Across street from beach
Nearest airport: Faro (64 km)
Nearest train station: Portimao (2 km)

Located within hailing distance of Cabo Sao Vicente (the most southwesterly point in Europe) is a tiny stone fortress. Careful inspection of a carved stone over the entryway reveals the number 1632 - the date it was constructed. Perched on a rocky promontory overlooking the craggy coast and the sea, it offers only four guestrooms, most of its traffic a result of its restaurant's reputation. The original fortress walls enclose two whitewashed buildings, one housing the reception, a small bar and the cozy dining room, which has a lovely wood ceiling. The other contains whitewashed bedrooms with brick-red tile floors and large baths. They vary only slightly: each is comfortably sized and simply appointed with regional dark-wood furniture and pale bedspreads. One bedroom has a clear view of the ocean while the others look onto the seaside terrace or into the interior garden, which is graced by a little white chapel. The dramatic setting is ideal for those seeking tranquility, but is still readily accessible for touring the Algarve. Best of all, it's only about half the price of its pousada neighbor (indeed, the Pousada do Infante books its overflow here).

CASA DE CHA DA FORTALEZA DO BELICHE
8650 Sagres
Portugal
Tel: 82 64124
4 Rooms - Double ESC 6,500-7,500
Credit cards: None accepted
Restaurant, romantic setting
Nearest airport: Faro (100 km)
Nearest train station: Lagos (35 km)

The picturesque coastal village of Sao Martinho, with its half-moon bay ringed with rocky cliffs, is an appealing destination for those seeking peace and quiet in a quaint setting. It has the additional attraction of offering a convenient base for excursions to nearby Obidos and Alcobaca. Its small semicircular beach is clean and looks over calm water dotted with colorful fishing boats. The Hotel Parque is just a block from the bay on a shady, tree-lined street. Originally an elegant turn-of-the-century manor, the red-roofed, cream-colored inn is accented with pretty pink and green azulejos outside, and is surrounded by luxuriant gardens featuring a tennis court. Inside, the large and lovely public rooms are well-maintained and furnished with period pieces. A broad hallway leads to spacious double rooms and a huge suite, all with 15-foot sculpted ceilings, tall windows overlooking the gardens and handsome furniture in traditional Portuguese style. We recommend you secure one of these charming lower-floor (planta baixa) rooms, since those upstairs are small, with low ceilings and utilitarian furniture. Not all have full baths, and some none at all, sharing hallway facilities. But they are clean and carry a shoestring pricetag.

HOTEL PARQUE
Avenida Marechal Carmona, 3
Sao Martinho do Porto
Portugal
Tel: 62 98505
34 Rooms - Double ESC 3,000-4,800
Credit cards: All major
Open: March to November
Tennis
Nearest airport: Lisbon (108 km)
Nearest train station: Sao Martinho do Porto

Imagine our surprise when, out of curiosity, we followed accommodation signs out of Tomar, through the village of Serra, and ended up at a small stone building on the shore of a lake with no more road to follow. Taking our next cue from an arrow, we went down a flight of stairs to find a small bar and a dock. When we inquired about the inn, we were informed that the boat was about to leave. It was then we noticed the small, pine-covered island in the middle of the broad blue lake and, on it, the inn. So we paid our 150 escudos (round trip) and took the launch to lunch. The whitewashed, red-roofed estalagem sits at one end of the island, wrapped around a large pool and grassy terrace. Through the airy reception area and upstairs is a cozy, rustic bar with a fireplace which leads to a bright, comfy lounge off the restaurant - all with wood-beamed ceilings and deep-red tile floors. The dining room offers good regional specialties and a lovely view across the lake. The bedrooms - all with lake views - are smallish and simply furnished in motel-modern style, with colorful flowered bedspreads. This is an ideal getaway spot offering nothing but peace and quiet, where you can unwind in the sun, or take a boat out fishing. The ferry goes between island and shore every hour until early evening.

ESTALAGEM DA ILHA DO LOMBO
2300 Serra de Tomar, Portugal
Tel: 49 37128
*15 Rooms - Double ESC 6,360 **
** includes boat ride from shore to island*
Credit cards: All major
Swimming pool
Unique island setting
Nearest airport: Lisbon (170 km)
Nearest train station: Tomar (16 km)

Between the quaint little towns of Canas de Senhorim and Nelas, watch for a sign saying Urgeirica-Hotel, and to the left you'll see the large stone and whitewashed hotel surrounded by verdant grounds, in which you'll later discover tennis courts and a pool. Currently Portuguese-owned, it was originally built in the 1930s by a British mining engineer who owned the nearby uranium mines until they were nationalized. From within and without it has the appearance and ambiance of a rambling hunting lodge - offering simple comfort in a beautiful mountain setting at a budget price. The lounge and restaurant are spacious and subdued, with high ceilings, hardwood floors and solid, well-worn furniture. Located off meandering hallways are bigger-than-average bedrooms, each distinct and appointed with a pleasing mixture of regional-wood and antique furniture. We especially liked the high, old-fashioned beds common to all the rooms. There are a few special rooms (a couple with terraces) that are nearly twice the size and have parquet floors and elegant antique pianos converted into dressing tables. For less than $5 more, these are a real bargain if available (rooms 123 and 124 are our favorites). The cool mountain air and the spectacular Serra da Estrela nearby make the Hotel Urgeirica an appealing budget choice.

HOTEL URGEIRICA
Canas de Senhorim
3520 Nelas, Portugal
Tel: 32 67267 Telex: 53535
53 Rooms - Double ESC 3,400-4,500
Credit cards: All major
Swimming pool, tennis
Nearest airport: Porto (165 km)
Nearest train station: Canas de Senhorim (4 km)

Scandinavia
Denmark - Finland - Norway - Sweden

Aeroskobing is a charming port village of cobbled streets lined by pastel-washed buildings with decorative front doors. Set back off one of Aeroskobing's main streets, facing onto its own inner courtyard, is the conveniently located Hotel Aerohus. The building, dating back to 1785, was converted to a hotel in 1936 by its owner, Johan Phillip Bonsack, whose name is inscribed above the hotel entry. It was purchased in 1954 by the Christensen family who have concentrated on restoring the Aerohus, building by building, ever since. The Christensens and their longtime staff try to - and succeed in - creating a homey atmosphere in this family-run hotel, serving especially good homemade food. The bedrooms are found either in the sienna red main building or in an annex tucked off at the back. The furnishings are a little too modern in style for my taste, but the location and friendly service cannot be surpassed, while the large gardens and quiet surroundings provide a most restful setting. The island of Aero lies an hour's ferry ride away from the main island of Funen. Although ferry service is frequent, car and passenger reservations are strongly recommended and can be made by telephoning (09) 52 10 18.

HOTEL AEROHUS
Owner: Birthe and Svend Christensen
Vestergade 38
5970 Aeroskobing
Aero, Denmark
Tel: (09) 52 10 03
35 Rooms - Double DKR 305-505
Closed: December 29 to January 20
Credit cards: AX
Charming village
Located S of Funen, on Aero island

The island of Aero is a distance of one hour's travel time by ferry from the coastal town of Svendborg. The Dunkaer Kro is a hotel sitting in the middle of this idyllic island, located just 4 kilometers from the quaint, picturesque port town of Aeroskobing. Licensed by the king in 1848, this simple inn has always been owned by the Clausens and is managed to date by the sixth generation of their family. The accommodation is basic and plain in furnishings and comfort (no room has a private bathroom), but is very inexpensive and children are extremely welcome. The feeling of a country inn pervades the lounge bar and restaurant: the decor of both is enhanced by a few cherished antiques and charming fabrics. The Dunkaer Kro is described by the owner as a "typical" Danish village inn, known for a very tasty meal with ample portions - a nice place to bring children. In the summer months guests dine in the garden and, year-round, at night the laughter of the local clientele, perched on stools at the bar, wafts through the halls. Although the English spoken by the management is limited, you are made to feel very welcome by the Clausens.

DUNKAER KRO
Owner: Ejvind Clausen
Dunkaervej 1, Dunkaer
5970 Aeroskobing
Aero, Denmark
Tel: (09) 52 15 54
7 Rooms - Double DKR 320
Open: All year
Credit cards: None accepted
Inexpensive inn
Located S of Funen, on the island of Aero

This is a delightful thatched inn set on a country road just half an hour's drive from Copenhagen, its location convenient to both the capital city and some of Denmark's most remarkable castles. Freddie Jacobsen, who bought the inn in 1974 after having worked there for a number of years as a waiter, is your host. He extends a gracious, warm, welcoming smile and is present to see that service and attention to detail remain excellent and personal. The Bregnerod Kro has existed as a restaurant for almost 200 years. The menu offers a large selection of regional specialties, from stuffed filet of plaice with creamed shrimps to a luncheon platter of herring, pickled salmon, tenderloin of beef and Brie cheese. An attractive wing of nine bedrooms has been built to accommodate overnight guests. These are tastefully decorated, with light oak furniture, cream walls, dark beams, rust highlights on door trims, bright airy print fabrics and fresh flower arrangements, and all are equipped with a mini bar and television. Room 9 is a large corner apartment that looks out the back onto an expanse of woods and parkland. A delicious, hearty, country breakfast of Danish pastries, boiled eggs, meats and crusty rolls is served in the same wing as the bedrooms.

BREGNEROD KRO
Owner: Freddie Jacobsen
Bregnerod, 3520 Farum
(Sealand) Denmark
Tel: (02) 95 00 57
9 Rooms - Double DKR 620
Open: All year
Credit cards: All major
Thatched inn
Located 25 km N of Copenhagen, 3 km outside Farum

Located north of Copenhagen, about 2 kilometers from Fredensborg Palace, the Pension Bondehuset is reminiscent of an inviting English bed and breakfast. Dating back over 180 years, the inn's thatched buildings nestle under trees set on 3 private acres of parkland whose sandy paths lead the short distance down to the shores of beautiful Lake Esrom. Karin Larsen, the Bondehuset's delightful hostess, offers accommodation for a rate inclusive of breakfast and dinner. Served around six, the delicious dinner includes soup or salad, a main entree, dessert and coffee. Wine and beer are available for an additional charge. Delightful views of Lake Esrom can be enjoyed from the dining hall as well as from the adjoining, tastefully decorated drawing rooms where one is welcome to linger either before or after dinner. In warm weather tables are set outside the restaurant on a delightful patio. Recently remodeled, the bedrooms are found in a neighboring building and are simple but sweet in their decor. Room 20 is the largest, a corner double that faces onto the water and enjoys the luxury of its own sitting area. Room 18, also a double room, looks out to the lake.

PENSION BONDEHUSET
Owner: Karin Juel Larsen
Sorup, 3480 Fredensborg
(Sealand) Denmark
Tel: (02) 28 01 12
15 Rooms - Double DKR 465
Full pension rate for two - DKR 820
Open: April 1 to October 15
Credit cards: None accepted
Lakeside setting
Located 50 km N of Copenhagen

One of Denmark's oldest inns, the Hvidsten Kro (built in 1634), was moved to Hvidsten in 1790. It has been owned and managed by the Fiil family for over 100 years. Marius Fiil, the grandfather of the present owner, was a key organizer of the Danish resistance movement during the Second World War. He, his son Niels, his son-in-law Peder, his daughters Tulle and Gerda were arrested by the Gestapo in March, 1944. The men were executed, the women sent to a concentration camp, while his wife Gudrun continued to run the inn, stating that "I certainly lost much, but I still think that those who lost their men and their means of subsistence were harder afflicted than I." Gudrun died in 1972. Always known for its good food, the Hvidsten Kro has five cozy dining nooks set under low beamed ceilings. It is an extremely charming inn with clocks, rust-painted timbered walls hung with copper, pewter mugs, and weathered paintings, tables paired with wooden benches worn smooth by years of use, a cupboard with a handsome bottled glass cabinet door set in a corner niche, heavy old trunks, plate racks, fresh flowers and dramatic fireplaces. There are eight simple, inexpensive bedrooms, none with private bathroom.

HVIDSTEN KRO
Owner: C. A. Paetch
Mariagervej 450, Hvidsten
8981 Spentrup
(Jutland) Denmark
Tel: (06) 47 70 22
8 Rooms - Double DKR 255
*Open: *All year*
** Except Mondays, September 15 to May 15*
Credit cards: DC
300-year-old inn, charming restaurant

In the 17th century King Christian IV chose this idyllic spot, on a forested peninsula almost surrounded by water, as an easily defendable site for a castle. You can see, through the trees, the copper tower roof and brick frame of the castle in the distance as you drive around the inlet at the end of Kerteminde Fjord to the castle's entrance. Impressive wooden doors with lion handles open to the tower's square entrance hall: take notice of the magnificent ceiling here, dramatic with its individually framed designs. Intimate in size, Ulriksholm Slot has lovely old rooms glimpsed through heavy wooden doorways. The dining room is regal in its decor and offers a tempting lunch and dinner menu for both residents and visitors. It was actually the chef who escorted us on a tour. The castle, now under the protection of the Danish Preservation Act class A, has 16 handsome bedrooms, each with a handbasin, though none has a private bathroom. The management is particularly proud of the bridal suite with its romantic four-poster bed.

ULRIKSHOLM SLOT
Owner: Anette Bastrup
Kolstrup, 5300 Kerteminde
(Funen) Denmark
Tel: (09) 39 15 44
16 Rooms - Double DKR 430-560
Closed: January
Credit cards: All major
17th-century castle
Located 25 km E of Odense

This is a delightful inn whose popularity is evidence of the Andersen family's high standard of service since 1949. The senior Mrs Andersen has written a cookbook entitled "Inn Food", a subtle indication of the fine dining you can expect to sample here. A lovely reception area serves as a wonderful introduction to the Kongensbro Kro and a salon warmed by a fireplace sits just off the entry. Drinks and light meals are served here in this lovely room which displays a handsome grandfather clock, some primitive pewter spoons, decorative Windsor chairs and wooden benches set against the wall. Up a staircase whose banister is charmingly carved with hearts and clubs is a wing of guestrooms running the length of the hotel. Recently remodeled, these bedrooms are comfortably equipped and look out through dormer windows to the river. The Kongensbro Kro is just outside Ans, set a short distance off the main road to Viborg - a surprisingly quiet location. Its back garden slopes down to the tree-lined Gudena River, where guests can enjoy the fine fishing and can also rent canoes to explore beyond the bend in the river.

KONGENSBRO KRO
Owner: Ole Andersen
Gl. Kongevej 70
Kongensbro, 8643 Ans
(Jutland) Denmark
Tel: (06) 87 01 77
16 Rooms - Double DKR 485-625
Closed: Christmas & New Year's Day
Credit cards: All major
Lovely riverside inn
Located 40 km NW of Arhus

The charming Hotel Postgaarden sits on the main square of Mariager behind an old timbered facade stretching along an uneven cobblestoned street. Concerned townspeople supervised the recent restoration of this inn and elected Kurt Clausen to manage the hotel - his efforts reflect their pride and interest. Heavy old beams, original to the house, add character to the hotel's many cozy rooms. Tea and light snacks are served at tables covered with brown checked cloths in what is the oldest part of the inn - the Vicar's Apartment, dating back to 1688. You can settle in any of the four snug dining rooms, the Marinestue, Almuestue, Mariagerstue and Jagstue, and enjoy a delightful dinner. Every third Thursday evening during the winter months you can hear local music played in what was once the old hotel salon. A corridor bounded by walls built in 1710 leads to the inn's superb bedrooms. With their light wood furniture, all the rooms are exceptional in their decor and outfitted with private, modern bathrooms. Tucked under the interesting angles of the inn's roofline, the Wedding Suite offers the most spacious accommodation. The bedrooms at the back overlook the hotel's herb garden.

HOTEL POSTGAARDEN
Manager: Kurt Clausen
Torvet, 9550 Mariager
(Jutland) Denmark
Tel: (08) 54 10 12
10 Rooms - Double DKR 475-525
Open: All year
Credit cards: All major
Timbered 18th-century inn
Located 58 km S of Alborg

At the junction of 13 roads, Randers has served for centuries as a thriving market town and its medieval quarter with its beautiful old houses, narrow streets and pavements has been lovingly preserved as a pedestrian district. The front door of the Hotel Randers opens up to the heart of this complex, while an underground parking lot, reached from Brodregade, provides direct driving access. Once you experience the kind hospitality and welcome of the staff, it is easy to understand why this hotel recently received the American Express award for outstanding service. Built in 1856, the hotel was the first in Jutland and has been owned by the same family for over 100 years. A large comfortable lounge is a popular gathering spot and you can enjoy international cuisine in the restaurant, or a less formal meal in the grill-room or the Kahytten, the bar. For the affordable price the accommodation is excellent value: you can stay in a quite luxurious suite for the cost of a standard double room in many hotels. The bedrooms' decor varies from antique to modern: you may choose the style you prefer when you make your reservations.

HOTEL RANDERS
Owner: Sonja Mtahisen
Manager: Alex Villadsen
Torvegade 11
8900 Randers, (Jutland) Denmark
Tel: (06) 42 34 22
85 Rooms - Double DKR 650
Open: January 2 to December 21
Credit cards: All major
Personalized service
Located 76 km S of Alborg

In 1648 Soren Anderson Weis came here from Itzehoe and built an inn offering food and accommodation to herdsmen taking their cattle from northern Jutland to Hamburg. Often, instead of paying for their shelter, the herdsmen payed with their belongings and today some of these are displayed at the inn. The Weis family owned the leaning half-timbered inn until 1915 when it was taken over by the local authority which has done a beautiful job preserving this pretty inn. The popular bar-restaurant, with its decorated beamed ceiling, dark wood panels painted with biblical scenes, farm tables, accents of brown and white Dutch tiles, a copper bed warmer, pewter plates and mugs and an old clock, is particularly memorable. A few smaller, more intimate, rooms serve as quiet niches for small groups around a clustering of one or two wooden tables and benches. Climbing up the short narrow stairway to the five bedrooms, with the assistance of the stairway's simple rope banister, is reminiscent of climbing into a loft. The floors creak, the ceilings are low and the rooms are extremely small, simple and without private bathrooms. But the price is reasonable, the furnishings are fresh and clean and an occasional antique piece and flowers set a very appealing mood.

WEIS STUE
Manager: Knud Nilsen
6760 Ribe
(Jutland) Denmark
Tel: (05) 42 07 00
5 Rooms - Double DKR 280-340
Open: All year
Credit cards: None accepted
Half-timbered 17th-century inn
Located 30 km SE of Esbjerg

A delightful alternative to a central hotel while visiting the Viking museum at Roskilde is the Svogerslev Kro, a charming thatched inn 6 kilometers from the outskirts of the city. The Svogerslev Kro has been welcoming guests into its cozy restaurant since 1772 and with the addition several years ago of two annexes of bedrooms the inn is now able to welcome overnight guests. The owner, Flemming Petersen, has done a splendid job with his bedrooms which with their beamed ceilings and delightful decor exactly match the mood and feel of the original thatched inn. The restaurant is the hotel's pride, its kitchen open daily from 11:00 am to 9:30 pm, except on days that private parties monopolize the facilities. The inn has proven so popular that private parties are required to book functions three years in advance.

SVOGERSLEV KRO
Owner: Flemming Petersen
Holbaekvej
Svogerslev, 4000 Roskilde
(Sealand) Denmark
Tel: (02) 38 30 05
13 Rooms - Double DKR 390
Closed: Christmas & New Year's Day
Credit cards: DC
Excellent restaurant
18th-century thatched inn
Located 30 km W of Copenhagen

Outside the lovely city of Silkeborg in a small farming village is a dear thatched inn, the Svostrup Kro. Tucked behind an arched entry with its own enclosed courtyard, set on the quiet banks of the Gudena River, this inn was built in 1834 to offer sustenance to passing bargemen. It is the Hilsens' hard work remodeling and decorating that has converted what they found as an empty timbered shell into a charming and inviting farmhouse hotel complex. This lovely inn has only nine bedrooms, none with private bathroom - though there are plans to build ten bedrooms with en-suite bathrooms. The restaurant is charming - intimate with soft lights, candles, lovely flower arrangements and countryside paintings framed in the ceiling beams. The menu is very reasonably priced and known for its fish courses. Every Saturday a wonderful buffet is offered. At the center of the inn the tavern remains, much as it was in the days of the bargemen, filled with conversation and atmosphere.

SVOSTRUP KRO
Owner: Karin & Niels Hilsen
Svostrup
8600 Silkeborg
(Jutland) Denmark
Tel: (06) 87 70 04
9 Rooms - Double DKR 320-360
Closed: January
Credit cards: MC
Riverside inn
Located 10 km N of Silkeborg

This small countryside inn was named after a knight, Niels Bugge, the owner of a neighboring estate during the 1350s whose crest is found on the sign of the inn. The Niels Bugge's Kro began life as the mill of Count Frederick Schinkel of Hovegaard, who was famous for his generosity in offering drinks to passing friends and travellers. Today, owned by the state, the inn is co-managed by Poul Nielsen and Claus Engmann and offers a fine menu in addition to a refreshing drink. The restaurant is small and very attractive, and popular with locals from the nearby city of Viborg. Accommodations are very simple and few in number: four bedrooms, none with private bath, are found on the second floor and, although plainly furnished, are very clean and quiet. Room 4, a back corner room, overlooks the lake.

NIELS BUGGE'S KRO
Manager: Claus Engmann & Poul Nielsen
Dollerup
8800 Viborg
(Jutland) Denmark
Tel: (06) 63 80 11
4 Rooms - Double DKR 350
Closed: December 22 to March 1
Credit cards: AX MC VS
Small, simple inn
Located 6 km S of Viborg

Voersaa is a tiny village south of the seaside/artist town of Skagen on the northeastern coast of Jutland. The hostelry is found on the country lane that leads from the village to the coast. A Danish flag flies proudly outside the blue-green shuttered building and serves as a promise of the fine Danish hospitality offered within. Usger Jensen is often present to offer a kind welcome. There are 22 bedrooms (9 with private bathroom) found in 3 buildings of this 300-year-old inn, all very simply furnished. The main building houses the pub and the restaurant where low, beamed ceilings are inscribed with old Danish sayings and lace curtains dress the windows. The pub is extremely inviting and the restaurant delightful. Guests return year after year to this spot on the edge of the Voer River for fishing and boating vacations. (A few rowboats are available for guests' use.) During the summer months the hardy can swim in the crystal clear sea water from the sand banks of the Kattegat.

VOERSAA KRO
Owner: Usger Jensen
Voersaa, 9300 Saeby
(Jutland) Denmark
Tel: (08) 46 00 06
22 Rooms - Double DKR 420
Open: All year
Credit cards: None accepted
On the Jutland coast
Located 45 km NE of Alborg

If you have children in tow, they will think the Messila Holiday Center is fabulous. The hotel, originally a farm dating from the 19th century, has been converted into a somewhat homespun fantasy land for children (and adults). Spreading throughout the old farm, beautifully situated on a sloping hillside above the lake, is a recreational area which includes a toboggan ride for winter or summer, horseback riding (with 30 horses available), 35 kilometers of beautiful trails through the forest, small motorized bumper-boats in the pond, Dancing Water (a large fountain whose eruption of lacy water is colored by a fantasy of lights), a sled ride with the dramatic conclusion of a splash into the water, eight ski lifts, saunas, plus swimming, boating and fishing in the lake. In addition, there are three restaurants and a handicraft center featuring a carpenter's shop, a jeweller's, a knitwear corner, a blacksmith's forge and a marvelous bakery. Here you can watch the skilled craftsmen at work and also buy beautiful handmade gifts. The old wood-frame, mustard-yellow farmhouse now serves as a restaurant, serving excellent food prepared with ingredients fresh from the farm. The one jarring note to this interesting hotel complex is the ultra-modern hotel-conference center, so when making reservations be sure to request one of the old farm cottages which have been converted into hotel rooms.

MESSILA HOLIDAY CENTER
Manager: Kyosti Toivonen
15980 Messila, Lahti, Finland
Tel: (918) 531 666
45 Rooms - Double FIM 200-420
Open: All year
Credit cards: All major
Horseback riding, lake, sauna
Located 104 km N of Helsinki

What a happy surprise to visit the Mukkula Manor House. The reviews I had read indicated a lovely setting, a romantic lake and a picturesque building, BUT a very simple inn with no private baths. Indeed, the pretty parklike setting has not changed, nor has the welcoming 18th-century mustard-yellow farm manor; however, this small hotel is not "basic" at all. Under the capable management of Heikki Kaija, the rooms have been completely remodeled and redecorated. Each now has its own private bath and the decor is some of the most attractive I found in all of Finland. Although not decorated with antiques, the guestrooms radiate a marvelous country ambiance. Sunlight streams through the large windows highlighting the spacious rooms with their print wallpaper, crisp-white furniture and wooden floors with a wash of blue accented by home-spun area rugs. The high-ceilinged dining rooms exude a romantic charm, with Wedgwood blue tieback drapes, wooden parquet floors, comfortable blue upholstered chairs, fine china with a blue print design and blue tablecloths. The food does justice to the decor. Not surprisingly, with rivers and lakes in every direction, fresh fish is always on the menu. The Mukkula Manor House is located beside the lake in Lahti City Park, with a sauna in a cabin by the shore.

MUKKULA MANOR HOUSE HOTEL
Manager: Heikki Kaija
15240 Lahti, Finland
Tel: (918) 306 554
14 Rooms - Double FIM 400-430
Open: All year
Credit cards: All major
Lake, park, children's playground, tennis
Located 104 km N of Helsinki

The Punkaharju Valtion has the honor of being Finland's oldest hotel. The idea evolved in 1803 when the Czar visited the area of Punkaharju, dotted with gorgeous lakes, and ordered that this paradise be preserved as a park. In 1845 a forester's lodge with three guestrooms was built - and so began the first inn in Finland. The setting of the hotel is superb - nestled amongst the trees on the knoll of a hill where the beauty of the lake far below can be glimpsed through the forest. A steep set of stairs cuts through the trees and winds down to the lake. The exterior of the hotel is like a cottage from "Hansel and Gretel" - a virtual gingerbread creation of beigey-pink wood siding enhanced by fancy carvings of white lacy design. The interior, however, definitely lacks the finesse promised by the sprightly facade. The main dining room is drab, although the adjacent porch-like dining room is quite cheerful, with rattan furniture and windows looking out through the trees. There are 18 bedrooms in the main building and 11 in a Victorian-style annex below the hotel near the lake. These guestrooms lack any of the touches that make a room warm and inviting, but they are clean and adequate for an overnight stay in this lovely part of Finland.

PUNKAHARJU VALTION HOTEL
Manager: Rauno Rinkinen
58450 Punkaharju, Finland
Tel: (957) 311 761 Telex: 5671
29 Rooms - Double FIM 410-480
(5 with private bath)
Open: June to September 15
Credit cards: DC MC VS
19th-century forester's lodge
Located 344 km NE of Helsinki

The Hotel Rauhalinna was built in 1897 by Nils Weckman, who, in spite of being a general in the Czar's army, must have been a romantic at heart. General Weckman brought craftsmen all the way from St Petersburg to build this fabulous gingerbread Victorian creation as a gift for his wife, Alma, for their 25th wedding anniversary. Perched on a knoll with a grassy lawn running down to the lake where in summer boats criss-cross back and forth to the bustling town of Savonlinna (about 4 kilometers away), the house is a fantasy of cupolas, dormers, little balconies and intricate wood detailing - truly a masterpiece of lacy Victorian-style architecture. Inside, the ceilings are high and richly decorated and there are fancy chandeliers and lovely ceramic stoves tucked into corners. Only one bedroom, actually a suite, has a private bathroom: all others share a common bathroom in the hall. Do not expect too much from any of the bedrooms because, although some antiques are used, the overall mood is one of very dated, rather shabby decor. Nevertheless, there are very few hotels in Finland with the olde worlde character and romance of this whimsical old building.

HOTEL RAUHALINNA
Manager: Leena Kosonen
Lehtiniemi
57310 Savonlinna, Finland
Tel: (957) 253 119 Season
(957) 228 64 Off-Season
7 Rooms - Double FIM 300-520
Open: June 1 to August 17
Credit cards: None accepted
Whimsical Victorian building
Located 340 km NE of Helsinki

The Augustin Hotel is the only small hotel I could find in Bergen with some olde worlde charm. This is not a luxury hotel, so those who want sophistication should stay across the harbor at the SAS Royal. But, frankly, I loved the Augustin and will probably choose it again. The lobby is small and a little drab in decor, but with a very gracious and warm reception. The lounge is a fussy Victorian-style room on the third floor. The breakfast room is also on the third floor and a real winner, with Wedgwood blue walls, white bentwood chairs, lacy white curtains, white hanging lamps and fresh flowers. By all means ask for one of the guestrooms overlooking the harbor, if possible a corner room. Our small room, 503, had two rather frumpy overstuffed chairs, a small writing desk and brass headboard. The bathroom was not very pretty, but quite adequate: its shower had no divider, but a curtain drew across the room and miraculously kept the room dry while the water was on. What made me fall in love with our snug little room was the view: the windows are low and while lying in bed you can watch the colorful parade of ships wind their way down the fjord and into the harbor.

AUGUSTIN HOTEL
Owner: Egil Smoeraas
C. Sundtsgate 24
5000 Bergen, Norway
Tel: (475) 23 00 25 Telex: 40923
38 Rooms - Double NOK 640-680
Open: All year except Christmas
Credit Cards: All major
Located in central Bergen near the harbor

The Elveseter Hotel is an extremely attractive mountain hotel cleverly incorporated into a very old wooden manor farm, the farm complex being grouped around a large central courtyard in the traditional style of the Gudbrandsdal Valley. Great care has been taken in the reconstruction to maintain the original peasant farmhouse atmosphere. The lounges are delightfully decorated with exceptionally fine country antiques: wedding chests, grandfather clocks, painted cupboards, leather saddles (made into chairs) and gleaming copper pots. Although the ambiance is very rustic, the amenities are conveniently modern: the various farm buildings are linked by heated corridors and each of the guestrooms has a private bathroom. There is even a large indoor pool built in the 400-year-old barn. The Elveseter family has owned the farm for five generations, and, in accordance with the old Norwegian custom, has taken its name from the farm. They have been not only farmers, but also renowned craftsmen, clock-makers and wood-carvers. Ommon, the great-great-grandfather, using the simplest of tools, turned out 104 clocks, 2 of which can still be seen at the hotel. Records show the land has been a farm for over 1,000 years and the oldest building now standing dates back to 1640 - beautifully preserved by the dry, pure mountain air.

ELVESETER HOTEL
Owner: Elveseter Family
2689 Elveseter, Lom, Norway
Tel: (062) 12 000
90 Rooms - Double NOK 460
Open: June 1 to September 27
Credit cards: None accepted
Indoor pool, old farmhouse
Located 348 km N of Oslo

The Roisheim, located in a glorious narrow valley south of Lom, is a superb tiny hotel. I fell in love with it immediately. The hotel has tremendous character, being incorporated into a 17th-century farmhouse complex of dark log buildings topped with sod roofs. The guestrooms are very simple (only a few have private baths), but they are extremely appealing, with a country-fresh ambiance created by the use of Pierre Deux-type fabrics, wood planked floors displaying simple rugs, and painted beds topped by plump comforters. One of the oldest cottages even has its own fireplace. The lounge brims with warmth and good cheer - nothing sophisticated; just a comfortable homey collection of furniture and some country antiques around a giant fireplace. The dining room is beautiful with antique chairs stripped to their original light color, tables covered with fine linen tablecloths set with gleaming silver and flickering candles. The greatest assets of the Roisheim are Unni and Wilfried Reinschmidt. They have recently bought this little inn and their warmth and friendliness permeate the air. Wilfried adds a special bonus: he is a gourmet chef. We felt quite smug to have "discovered" this beautiful, isolated little gem, so imagine our surprise when Crown Princess Sonja and a group of friends appeared in the lounge after a day of hiking.

ROISHEIM HOTEL
Owner: Unni & Wilfried Reinschmidt
2686 Lom, Norway
Tel: (062) 12031 or 12151
25 Rooms - Double NOK 460-520
Open: February 15 to October 31
Credit Cards: MC VS
Very old farmhouse
Located 340 km N of Oslo

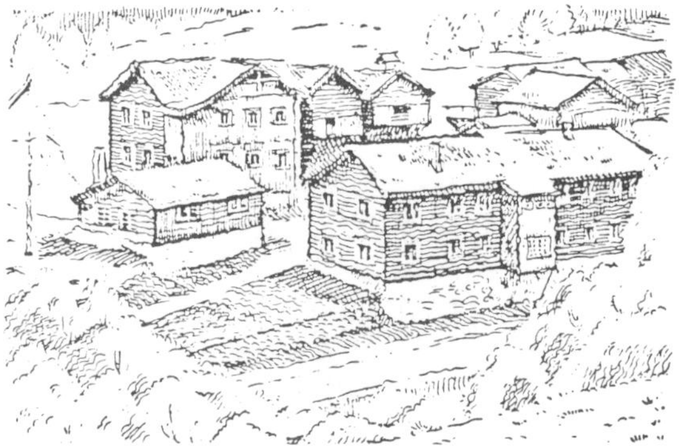

The Gabelshus is one of the most expensive hotels we have listed in Scandinavia. The reason it is included is because Oslo is such a popular tourist destination that we felt a hotel should be recommended and this is one of the least expensive good hotels we could find. The location is not perfect - a brisk 15-minute walk to the heart of town - but just near the hotel either a trolley or a bus will quickly take you into the city center for sightseeing and shopping. The three-story hotel with its mansard tiled roof is not very old but quite attractive, with a lawn in front and ivy creeping over the red brick facade. The interior is definitely olde worlde, with a cozy English country house ambiance. An especially attractive room is the lounge to the left of the reception area. Here white walls, a paneled ceiling, a fireplace flanked by old wooden chairs, gleaming copper knick knacks and bouquets of flowers create a very homey atmosphere. The guestrooms are pleasant, although with a modern, motel-like appearance. There is a large dining room, light and airy, with big windows looking out into the back garden. The Gabelshus is definitely a hotel with personality, quite different from any other in Oslo. If you don't mind being away from the town center, this might be just the hotel for you.

GABELSHUS HOTEL
Manager: Agathe Riekeles
Gabeles Gate 16
0272 Oslo 2, Norway
Tel: (02) 55 22 60
45 Rooms - Double NOK 1,400-1,800
Open: All year except Christmas & Easter
Credit cards: AX VS
About 15-minute walk to city center
Located in a residential area of Oslo

The Walaker Hotel has been in the same family since 1690 - it has been variously an inn, a posting station, a village shop and a bakery. The family tradition is richly maintained: Hermod Walaker is the cook, Oda Walaker the receptionist, the two sons waiters and gardeners, the two young daughters babysitters. The hotel is actually several buildings - one of which is a very plain 1940s-style motel cottage complex. But do not judge by this addition, because the main house is cozy in a Victorian way with beamed ceilings, open fireplace, red walls, green floor and lacy white curtains. This is where the family keeps its old furnishings and where guests frequently gather to sing around the piano. The guestrooms are very simple without any decorator touches. The location of the Walaker Hotel is enticing - just steps from the Sognefjord where small boathouses, brightly painted in reds, yellows and blues, reflect in the mirror-like water. Just across the fjord, easily reached in 15 minutes by boat, is the small, beautiful Urnes stave church - the oldest stave church in Norway. If you are looking for sophistication or elegance, this hotel would not be your "cup of tea", but if you want to find a family-style inn, rich with genuine warmth and hospitality, the Walaker Hotel has much to offer.

WALAKER HOTEL
Owner: Oda and Hermod Walaker
5815 Solvorn, Sognefjord
Norway
Tel: (056) 84 207
23 Rooms - Double NOK 360-580
Open: May 1 to October 1
Credit Cards: None accepted
Fabulous fjord location
Located 235 km NE of Bergen

Founded in 1722, the Utne Hotel is Norway's oldest inn. Undoubtedly this hotel also holds the record in continuity of ownership and management, for the same family has operated this small hotel for the last 200 years. With such a history, it is no wonder that the Utne Hotel is very special. The small white frame hotel sits snugly in its own little garden across from the pier where ferries constantly glide in and out - a most convenient location for exploring the Hardangerfjord. From the moment you enter, the snug ambiance envelops you in the cozy little lounges filled with antiques. My favorite room is the reception room, formerly the kitchen, with a large open hearth in the corner, a grandfather clock, antique country table - all accented by old wooden boxes, copper pots and beautiful old candlesticks. There are only 24 guestrooms, each varying in size and decor as befits such an old inn. The decor in the bedrooms is simple and old-fashioned, but comfortable and homey, with most having a small bathroom tucked into a corner or closet. Even if this were not such an appealing inn, the delicious food would certainly justify a detour to the Utne Hotel.

UTNE HOTEL
Owner: Hildegun Aga Blokhus
5797 Utne, Norway
Tel: (054) 66 983
24 Rooms - Double NOK 480-620
Open: All year except Christmas & Easter
Credit cards: All major
Small village on Hardangerfjord
Located 40 km S of Voss

The Hotel Rusthallargarden is located in the charming small fishing village of Arild, and although it sits directly on the main highway leading into town, across the street is a terrace for enjoying the sunshine and the view. The hotel is incorporated into a 17th-century farmhouse which was converted into a small hotel at the turn of this century. Since that time it has been lovingly operated by the Malmgren family, of which Peter and Eva are the fourth generation, and they have created an atmosphere of warmth and coziness. Downstairs there are several dining rooms, including a very attractive room like a sun-porch with windows on three sides. There are many nooks and crannies where guests can linger, including an especially charming library with beamed ceiling and walls lined with books. Upstairs each of the guestrooms varies, but all are attractively decorated, many with antique beds and desks. Instead of numbers, each bedroom has a name such as Grandmother's Room, The Major's Room, and The Poet's Room. It is just a short walk down the main road to the quaint harbor lined with old thatched-roofed cottages colorfully painted in blues, reds, pinks and yellows.

HOTEL RUSTHALLARGARDEN
Owner: Peter & Eva Malmgren
Box 5
26043 Arild, Sweden
Tel: (042) 46275
25 Rooms - Double SEK 590
Open: June to August
Credit cards: AX MC VS
Tennis, sauna, swimming pool
Located 35 km NW of Helsingborg

The Fjallnas, dating back over a hundred years, is the oldest mountain lodge in Sweden. Many wonderful photographs on the walls indicate that the mustard-yellow wood-frame building looks quite similar now to how it did in the days of old. And the tourists still come for the same reason - the enjoyment of being close to nature. The hotel consists of several buildings, with the main lodge situated on a tiny peninsula jutting into the lake. The large dining room has windows on three sides looking through the trees out to the water. My favorite room is the cozy lounge where the warmth of the fire invites one to nestle down with a good book. The walls are artistically decorated with an enormously long pair of narrow skis, very old ice skates, mountain traps, bugles and guns intermixed with a large assortment of hunting trophies. The guestrooms also have the mountain-lodge look, pine-paneled, with sturdy pine furniture: room 32 is especially nice, with a view out to the lake. Ulla and Nils Lundh are your warm and gracious hosts. Ask Nils about his fascinating hobby - he is Sweden's expert on the migration of the gigantic, beautiful musk ox. The Fjallnas is just what it is supposed to be - a simple mountain retreat.

FJALLNAS MOUNTAIN PENSION
Owner: Ulla & Nils Lundh
Fjallnas 10
82098 Tanndalen, Sweden
Tel: (0684) 23031
29 Rooms - Double SEK 400
Open: Feb to Apr & Jul to Sep
Credit cards: MC VS
Lakeside, boating, swimming
Near the Norwegian border
Located 556 km NW of Stockholm

If you are a lover of genuine castle hotels, Vastana Slott, open only during the summer months, is worth a detour. The castle, owned and managed by Rolf von Otter and his lovely wife, is far more like a home than a hotel, and indeed it is a home: Rolf von Otter was born here, as were many generations of his family before him. There is nothing commercial about this hotel. In fact, there are so few discreetly placed signs leading to the castle that, unless you are looking for Vastana Slott, you would never happen upon it. Once you find the road, it winds up the hill from the highway and ends in front of the hotel, a lovely white manor house with a red-tiled roof flanked by two small annexes which form a courtyard. The reception hall is on the first floor, with a fancy staircase leading to the upper level where there are a number of beautiful lounges superbly furnished with family heirlooms. There are seven bedrooms in the main building and two in the annex. Because the castle is so old, not all of the bedrooms have a private bathroom, but each is delightfully furnished with antiques. Breakfast is the only meal served at the castle, but there are several good restaurants just a short drive away. Staying at the Vastana Slott is like being a guest in a private home - of royalty, of course.

VASTANA SLOTT
Owner: Rolf von Otter
56300 Granna, Sweden
Tel: (0390) 107 00
9 Rooms - Double SEK 555
Open: June to August
Credit cards: None accepted
No restaurant
Wonderful castle above Lake Vattern
Located 186 km E of Gothenburg

For those who love boats the Kanalhotellet is a MUST. The hotel, a large brown Victorian mansion, is situated next to the Gota Canal. Most of the bedrooms are located in a new annex which stretches along the canal bank. From the outside, the annex is unassuming - a rather dull motel affair - but within, although simple and modern in decor, the rooms are pleasant and offer a stunning view. The wall facing the canal is almost entirely of glass and two strategically placed lounge chairs capture a magnificent panorama. The canal flows only a few scant yards from the guestrooms, separated by a narrow strip of grassy lawn. You will never need to attend another boat show. In summertime as many as 170 boats glide by each day - a fabulous display of vessels of every size and style. The Kanalhotellet has a history as romantic as its view. The hotel was built in 1894 by Anna and Johann Axelsson (grandparents of the present owner), who met at the White House where Anna was the housekeeper and Johann the butler for President Cleveland. They fell in love and Johann returned to Sweden where he built the Kanalhotellet along the Gota Canal, then sent for Anna to join him and become his wife.

KANALHOTELLET
Owner: Ann & Eric Axelsson Englinde
Storgatan 94
S-54600 Karlsborg, Sweden
Tel: (505) 12130
25 Rooms - Double SEK 300-450
Open: All year
Credit cards: All major
Overlooking Gota Canal

Mariefred, an endearing small village, is where Gripsholms Castle (with one of the finest portrait collections in the world) is located. Luckily, this quaint village is only a short distance from Stockholm and the favorite approach is by a nostalgic little steamer which departs from the capital regularly during the summer. A perfect combination is to arrive by boat and then take the train back to Stockholm. Although many people come just for the day, try to spend the night in Mariefred if you can squeeze it into your schedule. The place to stay is the Gripsholms Vardshus (one of the very oldest hotels in Sweden - dating back to 1623) located directly on the waterfront. There is a popular outdoor restaurant at the hotel, a favorite for tourists coming for the day from Stockholm. In addition, the hotel features a beautifully furnished restaurant on the second floor where elegant decor and fine food combine to make eating a memorable experience. Unfortunately the bedrooms are drab and none has a private bathroom. However, when I was at the hotel Bengt Eriksson's son, who showed me around, said that the family is planning to refurbish the guestrooms. But even if they have not been improved before you arrive, I think you will enjoy this historic old inn set in such a wonderful old village.

GRIPSHOLMS VARDSHUS
Owner: Bengt Eriksson
15030 Mariefred, Sweden
Tel: (0159) 100 40
10 Rooms - Double SEK 440
Open: All year
Credit cards: All major
Lakefront location
Located 82 km W of Stockholm

The town of Sigtuna is a gem - a truly beautiful lakeside town filled with colorful wood buildings lining a picturesque pedestrian street. The village is very popular with tourists who frequently come from Stockholm for the day. Sigtuna is about a 45-minute drive from Stockholm or an all-day excursion by boat. Stockholm's major airport is only about a 15-minute drive from the hotel, making this a convenient last-night stopover if you have been travelling around Sweden by car and want to spend one last night in a charming village before leaving by plane. Although the hotel is not especially charming or old, the village of Sigtuna is so conveniently located and so delightful that we wanted to be able to offer a hotel. The Stadshotellet is fairly new, having been built after the turn of the century. The dining rooms, two of which have large windows with a lovely view over the lake, are attractively decorated in a traditional style and serve most enjoyable food. The owner is very friendly and helpful. When I was at the hotel all of the bedrooms were being redecorated and the ones I saw were freshly painted and quite attractive - especially appealing were those with a view across the lake.

STADSHOTELLET
Owner: Lisbeth Wallden
Stora Nygatan 3
19300 Sigtuna, Sweden
Tel: (0760) 501 00
26 Rooms - Double SEK 430
Open: All year
Credit cards: All major
Charming old village
Located 40 km NW of Stockholm

The Lansmansgarden is located just 3 kilometers north of Sunne on Highway 234. This is Selma Lagerlof country, and the Lansmansgarden was supposedly mentioned in some of Selma's famous novels which were written about this part of Sweden where she was born and raised. Selma's home is nearby and has been turned into a very interesting museum. This lovely white frame farmhouse is now a modest hotel whose beauty lies in its simplicity. The decor inside is my idea of very Swedish, with light colors, white painted furniture, lots of windows letting in streams of sunlight, touches of blue in painted doors and awnings and handcrafted rugs. Nothing is fancy. Nothing is decorator-perfect, but the effect is one of a warm welcome and comfy caring. The guestrooms are small, but attractive - most with crisp-white painted furniture and accents of color in the throw rugs, bedspreads and curtains. Several of the guestrooms are on the grounds in small red cottages. Behind the hotel a field runs down to the lake where fishing and boating can be arranged. When I was looking for the hotel, I met some Americans at the tourist office who had "happened" upon the Lansmansgarden and loved it so much that they extended their stay for several days.

LANSMANSGARDEN
Owner: Ulfsby Herrgard
68600 Sunne, Sweden
Tel: (0565) 10301
30 Rooms - Double SEK 490
Open: May 2 to September 15
Credit cards: All major
Overlooking Fryken Lake
Located 358 km W of Stockholm

The Vadstena Klosters Guesthouse is located in the charming medieval town of Vadstena which is beautifully situated on the shore of Lake Vettern. As the name implies, the hotel is part of the old abbey founded by Saint Birgitta. Although the reception was not as personal as many others I experienced in Sweden, there is nothing austere about the little inn. The public rooms have warmth and charm created by the strategic placement of antiques. The bedrooms, although simple, are pleasant, with painted wood furniture and pastel colored walls. There is no restaurant, but a nice buffet breakfast is served each morning in the lounge. The cloisters are incorporated into the hotel and the arches are reminiscent of the early history of the inn as are the stone steps at the entrance - worn down through the ages by the feet of many nuns. The setting of the inn is perfect, adjacent to the lovely church designed by Saint Birgitta to her specifications: "plain construction, humble and strong". The effect is one of striking airiness and utter simplicity. From the church, a short stroll along the lake through a beautiful park brings you to the magnificent Vadstena Castle, certainly one of the most dramatic buildings in Sweden.

VADSTENA KLOSTERS GUESTHOUSE
Owner: The Birgitta Foundation
Lasarettsgatan
59200 Vadstena, Sweden
Tel: (0143) 11530
25 Rooms - Double SEK 515
Open: January 2 to December 20
Credit cards: AX MC VS
13th-century monastery, no restaurant
Located 265 km SW of Stockholm

In every research adventure, a few inns remain more than a memory of pretty rooms or a delectable dining experience. Instead, sometimes we lose our hearts completely, and fall in love we did with the Toftaholm Manor House Hotel. This delightful inn is really a dream. Not just a "dream" in that it is a picturesque mustard-yellow farmhouse perfectly situated on a grassy meadow stretching out to an idyllic lake, but also a dream of its young owners, Lisbeth and Jan Boethius. When they bought the property several years ago, the old farmhouse had become dilapidated and the lake had crept up to the house in marshland. But Lisbeth and Jan saw the potential for the inn they had always dreamed of owning. They dredged the lake in front of the manor and created a beautiful green lawn rolling gently to it. They replaced the ugly modern windows with beautiful old-fashioned ones. They freshly painted all of the guestrooms, lovingly placed their antiques throughout and added fresh flowers in every nook and cranny. The result of all their efforts is a delightful inn and a dream fulfilled.

TOFTAHOLM MANOR HOUSE HOTEL
Owner: Lisbeth & Jan Boethius
Toftaholm
34015 Vittaryd, Sweden
Tel: (0370) 44055 Telex: 70970
44 Rooms - Double SEK 570
Open: All year
Credit cards: All major
Lake, own island & beach, boats, playground
Located 190 km E of Gothenburg

Scotland

Ardvasar Hotel is a traditional country pub that has gained a reputation for good Scottish food. Bill Fowler loves to cook and changes his set dinner menu every evening depending upon what is fresh and locally available. He always offers a choice of starters and a choice of fish, poultry and meat for the main course. Overnight guests have the use of a simply furnished lounge for relaxing and enjoying after-dinner coffee. If you are in the mood to meet locals and other visitors to the Isle of Skye you can go into the adjacent pub. Bedrooms are not fancy in their decor and vary in size from small to quite large family rooms. The hotel is located just a short drive from the Mallaig to Armadale ferry at the southern tip of the Island of Skye. Although the crossing takes less than an hour it is a long, cumbersome procedure to load and unload cars onto and off the boat. As an alternative you can take the fast, very short ferry ride from Kyle of Lochalsh (for which no reservations are needed) and enjoy the hour's drive to Ardvasar.

ARDVASAR HOTEL
Owner: Bill & Greta Fowler
Ardvasar
Isle of Skye IV45 8RS, Scotland
Tel: (04714) 223
11 Rooms, 8 with private bathrooms
£20 per person B & B
Open: March to December
Credit cards: VS
Historic inn on the island of Skye
Located 1 mile S of the Armadale ferry

Arisaig Hotel lies on the "Road to the Isles" between Fort William and the port of Mallaig. It's an old-fashioned, comfortable coaching inn built about 1720 and greatly added on to over the years. There is nothing fancy or pretentious about this hotel and it has an atmosphere of utter tranquility. Every year George and Janice Stewart make improvements adding old-fashioned touches: over the 1987 winter season nine bedrooms are due to be refurbished, furnished with traditional-style furniture and given smart modern bathrooms. A meal at Arisaig Hotel is a pleasure. Janice and her son Gordon do the cooking and you can expect to see lots of well cooked traditional Scottish dishes on the menu. A typical dinner might include: venison pate, baked fillet of Loch Ness salmon with vermouth sauce and apple pie. The hotel stands on the shores of Loch Nan Ceal at the edge of the village of Arisaig. It's a perfect spot for visiting the Highlands and islands - Bonnie Prince Charlie country is all around you and the islands of Eigg, Rhum and Skye just a boatride away from the nearby port of Mallaig. From Fort William take the A82 north and turn left on the A830, Mallaig road, for the 35-mile drive to Arisaig.

ARISAIG HOTEL
Owner: The Stewart family
Arisaig
Inverness-shire PH39 4NH, Scotland
Tel: (06875) 210
12 Rooms, 9 with private bathroooms
£22 per person B & B
Closed: November and February
Credit cards: None accepted
Historic inn on the Road to the Isles
Located 35 miles W of Fort William

Braemar Lodge is a most attractive small hotel run by Vi Milne with the assistance of Carolyn Ridley. Carolyn's husband David is the chef who offers a tempting array of freshly prepared dishes from a short a la carte menu. The bedrooms are prettily decorated, with five having en-suite bathrooms with showers while two smaller bedrooms share a bathroom with a tub. Beyond the comfortable lounge and attractive dining room a small paneled bar with a blazing log fire is the focal point of this delightful hotel. On the first Saturday in September, Scotland's most famous Highland Games, the Braemar Gathering, draws thousands to the spectacle of kilted clansmen, pipe bands, caber tossing and the like. If you book a year in advance Braemar Lodge can offer you accommodation within walking distance of the games. But do not confine your visit to Braemar to this one famous week as the area around Braemar has much to offer: golf on the highest golf course in Scotland, Balmoral, the nearby home of the Royal family, fishing, skiing and beautiful countryside. Braemar is on the A93, 50 miles northwest of Perth.

BRAEMAR LODGE HOTEL
Owner: George & Vi Milne
Braemar
Aberdeenshire AB3 5YQ, Scotland
Tel: (03383) 627
7 Rooms, 5 with private bathrooms
From £25.50 single to £41.40 double
Open: All year
Credit cards: MC VS
Small hotel
Located 50 miles NW of Perth

Callander is a most inviting town close to the Trossachs - a picturesque area of hills and lakes. Situated just off the town's main street on a quiet side lane, East Mains House is an unusual, rather grand, stone home built over 200 years ago. Quite the nicest room in this bed and breakfast is the lounge - a Victorian addition on a grand scale. With its lofty, elegant plasterwork ceiling decorated in shades of blue and white with matching blue walls and blue flowered drapes and sofas toning with the soft beige and blue carpets, this room has a grand country house feel to it. Susie Lowden usually offers only bed and breakfast accommodation to her guests, suggesting restaurants and pubs in the town for evening meals, but if you give her advance notice she is happy to prepare one. A wide spiral staircase winds up to the bedrooms that are large enough to give travellers with the largest of suitcases lots of room. One of the attic bedrooms is an extremely large family room with two single and a double bed. Breakfast is served family-style in the kitchen. A casually furnished television room seems to be little used except for watching the news. From Edinburgh take the M9 to beyond Stirling, leaving at junction 10, the A84, for Crianlarich. On the main street of Callander turn left on the Glasgow road and East Mains House is signposted 200 yards from the bridge on your left.

EAST MAINS HOUSE
Owner: Susie Lowden
Callander
Perthshire FK17 8AG, Scotland
Tel: (0877) 30080
4 Rooms, 2 with private bathrooms
From £11 to £12 per person B & B
Open: All year
Credit cards: None accepted
Bed & breakfast
Located 50 miles NW of Edinburgh

This solid Victorian villa cannot be described as being a "countryside" bed and breakfast for it stands on the main Fort William to Inverness road, just to the north of town. But all the windows are double-glazed to reduce any sound from traffic and accommodation is quite the nicest in its category that I saw in Fort William so I decided to include it despite its position. Glynis Ross and her family came here a few years ago and have done a fine job stripping off layers of paint from the woodwork to expose the old pine beneath, papering prettily and adding homey little touches to all the rooms. A front parlor with comfortable chairs and lots of books is yours to use. Breakfast is the only meal that Glynis serves and she is happy to recommend restaurants and pubs in town at dinnertime. Upstairs one of the bedrooms enjoys a modern en-suite bathroom while the other two guestrooms share a large pine-panelled bathroom. Your arrival will doubtless be heralded by two Yorkshire terriers who summon Glynis to show you to your room. There is plenty of off-road parking behind the house. Fort William is a major touring center for the Western Highlands. Dalkeith Villa is on the A82 just north of town, next to the swimming pool.

DALKEITH VILLA
Owner: Glynis Ross
Belford Road
Fort William
Inverness-shire PH33 6BU, Scotland
Tel: (0397) 4140
3 Rooms, 1 with private bathroom
From £10 to £13 per person B & B
Open: All year
Credit cards: None accepted
Bed & breakfast
Located in the center of Fort William

Ranald and Margaret Laing are members of Wolsey Lodges, an association of selected members who offer hospitality in their homes. Margaret resigned from her job as head of the music department at an Inverness school to devote herself to her family, cooking and tending her large garden. She finds that her musical talents are quite often called for when she and Ranald gather with guests round the grand piano in the evening. Ranald is a Latin and Greek teacher with an intense interest in Scottish genealogy and the clans. The spacious sitting room has lots of books and armchairs gathered round the fireplace and the grand piano occupies a large portion of the room. Margaret cooks traditional home-style meals using local fresh produce and encourages guests to bring their own wine to accompany the meal. The bedrooms are large, light and airy - all are in the main house but one has its own private courtyard entrance. As to sightseeing, Loch Ness and Invernss are just down the road and there is an abundance of historic sights and castles within easy driving distance. From Inverness, go up Castle Street (B861) and continue until the suburbs end (2 miles). As the road goes up a hill Old Town of Leyes is signposted to your right down a narrow dirt lane.

OLD TOWN OF LEYES
Owner: Ranald & Margaret Laing
Culduthel
Inverness
Inverness-shire IV1 2AE, Scotland
Tel: (0463) 236394
3 Rooms with private bathrooms
£16 per person B & B
Open: All year
Credit cards: None accepted
Country home
Located 3 miles S of Inverness

The Falls of Dochart Cottage is a pretty little "doll's house" in a beautiful setting. Fronting the main road into Killin, the cottage faces the broad tumbling Falls of Dochart. The many intriguing craft shops of Killin are just a short walk away, the distance of a narrow stone bridge. Wanting to live closer to their daughter, Stan and Johnnie Mudd purchased this enchanting bed and breakfast which they run with great enthusiasm. Guests rave about the variety of menus Mrs Mudd plans for breakfasts, her homemade baking and her thoughtfully prepared evening meals. You dine in a homelike atmosphere around the large dining table. Guests have the use of a cozy lounge. There are only four small but prettily decorated bedrooms sharing a guest bathroom. Children are always given a warm welcome and Sona, the Mudds' sheepdog, is happy to keep them amused catching the ball they throw to her at the top of the stairs and rolling it back to them. From Edinburgh take the M8 to Stirling, the A84, then A85, to the A827 to Killin and as you see the falls Dochart Cottage is on your right before you go over the bridge.

FALLS OF DOCHART COTTAGE
Owner: Stan & Johnnie Mudd
1 Grey Street
Killin
Perthshire FK21 8SN, Scotland
Tel: (056 72) 363
4 Rooms sharing 1 bathroom
£8 per person B & B
Open: All year
Credit cards: None accepted
Bed and breakfast
Located 70 miles NW of Edinburgh

Surrounded by the quiet and peace of the countryside yet only a few minutes' drive from the center of Pitlochry, Auchnahyle is a complex of cottages and outbuildings set around a farmyard. The largest cottage is Alistair and Penny Howman's home and inside it's immaculate and comfortable. A snug dining room and lounge open off either side of the steep narrow staircase that leads to the two guest bedrooms set beneath the sloping eaves. These two rooms share a bathroom while a twin room downstairs has a private bathroom. All is country-cozy and Alistair and Penny find that quite often a group of friends takes over their home for a holiday. Penny cooks every dinner as if she were giving a dinner party, with menus such as avocado mousse with prawns, quail with almonds and fresh fruit pavlova. Often vegetables are homegrown. Guests are encouraged to bring their own wine to accompany the meal. Across the farmyard Rowan Tree Cottage is rented for family vacations: parents often prepare supper for their children and then slip across the courtyard to Alistair and Penny's for a leisurely meal. Three friendly dogs, two goats and an aged donkey complete the rural picture. To find Auchnahyle enter Pitlochry from the south (A9). Pass under the railway bridge, turn right up East Moulin Road and take the fourth turning right (by letter box). Continue on bearing right until you reach Auchnahyle.

AUCHNAHYLE
Owner: Alistair & Penny Howman
Pitlochry, Perthshire PH16 5JA, Scotland
Tel: (0796) 2318
3 Rooms, 1 with private bath
From £16.50 to £17.50 per person B & B
Open: Easter to October
Credit cards: MC
Country home
Located 30 miles N of Perth

Pitlochry developed in the latter half of the 19th century as a Highland health resort and remains today as an attractive town of sturdy Victorian houses standing back from the wooded shores of Loch Faskally. Knockendarroch House stands above the rooftops of the town isloated by its own little hill and surrounding garden. James McMenemie returned home from his job as a chef at Cromlix House to help his mum. Apart from being an excellent cook James has tremendous enthusiasm, which adds to the welcoming warmth of this small hotel. Intertwining flowers decorate the stained glass windows which filter sunlight onto the staircase which leads up to the spacious high-ceilinged bedrooms. All are crisply decorated and equipped with color television, coffee and tea makings and modern bathrooms with showers. If you have difficulty with stairs there is a small ground floor bedroom. We particularly appreciated the warmth of the central heating which kept the house snug on a chill August night. Pitlochry is 28 miles north of Perth on the A9.

KNOCKENDARROCH HOUSE
Owner: The McMenemie family
Higher Oakfield
Pitlochry
Perthshire PH16 5HT, Scotland
Tel: (0796) 3473
6 Rooms with private bathrooms
£28.50 per person dinner, B & B
Open: mid-March to mid-November
Credit cards: All major
Small hotel
Located 30 miles N of Perth

Medwyn House is the perfect place to stay for exploring Edinburgh (a 45-minute drive to the north) and the River Tweed Valley with its woollen mills, ancient ruined abbeys and grand variety of historic houses and castles. Anne and Mike Waterston fell in love with the house long before they realized what it would cost to heat its vast rooms. Undeterred by the expense, they ensure that central heating keeps guests warm so that they can enjoy the spaciousness of this lovely house. The pine paneled hall and lounge rise to the eaves of what was once a 14th-century inn - a blazing log fire with deep country-style chairs drawn around it give this room a mellow warmth. The adjacent large, sunny drawing room was added in the 1860s so it has large sash windows with views of the garden. Two of the bedrooms are spacious enough to be bedsitters, their adjacent bathrooms of equally large proportions - Anne adds nice little extras like sweets and shampoos. Anne enjoys cooking and a typical meal might include avocado and orange salad, homemade soup, roast beef and strawberry meringue. Mike and Anne are a particularly warm and genial couple. From Edinburgh take the A702 towards Abington, go through West Linton and take a righthand turn signposted Golf Club. The house is on your right.

MEDWYN HOUSE
Owner: Mike & Anne Waterston
Medwyn Road, West Linton
Peeblesshire EH46 7HB, Scotland
Tel: (0968) 60542
3 Rooms with private bathrooms
From £27 single to £36 double
Open: All year
Credit cards: None accepted
Country home
Located 20 miles S of Edinburgh

Spain

Perched on an overhang in one of the most perfectly preserved medieval towns in Spain you will find the Hotel Albarracin, situated in a 16th-century palace that was once the home of one of the leading ladies of the region. Recently acquired by an important Spanish hotel chain, the Albarracin retains some of its past elegance, most notably in the lobby with its heavy wood beams and staircase, in the hallways sprinkled with antiques, and in the restaurant, which serves very good regional specialties at very reasonable prices (the house salad and the migas, fried breadcrumbs with bacon, are particularly noteworthy). Unfortunately, in the effort to modernize, charm has been largely overlooked in the small, simply furnished bedrooms where linoleum now covers the original stone or wood floors. However, the Albarracin has a pretty little pool, is perfectly located at the edge of the old town (though this does make parking difficult) and is moderately priced, making it the best choice for the traveller who wishes to spend a full day wandering the tiny streets of this ancient town and exploring the archaeologically rich surrounding countryside.

HOTEL ALBARRACIN
Calle Azagra
Albarracin
Teruel
Spain
Tel: 74 71 00 11
36 Rooms - Double PTS 3,875-6,675
Credit cards: All major
Swimming pool
Nearest airport: Zaragoza (191 km)
Nearest train station: Teruel (38 km)

The Oromana is within easy driving distance of Seville but wonderfully isolated from the hubbub of the big city. Set in the countryside, surrounded by a cool, green pine grove, the white Oromana resembles an Andalusian villa, with lovely wrought-iron balconies, grillwork and the typical red-tile roof. The public rooms are tastefully furnished and casually inviting. The marble-columned sitting room with its vaulted ceiling is especially nice. The smallish guestrooms are simply furnished but comfortable and all have lovely views of the tranquil natural park on the Guadaira River: it is the setting that really makes this an outstanding choice of hotel. The hotel is air-conditioned throughout, a welcome touch in the heat of the Andalusian summer. The grassy pool area is very appealing and adds greatly to the restful atmosphere of the place. This is the hotel chosen by Spanish soccer teams that come to play Seville, and by NASA personnel when they come to man the nearby space-shuttle tracking station. They are all looking for peace and quiet and the manager, Senor Martinez, strives to provide it. Just a 15-minute drive from Seville, one can avoid city driving altogether by taking a bus that leaves the sleepy little suburban town of Alcala every half hour for the city.

HOTEL OROMANA
Avenida de Portugal, s/n
Alcala de Guadaira
Sevilla
Spain
Tel: 54 70 08 04
30 Rooms - Double PTS 5,200-6,300
Credit cards: AX VS MC
Swimming pool
Nearest airport: Seville (12 km)
Nearest train station: Seville (12 km)

The Colon is a stately hotel with some elegant touches, built in 1950 right in the middle of the enchanting Gothic Quarter (Barrio Gotico) of Barcelona. The lobby is entered up a broad, cream-carpeted stairway which passes through an impressive, square stone arch. The decor here, as throughout the hotel's public rooms, is perfectly lovely and makes you want to linger to watch the passersby in front of the massive cathedral across the street. On certain days local folklore buffs gather for a session of the regional dance, the sardanya (ask at the hotel desk for the current schedule). Some 34 of its rooms overlook the city's famous cathedral - a few have terraces. When making reservations request a room with a terrace, preferably a quieter location on one of the upper floors, and, if the budget allows, a suite or double room with a sitting area, for a little more money but also more space. All of the rooms have wonderful high ceilings and are accented with olde worlde touches which lend an intimate feeling to this fairly big hotel. The Colon is a good, middle-of-the-road choice between the other two hotels mentioned here, and enjoys an incomparable location.

HOTEL COLON
Avenida de la Catedral, 7
08002 Barcelona
Spain
Tel: 33 01 14 04 Telex: 52654
166 rooms - Double PTS 8,240-10,075
Credit cards: All major
Nearest airport: Barcelona
Nearest train station: Barcelona

Within easy walking distance of the "Ramblas" and the Gothic Quarter, this is a delightful hospice in the middle of the hustle and bustle of Barcelona. Originally the palace of a very wealthy 19th-century woman, the patron of San Juan Bosco, an Italian ambiance pervades the decor. It has a rooftop garden (a rare treasure) off a simply beautiful bar/lounge which boasts a sculpted ceiling, parquet floors and abundant antiques. Although the rooms are neither large nor lavish, each is unique in dimension and furnishings, has sculpted walls and a high ceiling. The rooms are centered around an interior arched gallery, topped with a beautiful old stained-glass skylight and accessed by an exquisite central staircase. To avoid street noise, you might want to request a room overlooking the terrace and, if you are there in the summertime, be sure to specify air conditioning. The Gran Via is a very special hotel in a special city, offering the intimacy and service that only a small, well-run family establishment can. It has no restaurant, but many excellent ones are nearby. And for a large city hotel the price is exceptional.

HOTEL GRAN VIA
Gran Via, 642
08007 Barcelona
Spain
Tel: 33 18 19 00
48 Rooms - Double PTS 6,000
Credit cards: All major
No restaurant
Nearest airport: Barcelona
Nearest train station: Barcelona

One of the most dramatic paradors in the country, the Duques de Cardona has dominated the fortified town of Cardona for centuries from its 1500-foot-high hilltop setting. This spot was chosen as a home by the Duke in the 10th century and, although much of the construction is recent, the period flavor and restoration have been faithfully attended to. Behind the hotel is a unique 2nd-century tower and 11th-century church along with a beautiful Roman patio from which a "bird's eye" view is obtainable of the unusual salt hills, the pueblo and the Pyrenees. The bedrooms are ample in size with wine-red tile floors, colorful woven bedspreads and dark wooden furniture. Room number 705 has "Catalan" beds with illustrated headboards, and overlooks the town and the ancient tower. Rooms 607 and 609 are semi-suites, and are divine, with curtained, canopied beds and wonderful perspectives onto the patio. The restaurant is spectacularly situated in a forever-long, stone-arched and wooden-beamed hall. Although out of the way, this parador offers a memorable night's stay in a carefully renovated historical setting with all the modern comforts of home.

P.N. DUQUES DE CARDONA
Castillo
Cardona
Spain
Tel: 38 69 12 75
71 Rooms - Double PTS 6,000-7,200
Credit cards: All major
Medieval castle
Nearest airport: Barcelona (99 km)
Nearest train station: Manresa (32 km)

In the foothills of the justifiably famous Picos de Europa, nestled atop the tiny mountain town of Covadonga, is the peaceful Hotel Pelayo. The hotel is sandwiched between the striking neo-Roman basilica and the cave of the Virgin of Asturias, which attract thousands of sightseers every year. Built in 1919 as a mountain retreat and hunting lodge, the inn is not elegant, but the rooms are comfortable and clean, and the setting unsurpassed in beauty. This is where Generalisimo Franco came to relax and hunt, and always reserved for him was the corner double, room 116, with views to both the basilica and the deep green mountains. The rooms are nicely decorated in red, green or gold, and have rustic wooden furnishings and floors and quite large, modern baths. All of the doubles have lovely vistas: a few rooms on the second floor have terraces, as do those on the third floor, but these are a bit smaller. There is an attractive lounge and a small bar on the first floor, but the restaurant is fairly ordinary. We suggest you head for the hills with a picnic as the scenery ranks among the most spectacular in the country.

HOTEL PELAYO
Covadonga
Asturias
Spain
Tel: 85 84 60 00
55 Rooms - Double PTS 4,200-6,800
Closed: Christmas to January 1
Credit cards: VS
Nearest airport: Aviles (110 km)
Nearest train station: Arriondas (15 km)

During its history, this charming hospice has been converted from a 16th-century wayside inn to a convent, to a farmhouse and most recently back to an inn. In typical Spanish fashion, the whitewashed building forms a square around a bright interior patio with fountain and flowers, and a wood-beamed gallery. A small dining room off the patio offers unusually good fare and on summer evenings there is music and a barbecue on the back terrace. It is located only 7 kilometers from the enchanting town of Cuenca, with its hanging houses, and only an hour and a half from Madrid, but the atmosphere is most definitely country, with cool breezes from the nearby Huecar River carrying the smell of pines and the sound of birds into every corner of the hotel. All of the bedrooms have countryside or patio views, and the tile floors, wooden ceilings and traditional, pale wood furnishings are much as they might have been over two centuries ago, the only discordant note being the rather flowery drapes and spreads. Room number 130 is particularly nice, a spacious suite with a fireplace and charming, old-fashioned sitting room. The ambiance is familial and the service personal in this intimate getaway.

HOTEL CUEVA DEL FRAILE
Carretera de Buenache, km. 7
16001 Cuenca
Spain
Tel: 66 21 15 71
54 Rooms - Double PTS 4,000-5,100
Closed: January 10 to March 1
Credit cards: AX MC VS
Swimming pool, tennis courts
Nearest airport: Madrid (165 km)
Nearest train station: Cuenca (7 km)

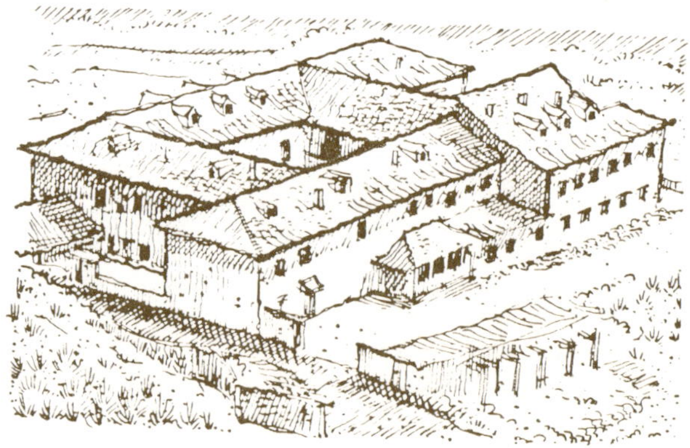

Recently added to the posh Entursa chain of hotels, the Victoria Palace, with its English country-manor flavor, is located a stone's throw from one of the most popular tourist attractions in Spain, yet offers a quiet and luxurious refuge from El Escorial's daytrippers and the fast-lane pace of Madrid. To see the whole monastery-cum-palace properly, you will need two visits, and this hotel will make that a pleasant prospect. A welcoming garden cafe in front (seemingly created for the turn-of-the-century tea-drinking crowd) entices you into the marble-floored lobby and up a graceful brass-railed double stairway to a spacious lounge with cozy brocade chairs, rich wood paneling and corner fireplace. Upstairs, past wide landings dappled with sunlight streaming through stained glass, are tastefully appointed bedrooms with lofty, high ceilings, polished wood floors and large windows overlooking the gardens. The service, though a bit formal, is correct and knowledgeable. By contrast, the warmly intimate, pub-style bar is charming and friendly. This impressive hotel, with its unique spired roof, will enhance a trip to Felipe II's palace.

HOTEL VICTORIA PALACE
Juan Toledo, 4
San Lorenzo de El Escorial
Madrid, Spain
Tel: 18 90 15 11 Telex: 22227
87 Rooms - Double PTS 4,400-6,700
Credit cards: All major
Swimming pool
Nearest airport: Madrid (46 km)
Nearest train station: El Escorial

Shadowed by the famous monastery's towers, this inn was a Hieronymite hospital and pharmacy in the 16th century, but, since the days of Ferdinand and Isabella, has sheltered those who came to worship. Until 1960 visitors exchanged a daily donation of a mere 50 pesetas (.30) for accommodation. Still today, for value received and atmosphere, follow the footsteps of the faithful here to this inn as there is nothing comparable in Guadalupe. Sharing and managing the edifice is an active Hieronymite religious order, whose guides regularly conduct an insider's tour of their monastery, museum and cathedral - a crazy and wonderful mixture of mudejar and Gothic architecture. The hotel rooms overlook the original stone-arched and paved hospital patio. Their decor varies wildly - some incredible, but all adequate and all with baths. To stay here is to live and breathe the history of Spain. Request a room on the gallery; number 112 is especially nice - given to visiting religious notables; the second-floor corner suite (no number) is baroquely elegant and many third-floor rooms boast original mudejar ceilings. Delicious fare and homemade wine is served under a high wooden ceiling in a richly paneled dining room.

HOSPEDERIA EL REAL MONASTERIO
Plaza Juan Carlos, 1
Guadalupe
Caceres
Spain
Tel: 27 36 70 00
40 Rooms - Double PTS 3,200-4,500
Credit cards: VS
Ancient monastery
Nearest airport: Madrid (225 km)
Nearest train station: Talavera (130 km)

This delightful hotel is on several floors of a large building in the heart of Madrid. Two elevators service the different floors, and the one on the right - a tiny, fire-sided affair - is unique, obviously having been constructed to fit the precise space available. Found on the third floor (Spanish second) are an extremely inviting reception, lobby and restaurant area whose decorative style could be called intense: pseudo-French with antique accents. But it is spacious, attractive and cozy, and a veritable oasis in the heart of town. The upper-floor bedrooms, each different in shape and size, are elaborately decorated with matching fabrics and offer olde worlde ambiance coupled with modern amenities. Manager Antonio Gil is justifiably proud of the frequent maintenance schedule - no chipped paint or worn carpet anywhere. The owners have gone to great lengths to soundproof the hotel from the noises of Madrid's central street, Gran Via. The hotel is a few blocks from the chic Puerta del Sol, a shopper's paradise, and the Plaza Mayor with its charming cafes. The Arosa is an excellent value for quality received.

HOTEL AROSA
Salud, 21
28013 Madrid
Spain
Tel: 12 32 16 00 Telex: 43618
121 Rooms - Double PTS 7,100-10,000
Credit cards: All major
Nearest airport: Madrid
Nearest train station: Madrid

Location and value are two of the best reasons for choosing this old-timer. It is located about halfway between the lively center of town at the Puerta del Sol and the elegant Paseo del Prado where the fabulous Museo del Prado awaits your visit. At the same time, the immediate vicinity of the hotel encompasses the relatively tranquil, pretty little plaza of Santa Ana, near the concentration of antique stores that line the Calle del Prado. Built in 1925, the hotel reflects its origins. The ground-floor entry from which the concierge efficiently directs the bustling scene is rather plain. The front desk, lobby and restaurant are found one floor up: removing the public rooms from city street noise. The bedrooms are on the floors above the lobby. They are all comfortable and the better rooms, facing the Plaza Santa Ana, are steeped with real olde worlde charm and style. A tiny, barely practicable, glassed-in terrace looks over the typical little plaza. The hotel is air-conditioned throughout - very welcome during a hot Madrid summer. The Gran Hotel Victoria is one of the best values in town and within walking distance of many of the highlights.

GRAN HOTEL VICTORIA
Plaza del Angel, 7
28012 Madrid
Spain
Tel: 12 31 60 00
120 Rooms - Double PTS 4,700-6,700
Credit cards: All major
Nearest airport: Madrid
Nearest train station: Madrid

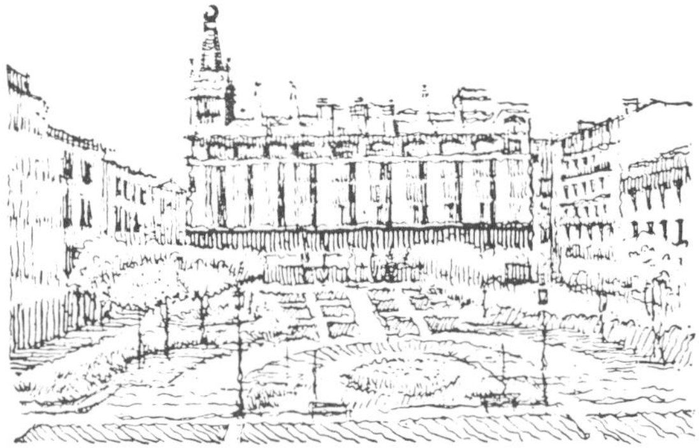

The ancient seignorial mansion which now houses the Emperatriz was constructed at the end of the 16th century, and has hosted such illustrious guests as the Empress Isabel of Portugal and Felipes II and III. The hotel is located on Merida's lively, stone-arcaded main square and, judging by the number of patrons, its pretty outdoor terrace cafe, with red-upholstered, white wrought-iron furniture, is a popular gathering spot. When you enter the manor, your first view will be of the wonderful cloistered central patio - with slender pillars and graceful arches - set up to allow you to dine in a truly noble setting. Everything about the hotel, from its fabulous historic facade, to its majestic stairway winding up to a stone-arcaded gallery, appears perfect for our taste. Unfortunately, due to "hotelocracy", in the absence of the director, we were unable to see the rooms personally. However, based on our impressions of everything else we feel confident that the integrity of the decor is maintained throughout, and this hotel offers such a good value that we have included it anyway. In this ancient city - Spain's richest in Roman remains - you cannot go wrong in the Emperatriz: the setting is charming and the location superb.

HOTEL EMPERATRIZ
Plaza de Espana, 19
06800 Merida
Badajoz, Spain
Tel: 24 31 31 11
41 Rooms - Double PTS 3,200-5,200
Credit cards: All major
Nearest airport: Badajoz (61 km)
Nearest train station: Merida

This hotel was originally a monastery, established by Cistercian monks in 1194, and active until 1835, when it was abandoned and tragically ransacked. For services rendered during the Carlist war of succession - and a nominal fee - General Prim came into this particular piece of property, and his descendants own it to this day. Curiously, because of the monastery's uninhabited period, neighboring villages can claim parts of it, too, as evidenced by some fabulous works of art (such as choirstalls, altars, furniture - even wine vats) that grace their otherwise relatively humble holy places. The site is large and rich in history, having fine architectural examples from the Gothic through the baroque periods. Wander at will, exploring every exciting corner, then enter the hotel from the beautiful cloisters. The antique-lined marble hallways must be 20 feet wide and 30 feet high, with arched ceilings, through which it seems the slightest sound echoes endlessly, and the incredible windows that appear to be covered with parchment are actually made of alabaster. The bedrooms are, not surprisingly, the original monks' cells, and therefore simply but nicely furnished, with wood floors and terraces overlooking a natural park, an interior patio or the cloister. Your stay here is guaranteed to be unforgettable.

HOTEL MONASTERIO DE PIEDRA
50210 Nuevalos
Zaragoza, Spain
Tel: 76 84 90 11
61 Rooms - Double PTS 4,200-4,900
Credit cards: All major
Tennis, swimming pool
Nearest airport: Zaragoza (118 km)
Nearest train station· Alhama de Aragon (20 km)

This hotel used to be part of the parador chain, but was recently ceded to the regional government of Andalusia. Its somewhat isolated location provides a delightful contrast to the cosmopolitan coastal area and is obviously a destination for travellers with a car. Everything here says relax and settle in for a few days. In keeping with its hunting-lodge origin, the decor is comfortably rustic with the emphasis on heavy wood furnishings. There are several cozy lounges, one especially attractive with a fireplace and numerous trophies. The restaurant is extremely inviting and specializes in excellent game dishes, which makes it popular with locals in Marbella, especially in the evening. The rooms are simple and attractive and offer every comfort, including large modern bathrooms. If you plan to be here between late fall and early spring, you might request room number 3, since it has its own little fireplace. But the stellar attraction of this hotel is its natural setting - a pine forest loaded with peace and quiet and, in the summer, a cool, shady terrace where you can breakfast to the scent of pine. There is also a small pool, made all the more pleasant by its surrounding towering pine trees.

REFUGIO DE JUANAR
Sierra Blanca
Ojen
Malaga, Spain
Tel: 52 88 10 00
19 Rooms - Double PTS 5,000
Credit cards: All major
Swimming pool
Nearest airport: Malaga (65 km)
Nearest train station: Cartama (38 km)

Back when you could cross the border between Spain and Gibraltar, the British residents of "the rock" used to come to Ronda for its cooler climate. In 1906, a hotel was built to house these British visitors and it was called the Queen Victoria. Although its interior has been remodeled and it is now a member of the extensive HUSA Spanish hotel chain, from the outside it betrays its non-Spanish origins. The public rooms are a mix of Victorian and modern decor. Some of the small sitting rooms are dominated by giant gilt-framed mirrors and boast Victorian furnishings, while the bar-cafeteria is decorated in rather ordinary contemporary Spanish style. The bedrooms are large and attractively fitted out with matching Victorian-style furniture. About 40 of them have views of the famous Ronda Gorge from their terraces, while the others look out on the pretty grounds whose paths lead down to the very edge of the gorge and whose gardens are shaded by giant trees. A large pool with its own tree-covered island and a smaller pool for children are surrounded by an expansive lounge area with a terrace overlooking the same spectacular view.

HOTEL REINA VICTORIA
Jerez, 25
Ronda
29400 Malaga
Spain
Tel: 52 87 12 40
90 Rooms - Double PTS 7,500
Credit cards: All major
Swimming pool
Nearest airport: Malaga (120 km)
Nearest train station: Ronda

Flanked by pretty gardens, the handsome stone facade of the Hotel Los Infantes blends beautifully with the medieval village of Santillana. The 18th-century facade of this typical moutain manor was moved stone by stone from the nearby town of Orena and faithfully reconstructed here. Over the doorway are two carved escutcheons - one bearing King Felipe V's coat of arms; the other that of Calderon, the original landlord. The reception area and the first-floor salon are filled with antiques and are perfectly charming, with wood floors and beamed ceilings. The breakfast room on the main floor, with its central fireplace, and the good dining room downstairs are not original, but are cozy and filled with olde worlde decor. Unfortunately, the bedrooms, with few exceptions, are small and rather plain, though consistently spotless and equipped with modern bathrooms and tiny terraces overlooking the gardens. The three front-facing doubles with sitting rooms, wooden balconies and antique touches cost a little more but are the best rooms in the house. Los Infantes offers reasonable accommodation with historical flavor.

HOTEL LOS INFANTES
Avenida Le Dorat, 1
Santillana del Mar
39330 Cantabria
Spain
Tel: 42 81 81 00
30 Rooms - Double PTS 5,200-6.800
Credit cards: AX MC VS
Nearest airport: Santander (30 km)
Nearest train station: Torrelavega (15 km)

The Linajes is (not easily) found down one of the tiny stone streets that crisscross Segovia's quaint old quarter, the barrio of San Esteban, which sits on a hill above the modern city. Known as "The House of the Lineages", the warm-stone and aged-wood facade of the hotel is beautifully preserved from the 11th-century palace of the noble Falconi family, whose escutcheon can still be seen over the arched entryway. Inside, with the exception of the pleasantly modern bar/cafeteria downstairs, the hotel conserves a charming old-Castile flavor, with dark wood, beamed ceilings and burnished-tile floors. A cozy alcove off the lobby, decorated with wonderful antiques, looks into a glass-enclosed garden patio on one side, and over the open terrace in back, sharing its panoramic views over the city's monumental skyline. There are lovely views from every bedroom, too. The rooms in the newer part are carpeted and comfortable, accented in golds and browns, with contemporary Spanish furnishings. However, those in the old part, though similarly furnished and decorated, remain favorites, with their wooden floors and views of the countryside through the original windows.

HOTEL LOS LINAJES
Dr. Velasco, 9
40003 Segovia
Spain
Tel: 11 43 17 12
55 Rooms - Double PTS 4,800-7,400
Credit cards: All major
No restaurant
Nearest airport: Madrid (89 km)
Nearest train station: Madrid (89 km)

Constructed on the 14th-century site of the church and convent of Santo Domingo, and next door to a 12th-century cathedral, this is nonetheless a parador whose byword is modern. But, as with all hotels in this government chain, the accommodations are something special. Of the original building, only the old cloister has been preserved, and converted into one of the most spectacular lounges we have come across. Graceful stone arches form the foundation of a square central room, several stories high, bedecked with hanging plants and decorated with soft contemporary furnishings. And the dining room, with its glass ceiling and wicker and chrome furniture, is sunny, bright and attractive, as is the indoor pool - a rarity in Spain. In interesting contrast to most other paradors, and certainly to its setting, the bedrooms are strikingly modern in decor, spacious with wine-red furnishings, pale woven bedspreads and black rubber floors. The demisuites, 121 and 221, are a few dollars more but offer enormous space for the price. Situated in a fertile valley, Seo de Urgel is surrounded by the sierras of Arcabell and Cadi.

P.N. DE LA SEO DE URGEL
Santo Domingo
Seo de Urgel
25700 Lerida
Spain
Tel: 73 35 20 00
84 Rooms - Double PTS 5,600-6,700
Credit cards: All major
Indoor swimming pool
Nearest airport: Barcelona (200 km)
Nearest train station: Puigcerda (51 km)

Seville is famous for its enchanting Santa Cruz Quarter (barrio), and the Murillo, a budget hotel, is situated within it. Only pedestrians can navigate the maze of streets in the barrio, so it is necessary to park outside the quarter - but a porter with a handcart will accompany you back to your car for your luggage. Built in "barrio" style by the owner, Don Miguel, the whitewashed hotel faces a narrow stone street overhung by iron lanterns and balconies, a setting which offers incomparable tranquility in this bustling city. Prior to his reincarnation as a hotelier over 20 years ago, Don Miguel was an antique dealer and wood craftsman, both apparent from the moment you arrive. The doors and ceiling are hand-carved, and the lobby is chock-full of antiques, including suits of armor. However, the Murillo's charm is almost spent in the lobby. The hallways above are dotted with antiques, but the bedrooms are nothing fancy, just simple, clean accommodations with white marble-tiled floors and pseudo-traditional Spanish wood furniture. Request an exterior room to take best advantage of the setting, and if one should fit your needs, there are a couple of small singles on the top floor that have terraces.

HOTEL MURILLO
Lope de Rueda, 7 y 9
41004 Seville
Spain
Tel: 54 21 60 95
61 Rooms - Double PTS 4,300-6,800
Credit cards: All major
No restaurant
Nearest airport: Seville
Nearest train station: Seville

Next to the ramparts, in the ancient fortified town of Sos, birthplace of the Catholic King Ferdinand, is the new parador which bears his name. Despite its recent construction, the hotel blends harmoniously with the centuries-old buildings around it. The setting is enchanting - surrounded by the fertile Campo Real, resplendent with corn, wheat and hay. The serenity is interrupted only by the chirping of swallows and the clanking of cowbells. The hotel's location is convenient for exploring the narrow maze of streets lined with low, sunken doorways and stone escutcheons, and for venturing up to the Sada palace where Spain's most renowned king, and Machiavelli's model prince, was born. In the lobby is a statue of the "reyito" (little king) alongside his mother, Juana Enrique. Upstairs, the view can be enjoyed over coffee or cocktails on an outdoor terrace, and the dining room is cozy, with leather chairs, wood-beamed ceiling and elaborate iron chandeliers. The bedrooms have brick-red tile floors, colorful woven spreads and drapes, pretty brass and glass lamps, and simple iron and brass bedsteads. A few have terraces.

P.N. FERNANDO DE ARAGON
Sos del Rey Catolico
50680 Zaragoza
Spain
Tel: 48 88 80 11
65 Rooms - Double PTS 5,600-6,700
Closed: December 15 to January 15
Credit cards: All major
Nearest airport: Pamplona (59 km)
Nearest train station: Pamplona (59 km)

Almazara translates as olive-oil press and identifies the purpose of this building before it was turned into a hotel in 1950. It once also served as a convent and, when built in 1560, it was the residence of Cardinal Mendoza, called the "Third King" because of his behind-the-scenes power during the reign of Ferdinand and Isabella. The owner has gone to great lengths to maintain the atmosphere - even to the point of constructing his own nearby residence in the same style. Like the parador, this modest hotel is outside of town on a hillside across the Tagus River, and thus requires a car, especially since the only meal served is breakfast. If you like a rural setting, however, and a good value, it is an excellent choice. The public areas are nicely appointed with regional decor and inviting with a cozy fireplace in the handsome lounge. The bedrooms are plain, but comfortably furnished, and seven of them have heart-stopping views of the city from large terraces. The view of one of Spain's most beautiful cities is not quite as all-inclusive as the parador's since this hotel is farther from town, but the terrace at sunset is lovely, and a room here is less than half the price.

HOTEL LA ALMAZARA
Apartado Postal, 6
48080 Toledo
Spain
Tel: 25 22 38 66
21 Rooms - Double PTS 3,400-5,200
Open: April to October
Credit cards: VS MC DC
No restaurant
Nearest airport: Madrid (80 km)
Nearest train station: Toledo

Originally only an exquisite restaurant, the hostal now also provides similarly wonderful lodgings in a former archbishop's summer home. The mansion is a real jewel, located only a stone's throw from the main city gate (Puerta de Bisagra). Enter from the parking lot through an 11th-century-wall to find a marvelous garden with the outdoor restaurant on the left. Climb the stairs on the right to reach the tiny foyer of the hostal. This is the one negative about the place - it is something of a hike with luggage. Reflecting its 18th-century heritage, the stunning stairway, the patio with its lovely fountain, and the cozy sitting rooms, embellished with antiques, are harmonious and tranquil. The indoor dining rooms (which are used only in the winter) are fabulous with their heavy wood beams and fireplaces. In warmer months dine outdoors in the shadow of the medieval walls on succulent Castilian specialties such as suckling pig. The period furnishings in the inviting guestrooms seem to blend into a tasteful whole. Although smallish, the rooms provide modern comfort with an unbeatable ambiance of past centuries all for a modest price, particularly when considering the quality and location.

HOSTAL DEL CARDENAL
Paseo Recaredo 24
45004 Toledo
Spain
Tel: 25 22 49 00
27 Rooms - Double PTS 4,300-6,600
Credit cards: AX
Nearest airport: Madrid (80 km)
Nearest train station: Toledo

This truly delightful small country inn is located just west of the sleepy village of Villalonga and only 3 kilometers from La Lanzada, one of the finest white-sand beaches in Spain. The ivy-covered, 16th-century, Galician manor house (pazo) is made of square-cut stone blocks, and is surrounded by verdant countryside and lovely gardens which shelter the hotel's pretty pool and tennis courts. It looks just like all the other farmhouses in the area, but you are invited to stay here. The arched stone entryway leads to a charming interior courtyard where meals are served "al aire libre" on the awning-covered patio off the dining room which features a wood-beamed ceiling and massive bare stone walls. The lobby and lounge retain an olde worlde country flavor down to the last detail, with wood floors and ceilings and whitewashed walls. The bedrooms are simply furnished, but appealingly decorated, with red-brick tile floors and warm wood furniture. If you are looking for a "getaway" spot, with the feeling of being in the middle of nowhere, while still within walking distance of the ocean and easy driving distance of an exciting city - Santiago - this inn is hard to beat.

HOTEL PAZO EL REVEL
Camino de la Iglesia
Villalonga
36990 Pontevedra
Spain
Tel: 86 74 30 00
21 Rooms - Double PTS 5,800
Closed: September 1 to June 15
Swimming pool, tennis
Nearest airport: Santiago (64 km)
Nearest train station: Pontevedra (25 km)

Switzerland

We were enchanted by the Schloss Hagenwil a few years back but sadly decided the facilities too basic to include the hotel in an edition of *Swiss Country Inns & Chalets*. However, *Best on a Budget* affords us the opportunity to qualify the attributes of this castle-hotel and share our discovery. Surrounded by a moat that is bounded by endless stretches of lush Appenzeller farmland, the Schloss Hagenwil dates from the 11th century. Its handsome timbered facade crowns an imposing stone base whose massive wood door once opened up to a drawbridge and now to a small, narrow bridge. Although a medieval fortress, the Schloss's purpose on a first weekend in May seemed to be to host a multitude of wedding parties. Above a lofty and barren entry hall, the Schloss Hagenwil has a few banquet rooms and an inviting popular, local restaurant. The menu is traditionally Swiss in its offering of delicious veal dishes, noodles, pastas, hearty soups and regional wines. It is in the restaurant that you will most likely meet the family who owns and manages the Schloss Hagenwil. The Angehrns are charming, and although Alfons and his wife are generous with smiles and warm greetings, they speak a heavy German dialect and understand very little English. Their daughter, however, is often present and has a good command of the English language. Under timbered beams of the upper floors are numerous rooms of which only two are offered to overnight guests. Although without private bathrooms (one must use the public toilets located on the first floor) the bedrooms are handsomely decorated and very comfortable.

SCHLOSS HAGENWIL
Owner: Alfons Angehrn family
CH-8580 Hagenwil bei Amriswil
Switzerland
Tel: (071) 67 19 13
2 Rooms - Double SFR 75
Credit cards: None accepted
Located 25 km SE of Konstanz

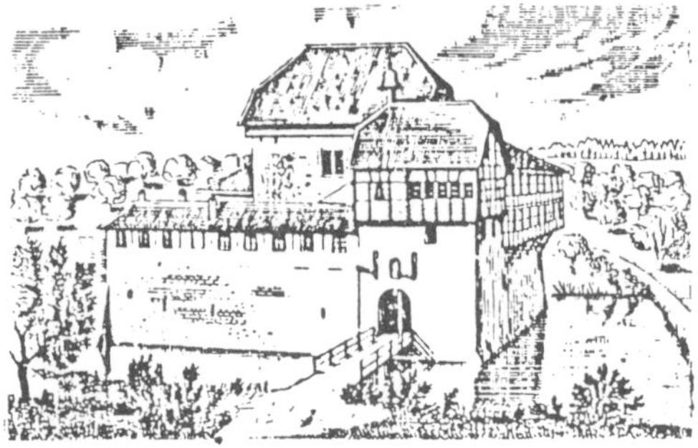

On my first visit to the Star and Post Hotel my heart was won by Faro, an enormous Bernese mountain dog napping in the middle of the lobby. Faro was such a fixture that postcards of this gentle, affectionate overgrown "puppy" were sent to his many admirers. Unfortunately Faro has died, but Haro, an equally gentle, loveable Bernese moutain dog is winning the hearts of guests of all ages. The Star and Post has been in the Tresch family for several hundred years and Rosemary Tresch is the hostess, warmly greeting her guests. When first we met, I asked her if she were the owner. She replied, with a twinkle in her eye, that in Switzerland the woman is not the "owner", she is always the "owner's wife". The Star and Post Hotel's history dates back many years to when it was a strategic post station giving shelter to those going over the St Gottardo Pass. About one-third of the rooms have an antique decor, but the majority are modern, so be sure to specify your preference at the time you make your reservation. The public areas abound with antiques and are very cozy.

STAR AND POST HOTEL
Owner: Tresch-Gwerder family
CH-6474 Amsteg, Switzerland
Tel: (044) 6 44 40 Telex: 78445
35 Rooms - Double SFR 55-150
Open: All year
Credit cards: AE VS DC MC
Old postal stop for St Gottardo Pass
Located 110 km S of Zurich

The Hotel Tamaro, ideally situated across the street from Lake Maggiore, has cheerful little tables set out in front of the hotel attracting many who gather to enjoy a cup of coffee or an ice while leisurely watching the boats gliding in and out of the harbor. As you enter the hotel the reception lounge, with an inviting array of comfortable antiques, is to the right. To the left is one of the most charming features of this small hotel, an interior courtyard crowned by a glass ceiling for protection against the weather. In this small inside patio tables are set gaily amongst many plants, giving the feeling that you are dining in a garden. The guestrooms are situated on many various levels - sometimes it is like a game to find your room. Although each of the bedrooms varies greatly in style of decor and size, they are all quite pleasant and immaculately clean. I prefer the rooms in the front with a view of the lake - some even have small balconies. However, the lakeside rooms are noisy, so if you prefer quiet, ask for a room in the back. Annetta and Paolo Witzig are the owners of the Tamaro and they are very involved in the management of this delightful old Ticino-style patrician house: the charming and attractive Annetta is frequently at the reception desk greeting guests as they arrive.

HOTEL TAMARO
Owner: Annetta & Paolo Witzig
CH-6612 Ascona, Switzerland
Tel: (093) 350 282 Telex: 846132
56 Rooms - Double SFR 90-170
Open: February to November
Credit cards: All major
Across the street from Lake Maggiore
Located 200 km S of Zurich

Every aspect of the Hotel Stern has been designed and managed with the guest in mind. This is not a glamorous hotel, yet it is obvious that behind every detail is someone who cares and works very hard to achieve the greatest comforts. Mr Pfister, the owner, is a true professional in his field. He and his wife oversee every detail of management: Mrs Pfister is in charge of the bookkeeping and the hotel staff while Mr Pfister tends the front desk and the kitchen. Located in the old section of Chur, the Hotel Stern dates back 300 years and is a wonderful blend of traditional decor and modern conveniences. In the 20 years that the Pfisters have owned the Hotel Stern they have been dedicated to providing choice accommodations and an excellent restaurant, and they have done a tremendous job bringing this old hotel into the 20th century. The bedrooms are simply furnished and comfortable, although not as attractive as the dining rooms and lounges which have more antiques. The furnishings are principally of the light pine wood so typical in the Grison area of Switzerland. The decor also profits greatly from the fact that Mr Pfister is an avid art collector and throughout the hotel are many skillfully displayed works of original art. There is a wonderful collection of the paintings of the famous Swiss artist, Carigiet, whose whimsical scenes are inspired by his own childhood in a small country village.

Another interesting collection of the Pfisters' is a fabulous assortment of horse-drawn carriages and sleds stored in a garage behind the hotel. The collection, which is like a tiny museum, ranges from simple country sleds to gorgeous carriages fit for nobility. Mr Pfister's father owned these marvelous carriages for use in his profession as a driver. Mrs Pfister told a wonderful story about her father-in-law who must be quite a man. A few years ago, when in his seventies, he agreed as a favor to a friend to drive one of the carriages all the way to Germany for a political celebration. En route he had an accident, was hospitalized, and ordered by the doctor to remain in bed and not continue the journey. Undaunted, the senior Mr

Pfister "escaped" from the hospital, caught up with his carriage, and arrived on time in splendor and style. Any car buff would also envy a more modern counterpart, Mr Pfister's 1932 Buick Sedan. With a brown exterior and dusty rose colored velvet interior, it is truly gorgeous and in mint condition. As the city fathers were opposed to the use of horse and carriages on public roads, the Pfisters instead use the Buick on special occasions. On request, he can meet guests arriving by train. (Note: Speaking of trains, Chur makes an excellent choice for a town to stay in when either arriving or departing on the Glacier Express - one of Europe's most fabulous rail journeys.)

The town of Chur is one of the oldest cities in Switzerland and has many excellent medieval buildings. A new addition to the town is a wine museum featuring an enormous antique wine press plus showcases displaying the history of wines. Mr Pfister has been one of the sponsors of this extremely interesting museum and (with a little persuasion) can probably give you a short tour should you happen to arrive when the museum is closed.

HOTEL STERN
Owner: Emil Pfister
Reichgasse 11
CH-7000 Chur
Switzerland
Tel: (081) 22 35 55 Telex: 74198
55 Rooms - Double SFR 124-134
Open: All year
Credit cards: All major
In heart of Chur
Located 120 km E of Zurich

Sometimes I will include a town because of an inn's location, but, in this case, I've included an inn because I fell in love with the town. The mountain village of Grimentz is a bundle of old, storybook, darkened wood timbered chalets, brilliantly accented with colorful flowers. This village deserves to be explored and its appeal demands that you linger. Tucked at the entrance to the village is a pretty little whitewashed inn, with handsome wood shutters. Although a simple inn, the Hotel de Moiry has some especially inviting rooms. On the top floor and in the little "chalet" in front of the hotel you find the choicest rooms, each with its own private bathroom and with windows opening onto the most refreshing mountain views imaginable. Marvelous sunshine blessed our visit and we were able to dine on the patio in front of the hotel enjoying a memorable meal of fondue, salad, crusty, dark bread and beer. The dining room inside is warmed by a cozy fireplace, and the tables are set with fresh cloths and flowers. Be sure to notice a mural on one of the walls which portrays an annual competition between the cows of the area to determine the leader. (I am happy to report that the cows belonging to the Hotel de Moiry are consistently the winners.)

HOTEL DE MOIRY
Owner: Aurel Salamin
CH-3961 Grimentz
Switzerland
Tel: (027) 65 11 44
25 Rooms - Double SFR 70-90
Open: All year
Credit cards: None accepted
Charming high mountain village
Located 200 km E of Geneva

The Berghaus Marmorbruch is a cozy mountain chalet located high on a hillside above Grindelwald. To reach it, wind up a beautiful forested road, the trees broken only by small green pastures and occasional grazing cows. A very small inn, open only in the summer months, the Marmorbruch has just four plain, but very clean rooms. All have beautiful views of the mountain climber's dream (and nightmare), the infamous "Eiger". None of the bedrooms have private bath, but all have a sink and mirror area, and towels are provided. Downstairs, the small, homey restaurant has only seven tables, but during daylight hours the outdoor terrace offers additional seating, and welcomes hikers and sightseers alike. Many hiking trails begin near here, and in the evening fondue parties and folkloric entertainment liven the atmosphere of the cheerful restaurant. Children will be enchanted by the sheep, donkeys, goats and cows who live nearby. The Marmorbruch is a perfect retreat for avid hikers or travellers in search of peace and quiet, Swiss Alps style.

BERGHAUS MARMORBRUCH
Owner: Peter Markle
Berghaus "Marmorbruch"
CH-3818 Grindelwald
Switzerland
Tel: (036) 53 13 18
4 Rooms - Double SFR to 70
Closed: October 13 to May 30
Credit cards: None accepted
Restaurant, hiking trails, outdoor terrace
Mountain setting - 4 km above Grindelwald
Located 77 km SE of Bern

Overlooking the lovely little Grindelwald church is the small, shuttered chalet-style Hotel Fiescherblick. The hotel is not fancy but does possess a most inviting atmosphere. As you enter the lobby the mood is set by a great old Swiss clock, a painted Swiss wall cupboard, a little table joined by a regional Alpine chair and a few very old milking stools. The dining room is decorated with modern furniture but the flowers on the tables, and the pewter mugs and antiques that adorn the walls add warmth to the area. (The food is quite well known locally). In addition to the main room, there is an outdoor restaurant at street level. A small terrace, one level up, is reserved for the use of hotel guests only. I was intrigued with the many little niches throughout the hotel artistically displaying antique farm implements. Mr Brawand explained that the inn was originally his family's home and the collection of various farm tools were used on his father's farm. In one area are a number of cheese-making utensils, churns, a milking stool, the sieves and the wooden frames. Upstairs the olde worlde feeling vanishes, but the rooms are clean and tidy. Some of the bedrooms have a small balcony and the views are so startling that the simplicity of the rooms, by contrast, seems only appropriate.

HOTEL FIESCHERBLICK
Owner: Mr Johannes Brawand
CH-3818 Grindelwald, Switzerland
Tel: (036) 53 44 53
23 Rooms - Double SFR 110-144
Closed: November & May
Credit cards: All major
Gorgeous mountain views
Located 190 km S of Zurich

We were exploring the valley beyond Gstaad, heading south toward the soaring mountains, when we discovered the picturebook-perfect hamlet of Gsteig. In the middle of the village near the church is the Hotel Baren with what must be one of the prettiest facades in Switzerland. The Hotel Baren is what is termed a typical Saanen-style house and this original 17th-century wooden inn is such an outstanding specimen it is protected under special Swiss law. The heavy, sculptured beams and intricately carved exterior walls are exquisite. In summer the cheerful geraniums at each window, red checked curtains peeking through the small window panes, plus the jaunty Swiss flags hanging from the upper windows enhance the image of the perfect Swiss inn. The decor in the dining room continues with the regional flavor. This cozy room is richly paneled and furnished with country style wooden chairs and tables. Red checked tablecloths and fresh flowers on the tables add further charm. The inn is largely famous for its cuisine. However, there are several very simple, moderately decorated bedrooms whose beds are decked with inviting traditional soft, down comforters. When requesting a room, please note that only one guestroom has a private bath.

HOTEL BAREN
Owner: Ambort family
Manager: Sonja Ambort
Ch-3785 Gsteig, Switzerland
Tel: (030) 51 033
7 Rooms - Double SFR 80-95
Closed: November
Credit cards: None accepted
Located 170 km E of Geneva

Clinging to a narrow shelf, the old town of Guarda seems to reach out precariously over the Unter-Engadin valley. The day was gloriously sunny and warm, a moment of autumn perfection, as we entered this town of twisting streets, characteristic old homes colored with flowerboxes at every window, intricately carved old hay barns and spectacular views. Influenced by this absolutely magnificent day, I was in the mood to find a gem of a hotel to match the charm of the village. Almost the first hotel I saw was the Hotel Meisser, beautifully situated on a promontory overlooking the expanse of green valley below. On the lawn were tables set in the warm sunshine while waitresses in bright Alpine costumes were busy serving the happy guests. I could not have imagined a more blissful scene. Although the hotel does not appear to be extremely old, it does have some antiques used throughout the public areas and pieces of old copper, baskets of flowers and heavy chests to add further cozy touches. The dining room is especially appealing with large windows capturing a splendid view of the moutain vista. Most of the guestrooms are simple, but several are outstanding, with wonderful mellow wood paneling and country antique furniture.

HOTEL MEISSER
Owner: Ralf Meisser
Ch-7549 Guarda, Switzerland
Tel: (084) 9 21 32 Telex: 74637
25 Rooms - Double SFR 110-140
Open: June to October
Credit cards: DC AE VS
Marvelous mountain village
Glorious views from terrace
Located 210 km E of Zurich

A long alpenhorn and a front porch full of flowers welcome guests into the Hotel de la Paix, a former private home on a quiet side street in Interlaken. The welcome continues as one enters the tasteful entryhall, furnished with striped antique chairs and fresh flowers, and as one is met by gracious young hosts George Etterli and his British-born wife, Gillian. The Hotel de la Paix has been run by the Etterli family with an emphasis on personal service for 40 years. George's passion is collecting all kinds of clocks, which are happily displayed throughout the halls, sitting rooms and restaurant of the hotel. The spotlessly clean and highly comfortable bedrooms all have private bath or shower. The cozy rose-toned bar area is an inviting spot for an aperitif before a delicious Swiss meal available to guests only. The menu changes daily and we were treated to a delicious potato leek soup, followed by tender wienerschnitzel, fresh pasta and mixed garden salad, topped off by an ice cream sundae. This hotel is in the upper price range for a budget hotel, but it offers a high level of comfort at a reasonable price in this tourist town where a good value is hard to find.

HOTEL DE LA PAIX
Owner: Etterli family
24 Bernastrasse
CH-3800 Interlaken
Switzerland
Tel: (036) 22 70 44
26 Rooms - Double SFR to 140
Open: All year
Dinner offered only May through October
Credit cards: All major
Elevator, parking lot
Located 60 km SE of Berne

After a frustrating day of visiting inn possibilities which all turned out to be not charming, and worse, not clean, we found the picturesque Gasthof Hirschen in Matten, a small "suburb" of Interlaken. We were greeted by Frau Sterchi-Barben who explained to us than the Gasthof Hirschen was built in 1666 as a farmhouse which also had a tavern, actually the first registered tavern in Interlaken. The original walls are still intact, along with engraved leaded windows in the front bedrooms which look out onto the famous mountain peak, the Jungfrau. The 21 bedrooms are all comfortable, although only 4 have private bath or shower. Breakfast and dinner for guests is served in the cheerful, pine paneled dining room on the second floor which has superb views of the Jungfrau and surrounding mountain scenery. Antique chests and armoires decorate the hallways while the guest sitting area offers tasteful contemporary tables for playing cards and comfy chairs for relaxing. A possible disadvantage is traffic noise heard from the front bedrooms, but in all other respects the Gasthof Hirschen is a find: a reasonably priced, wonderfully friendly and atmospheric Swiss inn.

GASTHOF HIRSCHEN
Owner: Alfred Sterchi
CH-3800 Matten-Interlaken
Switzerland
Tel: (036) 22 15 45
21 Rooms - Double SFR to 95
Closed: October 15 through December 15
Credit cards: All major
Restaurant with terrace seating
Children's play area in garden
Located 1.5 km S of Interlaken - toward Grindlewald

Wilderswil is an unspoilt, picturesque village dating from 1315, full of old, flower-bedecked chalets, and blissfully removed from the tourist hubbub of Interlaken. The friendly Hotel Baren has been in the Zurschmiede family for five generations, and its tavern license dates from 1706 when the hotel began as a blacksmith shop offering rooms to travellers with horses. Today Fritz Zurschmiede is the charming host who proudly points out the original license and old family photos as he leads guests up the wide wooden stairway to the airy and spacious bedrooms. All rooms have private bath or shower, telephone, radio and minibar, and are furnished either in traditional antiques or pretty pine reproductions. Many have magnificent views of the Jungfrau and the surrounding mountains. Dining is a wonderful and varied experience at the Hotel Baren. A sumptuous buffet is served at breakfast, and a wide variety of regional specialties are offered at lunch and dinner. Fall brings game dishes to the Baren's table and winter prompts the traditional fondues and raclettes. Fresh pastas are always featured, created daily by the talented Swiss-Italian chef and his crew. In all ways, the Hotel Baren is a wonderfully atmospheric and welcoming base from which to explore the Interlaken and Grindelwald areas. An added bonus is the free bicycles that Fritz offers for the use of his guests.

HOTEL BAREN
Owner: Fritz Zurschmiede
Barenplatz
CH-3812 Wilderswil-Interlaken, Switzerland
Tel: (036) 22 35 21 Telex: 923137
50 Rooms - Double SFR to 120
Open: All year except November
Credit cards: All major
Apartments also available in historical annex
Located 5 km S of Interlaken

The Hotel du Lac Seehof is located on Lake Lucerne at Kussnacht. Many steamers that ply the lake stop here, and as the hotel is ideally situated directly on the waterfront where the boats dock, it serves as a popular luncheon spot. The town of Kussnacht is rather noisy and bustling with tourists, but you have a feeling of tranquility in the oasis of the hotel's terrace restaurant. (The garden restaurant is a very popular attraction for tourists who have taken the boat for a day's adventure from Lucerne.) The Hotel du Lac Seehof has been in the Trutmann family for five generations and is now managed by Albert Trutmann and his attractive wife, Joan. Albert Trutmann lived in the United States for a number of years, speaks perfect English and understands American tastes. Downstairs, the dining room to the left of the front hall is delightfully decorated with antiques. It has a certain elegance, but is not pretentious. Mr Trutmann showed me the bedrooms which have been redecorated. Recently a few private bathrooms have been added. The Trutmanns told me they are expecting to continue slowly in the remodeling of the hotel.

HOTEL DU LAC SEEHOF
Owner: A. Trutmann
CH-6403 Kussnacht am Rigi
Switzerland
Tel: (041) 81 10 12
17 Rooms - Double SFR 65-95
Open: All year
Credit cards: None accepted
Lakeside setting - next to pier
Located 13 km NE of Lucerne

Kussnacht is a main stop for the ferry boats which ply Lake Lucerne. The town is a favorite for tourists who want to make a luncheon stop while exploring the lake on a day's excursion from Lucerne. Should you opt to overnight here you would enjoy the Gasthaus Engel which is much less expensive than comparable hotels in Lucerne. The oldest part of the inn dates back to 1405. In 1552 a second section was constructed and from that period its appearance has remained unchanged for over 400 years. The atmosphere of the hotel is established by the cream colored facade textured with a cross work of old beams and green shutters. The charm of the outside is reinforced inside. The dining room is ornately paneled in walnut, which, interestingly, came from one tree, also centuries old. The tables are laid out with cheerful country checked cloths. When I visited the Gasthaus Engel I saw most of the guestrooms which vary tremendously: some are extremely drab, with plain modern decor, but some are extremely attractive, with mellowed wood paneling and antique furniture. So, unless you are on a budget, request one of the best rooms and indicate you want one with an olde worlde ambiance.

GASTHAUS ENGEL
Owner: Hans Ulrich
CH-6403 Kussnacht am Rigi
Tel: (041) 81 10 57
12 Rooms - Double SFR 85-117
Open: March to November
Credit cards: None accepted
Very old country inn
Located 13 km NE of Lucerne

Meandering through the serenely beautiful Emmental Valley when researching the first edition of our Swiss guide, I had happened upon the Hotel Hirschen. I remember being captivated by the small inn's wonderfully cozy facade of many little shuttered windows sheltered by a deeply overhanging roof - a typical Emmental chalet. But on my first visit I thought the guestrooms needed a "touch up". Happily, the hotel has been refurbished and now, outside and inside, it is quite delightful. There are several dining rooms, extremely popular, especially on Sundays when the rooms are bustling with the warmth of families sharing the noonday meal. And the food is excellent: the kitchen has earned many honors, including Officier Maitre Chaine des Rotisseur and Commandeur des Cordons Bleus de France. There are only a few guestrooms. These are simply decorated, but pleasant, with light wooden built-in furniture, good reading lights and modern bathrooms. The town of Langnau is one of the most charming in the Emmental Valley.

HOTEL HIRSCHEN
Owner: Birkhauser family
Dorfstrasse 17
CH-3550 Langnau im Emmental
Switzerland
Tel: (035) 2 15 17
16 Rooms - Double SFR 85-140
Open: February to December
Credit cards: All major
Cozy Emmental-style chalet
Located 110 km W of Zurich

The Hotel Beau Sejour enjoys an extremely scenic location away from the city center, set back and across the street from a lovely little park and splendid lakeside promenade. Built in 1874 as a grand home, the Beau Sejour has been a family run hotel with a faithful returning clientele for 20 years. Madame Binggeli is the extremely helpful and accommodating hostess, offering whatever services are necessary for guest comfort, even babysitting. The 30 scrupulously clean bedrooms all have private bath or shower and phone. They are decorated in very good taste with soft colors, brass or antique beds with lace or pretty print bedspreads. Madame Binggeli is especially proud of the high quality of all the mattresses and boxsprings in her house, thus assuring her guests of a very good night's rest. The bedrooms in the front of the house are light and airy with spectacular views of the mountains surrounding Lake Lucerne. Down the wide staircase, the sitting area and salon are furnished in family antiques and display large, elaborate Swiss clocks. Breakfast is the only meal served, but the neighborhood offers fine restaurants within easy walking distance. It is slightly more expensive than most budget hotels, but the Beau Sejour offers a restful respite from the sometimes noisy, cramped and impersonal atmosphere of many European city hotels.

HOTEL BEAU SEJOUR
Owner: Frau P. Binggeli
Haldenstrasse 53
CH-6006 Lucerne, Switzerland
Tel: (041) 51 16 81 or (041) 36 84 88
30 Rooms - Double SFR to 140
Closed: November
Credit cards: VS
Past the spa on the shoreline of Lake Lucerne
Located 1 km from the city center

The atmospheric Hotel Schlussel is a wonderful "find" offering a very good value in the pretty, but expensive, city of Lucerne. A large golden key and a Swiss flag hang from the flower-adorned facade to welcome guests here. Located off a small side street on a tiny historical square, the Hotel Schlussel faces an old church and enjoys a relatively quiet corner in this bustling city. The hotel is a pretty medieval house which has been converted into a refreshing little city hotel. The Schlussel's historic beer-stube restaurant has beamed ceilings, old leaded glass windows, and is often frequented by locals for an afternoon drink. There are also cozy nooks where guests enjoy traditional home-cooked meals. Freshly painted white hallways lead to the newly renovated bedrooms, almost all of which have private bath or shower. The airy rooms are furnished with light-colored, modern furniture and tasteful fabrics with a greenery motif. Frau Gressner tends to all aspects of the hotel with care and provides a warm welcome to her guests. Offering only 11 rooms, the Schlussel is an intimate little hotel, and reservations should be made well in advance in order to enjoy a stay here.

HOTEL SCHLUSSEL
Owner: Frau M.M. Gressner
Franziskanerplatz 12
CH-6000 Lucerne
Switzerland
Tel: (041) 23 10 61
11 Rooms - Double to SFR 90
Open: All year
Credit cards: None accepted
Elevator, restaurant and bar
Located in the historic old part of the city

The Pension Villa Maria is truly a "home away from home", complete with Frau Winkler to solicitously attend to her guests' every need. She is fluent in several languages, as she demonstrated during our visit, rapidly changing from Italian to German to English with amazing ease. Her house is modest and only half the rooms have private bath, but all are comfortably furnished with homey touches. Located on a relatively busy street off Lucerne's lakeside promenade, the slight traffic noise is more than made up for by the gorgeous walks and views a stone's throw from this pretty, mustard colored house. The small, friendly breakfast room is a welcome way to begin the day, and the inviting living room with its fresh flower arrangements and old grandfather clock is a relaxing spot in which to enjoy an evening aperitif. French doors lead out to a pretty back garden: a calming retreat after a busy day of sightseeing in the city. A mix of family antiques and modern pieces adorn the living room, creating the "private home" feeling that can only be found in a pension. Do not expect luxury, but a comfortable and homey atmosphere, and you will not be disappointed in the Villa Maria.

PENSION VILLA MARIA
Owner: Winkler family
Haldenstrasse 36
CH-6000 Lucerne
Switzerland
Tel: (041) 31 21 19
10 Rooms - Double to SFR 103
Closed: November 1 through March 15
Credit cards: None accepted
Garden
Lakefront setting, past the spa
Located 1.3 km from center of Lucerne

The Elvezia al Lago is an extremely attractive small budget hotel located along the lakeside footpath joining the towns of Castagnola and Gandria. There are four bedrooms without private bath plus four more bedrooms being added which will each have a balcony and a private bath. I have not yet seen the new addition, but even the "budget rooms", although snug, are pleasantly furnished and have lovely views overlooking the lake. There is a cozy small restaurant on the first floor of the hotel, but the favorite place to eat is the terrace restaurant on the edge of the water. The Elvezia al Lago is pretty, with a white facade cheerfully enhanced by blue and white awnings - a color scheme repeated in the blue striped awning over the waterside terrace and the blue checked tablecloths. Because the hotel is so small, Mr Lucke cannot accept reservations for less than five days, but if you call him upon your arrival in Switzerland, he will be delighted to arrange a room for a shorter stay if space is available. To reach the hotel, park your car in the last car park leading along the road to Castagnola, then ring the hotel from the phone in the parking lot and Mr Lucke will send a boat to pick you up at the adjacent dock.

ELVEZIA AL LAGO
Owner: Herbert & Doris Lucke
CH-6976 Lugano-Castagnola, Switzerland
Tel: (091) 51 44 51
8 Rooms - Double to SFR 120
Open: January 4 to October 24
Credit cards: None accepted
Lovely views from the guestrooms
Delightful setting on the lake
Located 6 km E of Lugano

The Hotel Chasa Chalavaina, although quite a simple little inn, has a remarkably sophisticated charm. Fresh white walls and an open, uncluttered decor give the hotel a crisp, airy atmosphere. The dining room is decorated with wonderful wooden country-style furniture and has a beautiful antique ceramic stove - in bygone days the only source of heat. I struggled to explain to the owner, Mr Jon Fasser, who unfortunately for me did not speak English, that I would like permission to take photos and to see some bedrooms. We were not communicating too well when I was approached by a charming Swiss lady, obviously a guest at the hotel, who had been listening to the conversation and offered to assist. She delayed her departure for a day's excursion to take me under her wing and show me the entire hotel. First we saw her room, delightful with country-style decor and a beautiful balcony overlooking the valley. My new-found friend and I then peeked into every nook and cranny (luckily most of the guests were already out for the day), including the kitchen, dining rooms and bar. The guest rooms I saw were extremely pleasant - bright and airy with nice views from the windows. After the "tour", my friend rejoined her husband whom she had deposited at the hotel's arched entrance, said goodbye and was on her way.

HOTEL CHASA CHALAVAINA
Owner: Jon Fasser
CH-7537 Mustair, Switzerland
Tel: (082) 8 54 68
20 Rooms - Double SFR 65-95
Open: All year
Credit cards: None accepted
Delightful small inn
Located 250 km E of Zurich

The Hotel Kreuz, a few blocks off the main highway, does not look too promising from the outside. It is a stately old manor home behind which is a rather uninteresting motel section. However, what a surprise inside. Although a large hotel, it is decorated with great charm. The hotel has been in the same family since 1489 and family antiques are used throughout - old chests, wonderful clocks, cradles, armoires, paintings, antique tables, beautiful old chairs, and other heirlooms highlight the tasteful decor in all the public rooms. Although some of the guestrooms are uninterestingly situated in a motel-like annex, others are outstanding. I was shown an old wooden Swiss chalet located next to the main hotel. Rooms 1 and 2 in this little cottage are lovingly restored and decorated in simple country style, very appropriate for a house dating back 400 years. This little wooden chalet is called the "colored house" because it used to be painted red, which signified that this was the home of the magistrate - the most important man in town. In the rear of the main residence is an old mill which has also been converted into hotel rooms. Here, suite 73, is one of the most beautifully decorated rooms I had seen in Switzerland. If you want to splurge ask for this divine suite. As an added bonus, the hotel has its own small garden area on the lake.

HOTEL KREUZ
Owner: Mr E.H. Lotzing
CH-6072 Sachseln, Switzerland
Tel: (041) 661 466 Telex: 866411
50 Rooms - Double SFR 75-117
Open: June to April
Credit cards: All major
Located 80 km S of Zurich

The Chasa Capol is a unique hotel located on the main street of the small town of Santa Maria in the beautiful Mustair Valley. The colorful background of the inn given to me by the owner stated: "The foundation of Chasa Capol dates back to the 8th century. Over the centuries, it was the property of the noble family De Capol as well as the valley governor's residence. The Capol's genealogical tree has been traced back to the Venetian, Marco Polo." The hotel's history piqued my imagination, and it alone would have merited a visit to this beautiful remote valley. I loved the Chasa Capol from the moment I walked into the small lobby and was warmly welcomed. The owners, Mr and Mrs Ernst Schweizer, speak no English, but their smile of welcome is an international language. Fortunately for the guests, a most delightful young lady, Karin Hansen, speaks English fluently. She has been with the hotel for many years and can answer your questions, offer sightseeing suggestions, or even arrange a chauffeur-driven car, should you so desire. I became friends with Karin on my first visit and am pleased to find she is still with the Schweizers - and as gracious as ever.

The bedrooms have names which represent famous guests. Our room, "Guerg Jenatsch", overlooked the back garden. It had twin beds joined by a wooden headboard painted green with reading lamps on either side. On the beds are the ever-present fluffy down comforters covered with a delightful red and green provincial print fabric, and each room has a small writing table with chair and lamp. Rag rugs on the floor and cheerful green print draperies on the window complete the scene.

The dining room is charming, with light antique wood furniture, flowers everywhere and wonderful food. Mrs Schweizer is an accomplished chef who adds her talents in personally supervising the kitchen. To complement the meal the Chasa Capol has its own vineyards and serves an excellent Gewurtztraminer house wine. The hotel even has its own casks of wine stored in the cellar. The hotel has many other special features including a wonderful little theater, a small museum and a small pool in the rear garden (a welcome addition on a warm summer day, especially if travelling with children).

The Schweizers are lovingly restoring this wonderful historical building. The hotel almost has a museum quality, with a small chapel in the basement with precious icons, a little theater in the attic where special concerts are still given, plus artifacts throughout such as antique costumes and old sleds. Staying at the Chasa Capol is truly like stepping back in time to enjoy the ambiance of yesterday with the amenities of today.

Note: The Schweizers have opened a small "bed and breakfast" across the street in an old house called "Villetta Capolina" for those on a budget. Although the rooms do not have private bathrooms, they are decorated in a romantic style and cost only Sfr 35 per person. There is also an apartment available which has a kitchenette.

THEATER-HOTEL CHASA CAPOL
Owner: Mr & Mrs Ernst Schweizer
Receptionist: Karin Hansen
CH-7536 Santa Maria, Switzerland
Tel: (082) 8 57 28
20 Rooms - Double SFR 120-172
Open: All year
Credit cards: None accepted
Inn dating from the 8th century
Small museum, family chapel
In-house theater, wine cellar
Small swimming pool in garden
Located 230 km E of Zurich

Soglio is a picture-perfect village, perched on a narrow mountain ledge overlooking the beautiful Bregaglia Valley. The almost too-perfect image is completed by a church spire stretching into the sky and cows lazily grazing in the mountain meadows. When finally I visited Soglio, I found it in reality even more beautiful than anticipated. The Hotel Palazzo Salis, an imposing box-like mansion, sits smack in the middle of the village in its own square. Although the name implies a "palace", this is really quite a simple hotel, but very nice. The guestrooms are upstairs and only a few in the hotel have a private bath. To accommodate extra guests, various rooms are also scattered throughout the village in annexes. The guestrooms, although simple, are clean and very adequate for an inexpensive hotel. The Palazzo Salis dates back several centuries and maintains the character of yesteryear. A number of hunting trophies proudly decorate the reception area, and a collection of antique spears are artistically arranged on the third floor walls. Settle here and days can be spent following an endless number of paths that explore this gloriously beautiful region. I fell in love with Soglio and consider it one of Switzerland's most picturesque villages and well worth any detour.

HOTEL PALAZZO SALIS
Owner: Cadisch family
CH-7649 Soglio
Switzerland
Tel: (082) 4 12 08
15 Rooms - Double SFR 90-150 (with 2 meals)
Open: May to October
Credit cards: None accepted
Spectacular mountain village
Located 210 km SE of Zurich

The picturesque village of Stein am Rhein dates from the 1500s and is a well preserved, gem-like little town full of traditional architecture and frescoed buildings. The half timbered facade of the Zur Ilge is well located on the historic market square amidst traditional Swiss shops and across from the characterful old town hall built in 1539. The Gasthof zur Ilge is a very simple and traditional, family-run guesthouse offering only four rooms, all with private shower and toilet. Rates are reasonable and rooms are fresh and very clean, furnished with contemporary pieces. A friendly welcome is extended by the Benker family, including their daughter who speaks English. The family's main occupation is the small ground floor restaurant, frequented by locals and visitors alike for savory lunches and dinner. Herr Benker cooks all the hearty home-style meals, while his wife and daughter serve the guests. Just a few steps away from the Gasthof is a pleasant riverside promenade, as well as an abundance of shops and restaurants. Stein am Rhein is also known for Roman fortification remains, a nearby castle, and an ancient Benedictine monastery and cathedral, now a museum open to the public. This pleasant little town on the lower Rhine is well worth a visit, and if staying overnight, the Gasthof zur Ilge offers inexpensive and spotless accommodation.

GASTHOF ZUR ILGE
Owner: Benker family
CH-8260 Stein am Rhein
Switzerland
Tel: (054) 41 22 72
4 Rooms - Double SFR to 85
Closed: first two weeks of Nov and Jan
Credit cards: All major
On the southeasternmost tip of Lake Constance
Located 55 km NW of Zurich

In the small town of Worb, just a few miles east of Berne, is the Hotel Lowen. This hotel is positioned at the junction of two busy streets, but, even so, a country charm radiates from its colorful, shuttered exterior. On the entry level the inn has a number of small, beautiful dining rooms. Each varies in decor, but all abound with antiques. Dining is famous in this little inn - attracting dinner guests from all over Switzerland. (If your base is Berne and Worb proves to be just a day excursion, arrange your trip to include a lunch or dinner stop at the Hotel Lowen). The accommodations are simple but pleasant. Antiques adorn the halls and lobbies giving a cheerful, cozy ambiance. The Hotel Lowen was established over 600 years ago and incredibly has been in the same family for over 11 generations, so it is not surprising that the service and quality of this small inn is so special - a perfect example of one of Switzerland's most highly regarded professions, the hotel business.

HOTEL LOWEN
Owner: Bernhard family
Enggisteinstrasse 3
CH-3076 Worb, Switzerland
Tel: (031) 83 23 03
14 Rooms - Double SFR 77-125
Open: All year
Renowned for its restaurant
Located 105 km W of Zurich

The Hotel Eos is a wonderfully warm and comfortable spot to spend one or several nights. It is located in a quiet, upper class neighborhood just a few minutes from the noisy hustle and bustle of downtown Zurich. The atmosphere of a gracious home is present throughout; from the basket of umbrellas and fresh flowers in the entry hall to the comfortable living room with its writing table offering daily newspapers in three languages. The room's fine old drapes and upholstery invite one to sit beside the large picture window framed by wisteria vines. A piano and television offer entertainment in the evening. The wide stairway clad in an Oriental rug runner leads the way to the upper hallways, decorated with antique painted chests and armoires, as well as old vases and other antique artifacts. Of the 25 bedrooms, only 16 have private bath or shower, but all are clean and very adequately furnished. Many rooms have scenic views over the rooftops to the city of Zurich and the mountains beyond. The feeling of being a guest in a private home continues in the lovely breakfast room, where fresh coffee, croissants and jam are watched over by a ticking grandfather clock, and a pretty lace tablecloth covers the central, round table. Colorful paintings adorn the walls and a sunporch offers two private tables surrounded by windows and greenery. The Hotel Eos is a refreshing change from the impersonal hotels so often found in large cities.

HOTEL EOS
Owner: Carmen Immobilien
Manager: Veronika Zaverojiev
Carmenstrasse 18
CH-8032 Zurich, Switzerland,
Tel: (01) 47 10 60
25 Rooms - Double SFR to 140
Open: All year
Credit cards: All major
Located in the Hottingen section of Zurich

Geranium-filled windowboxes soften the stark city facade of the Hotel Vorderer Sternen, located on the busy Bellvueplatz across the street from Lake Zurich's shoreline. As in many smaller and more inexpensive European hotels, the reception area is not found on the ground level and here actually not until the third floor. But, once found, a warm welcome is assured. Eduard Rosenberger is the host who speaks very good English, French, German and Italian. Dining at the Hotel Vorderer Sternen is varied as there are three different restaurants to choose from. For fast, lighter meals, there is a casual, open-air "snack bar" where mouthwatering "wurst" are always on the grill. Inside on the ground floor, a bustling and atmospheric restaurant offers sit-down meals at reasonable prices. For slightly more formal dining, the second floor restaurant serves delicious Swiss specialties in a cheerful atmosphere. Do not expect imaginative decor in the ten bedrooms as all are simple, yet comfortable. None have private bath, but all are spotlessly clean. The Vorderer Sternen is for the traveller seeking to be centrally located in downtown Zurich, looking for bargain prices, and willing to forgo conveniences such as elevators, private baths and gracious lobby areas.

HOTEL VORDERER STERNEN
Owner: Eduard Rosenberger
Bellevueplatz
CH-8001 Zurich
Switzerland
Tel: (051) 32 49 49
10 Rooms - Double SFR 80
Open: All year
Credit cards: All major
3 restaurants
Located at the eastern end of the Limmatquai

Wales

Hidden away down a country lane in the south of Snowdonia National Park, Llidiardau Mawr is a picturesque gleaming-white 17th-century farmhouse and watermill with flower-filled gardens and a gurgling little stream. The interior is country-cozy: tiny cottage-sized rooms where the old plaster and stonework is painted bright white contrasting with the blackened beamed ceilings and pine plank doors, low doorways and creaking floorboards. Up the narrow steep flight of stairs are two adorable bedrooms named after their color schemes - The Green Room and The Pink Room. A third bedroom, The Hayloft, is a few paces away from the house, entered by rough-hewn steps and a low door. The hayloft has a double bed and long low windows that offer views across sheep in the pasture to the distant mountains. Shirley May loves to cook and to encourage guests to bring along their own drinks she provides them with a refrigerator, glasses and ice in a little nook just off the sitting room. If you are arriving late in the evening Shirley will happily prepare a late supper for you. The nearby town of Bala is a lively place and the terminus for the Bala Lake Railway that runs along the picturesque Lake Bala to Llanuwchyllyn. And all around you the many beauties of Snowdonia National Park await your exploration. From Bala take the A4212 towards Ffestiniog for about half a mile. Turn left at the signpost for Rhyduchaf, drive for 3 miles and the cottage is on the left.

LLIDIARDAU MAWR
Owner: Shirley May
Llidiardau, Bala, Gwynedd LL23 7SG, Wales
Tel: (0678) 520555
3 rooms sharing 1 1/2 bathrooms
£11 per person B & B
Open: Easter to October
Credit cards: None accepted
Country home
Located 50 miles SW of Chester

"This small Welsh manor house is our own home," writes Susan Jones of the small hotel she and her husband run on the outskirts of Cardigan. "Our aim here is to entertain customers as we do our friends and family in a traditional British way." In this Huw and Susan succeed admirably. When I arrived, Susan was at the door to welcome me. I was immediately made to feel at home and shown upstairs to my room. There are only three bedrooms - thoughtful little touches such as sewing kits and piles of interesting magazines are provided. Bathrooms are en suite or across the hall. Visitors should be aware of the rookery outside the bedroom windows - their concert starts early - and that heat during chilly spells is provided by individual heaters. Guests gather for drinks in the small bar to discuss with Huw the wine which will best complement dinner: meanwhile Susan is busy in the kitchen putting the finishing touches to the five course meal. The menu is changed each day and based upon seasonal local fresh produce. The whole atmosphere is that of a friendly house party with Susan and Huw as your charming hosts. Rhydgarnwen is 3 miles from Cardigan. Take the A487 (signposted Fishguard) and after crossing the River Tefi turn left at the first crossroads (signposted Cilgerran). The entrance to the house is on your right.

RHYDGARNWEN
Owner: Huw & Susan Jones
Cardigan
Dyfed SA43 3NW, Wales
Tel: (0239) 612742
3 rooms with private bathrooms
£33 per person dinner, B&B
Open: Easter to September
Credit cards: None accepted
Country home
Located 3 miles SW of Cardigan

Long ago this was the spot where two gated country roads met and thus the village got its name - now busy "A" roads have replaced the lanes. Standing beside the roundabout that has replaced the gated crossroads is Guidfa House, an extremely comfortable guesthouse run by Roy and Nancy Stevens. The bedrooms are particularly pretty, with matching small print papers and curtains, and four have nice en-suite bathrooms. A small sitting area on the landing has books and games. Downstairs a bar is tucked into the corner of the lounge so guests can relax with a drink before or after dinner. Nancy produces good, homey meals such as her own mushroom soup, roast beef with Yorkshire pudding and vegetables, and lemon coconut meringue which Roy serves to their guests. At breakfast their roles are reversed and Nancy serves the breakfast of sausage, bacon, egg and tomato that Roy has prepared. Roy and Nancy enjoy guests staying for several nights and have outlined trips to Dollgellau, Brecon, Hereford, Ludlow and Shrewsbury and some circuitous, scenic mountain routes. Guidfa House is at the junction of the A44 and A483 3 miles north of Llandrindod Wells.

GUIDFA HOUSE
Owner: Roy & Nancy Stevens
Crossgates
Llandrindod Wells
Powys LD1 6RF, Wales
Tel: (059787) 241
7 rooms, 4 with private bathrooms
From £11 to £14 per person B & B
Open: All year
Credit cards: None accepted
Guesthouse
Located 3 miles N of Llandrindod Wells

The Old Rectory was very run-down when Michael and Wendy Vaughan took it over a few years ago. Now it is a lovely place in an equally lovely setting on a bluff overlooking the River Conwy estuary. Standing on the terrace you have the most magnificent view across the broad river to Conwy Castle. On the recommendation of a reader I stopped at The Old Rectory, only to find that no-one was home. I was glad of the house having no near neighbors as I peeked in the windows to evaluate the facilities of this small family establishment: a long dining table elegantly set with crystal and silver, the polished wood floors covered with lovely patterned carpets, fine watercolors hanging on the walls; deep velvet sofas with plump cushions beckoning a welcome to the drawing room and warm pine panelling adding coziness and warmth to the small sitting room. I was unable to see any of the second floor bedrooms - it did not seem wise to attempt the climb - but have subsequently seen photos showing one of the rooms to have a beautiful half-tester bed romantically draped with lace against a background of pastel flowered wallpaper. Michael and Wendy Vaughan run their home as a country house where guests dine together as at a dinner party. The Old Rectory is on the A470 half a mile south of the junction with the A55.

THE OLD RECTORY
Owner: Michael & Wendy Vaughan
Llanrwst Road, Glan Conwy
Gwynedd LL28 5LF, Wales
Tel: (0492 68) 611
3 rooms with private bathrooms
From £20 to £25 per person B & B
Open: All year
Credit cards: None accepted
Country home
Located 1 mile S of Conway

A soft pink colorwash brightens the exterior of this spacious home in the village of Newport. Cnapan House is very much a family-run affair, with John and Eluned Lloyd, their daughter Judith and her husband Michael Cooper. John and Michael are your genial hosts while Eluned and Judith work together in the kitchen. Lunchtime fare emphasises wholefood cooking with old-fashioned hearty soups and puddings. Tables are covered with lace cloths for dinner - adding a romantic touch to a special meal where the main course is always served with five or six vegetables. Guests can enjoy before dinner drinks in either the sitting room or the bar: both snug rooms filled with country antiques and overflowing with charm. The bedrooms are superb, artfully decorated in a light, airy style and immaculately furnished, with every nook and cranny filled with old family treasures. One guestroom is a family room with a small adjoining bunk-bedroom for the children. (Nursery teas are served in the early evening so that parents can put the children in bed or in front of the TV before coming down to dinner.) You will love the welcoming, free and easy atmosphere that pervades this home. Newport is on the A487 between Cardigan and Fishguard.

CNAPAN HOUSE
Owner: The Lloyd & Cooper families
East Street
Newport
Pembrokeshire SA42 0WF, Wales
Tel: (0239) 820575
5 rooms with private bathrooms
£14.50 per person B & B
Closed: February
Credit cards: MC VS
Guesthouse
Located 7 miles SW of Cardigan between Fishguard & Cardigan

Overview Map of Europe

AUSTRIA - MAP I
Index of Places to Stay by Map Number

Austria - Map I

BENELUX COUNTRIES - MAP II
HOLLAND - BELGIUM - LUXEMBOURG
Index of Places to Stay by Map Number

Holland

Belgium

Luxembourg

Benelux Countries - Map II
Belgium Holland Luxembourg

ENGLAND - MAP III
Index of Places to Stay by Map Number

England - Map III

FRANCE - MAP IV
Index of Places to Stay by Map Number

France - Map IV

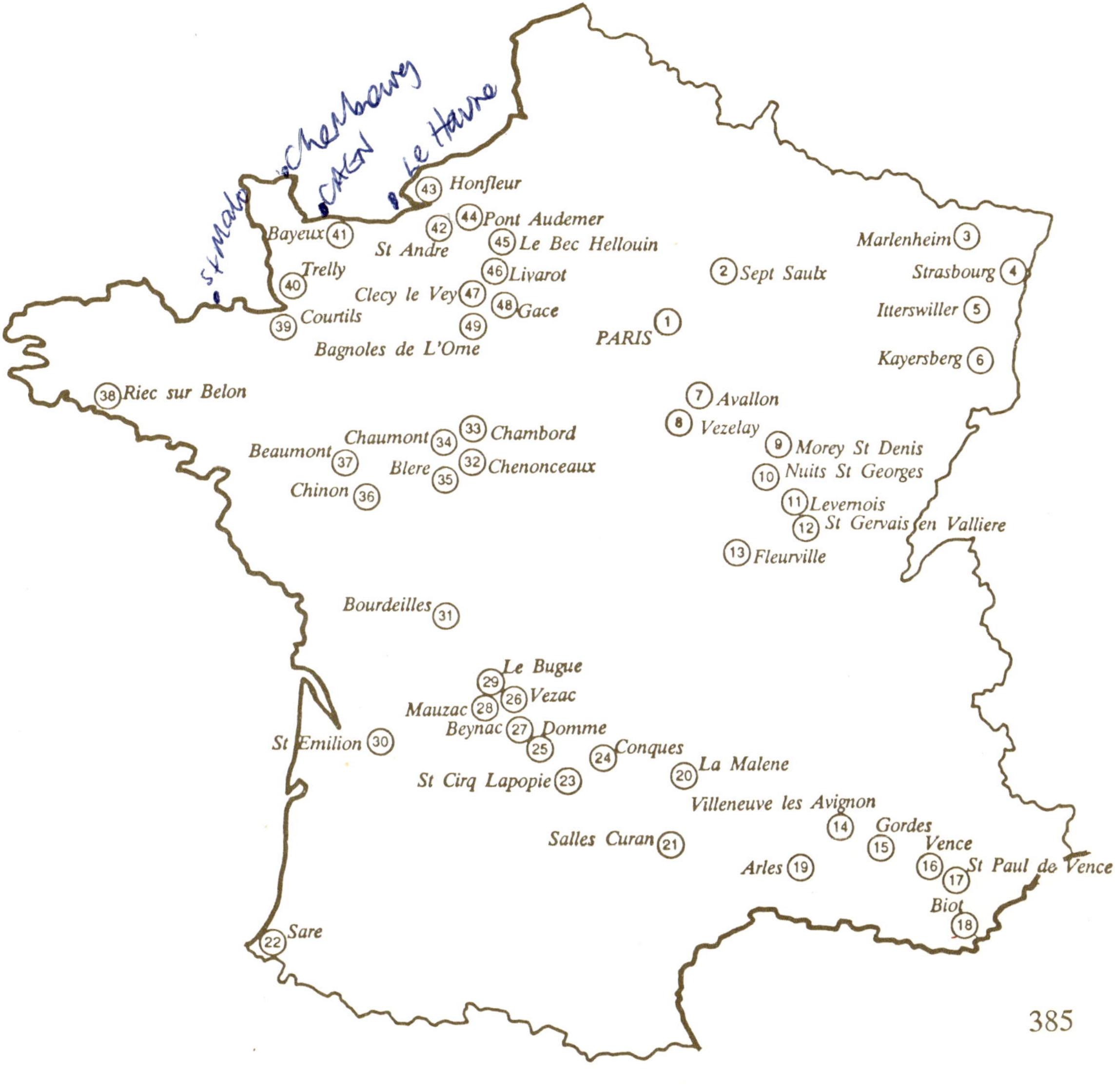

GERMANY - MAP V
Index of Places to Stay by Map Number

Germany - Map V

IRELAND - MAP VI

Index of Places to Stay by Map Number

Ireland - Map VI

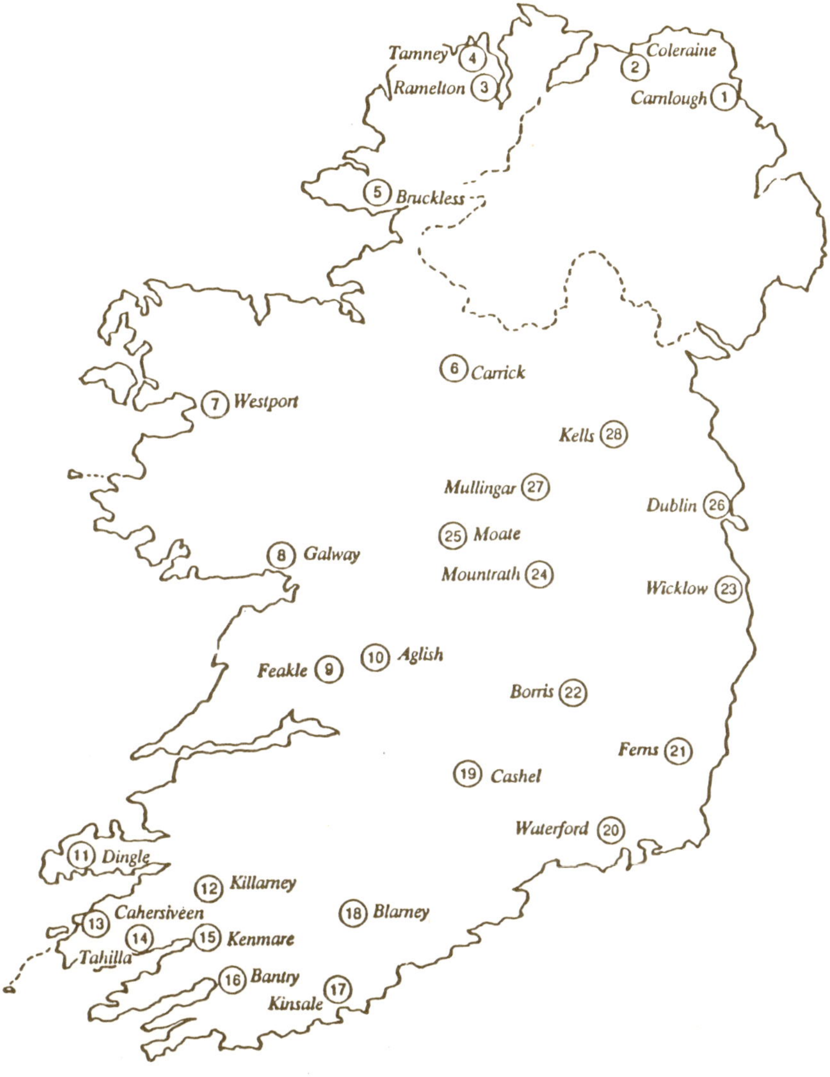

ITALY - MAP VII
Index of Places to Stay by Map Number

Italy - Map VII

PORTUGAL - MAP VIII
Index of Places to Stay by Map Number

Portugal - Map VIII

SCANDINAVIA - MAP IX
NORWAY - SWEDEN - FINLAND
Index of Places to Stay by Map Number

Norway

Sweden

Finland

Scandinavia - Map IX
Norway Sweden Finland

SCANDINAVIA - MAP X
DENMARK
Index of Places to Stay by Map Number

Denmark

Scandinavia - Map X
Denmark

SCOTLAND - MAP XI

Index of Places to Stay by Map Number

Scotland - Map XI

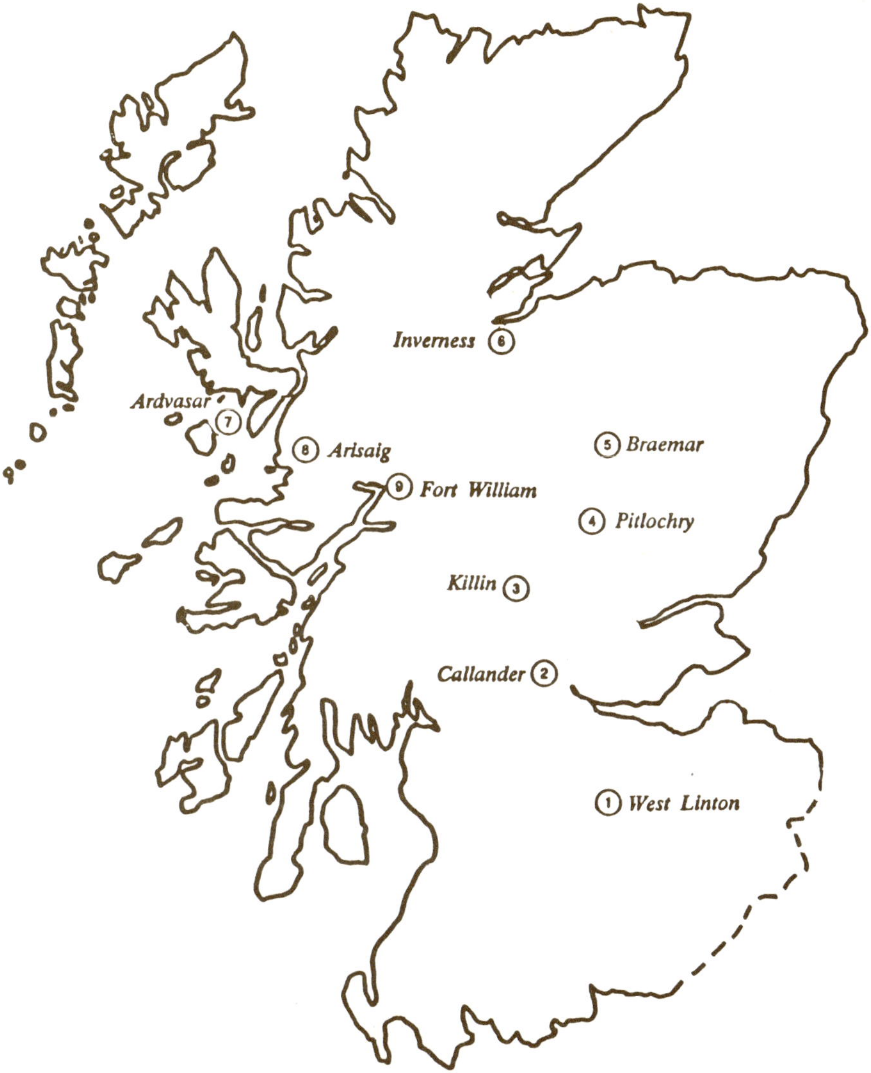

SPAIN - MAP XII
Index of Places to Stay by Map Number

Spain - Map XII

SWITZERLAND - MAP XIII
Index of Places to Stay by Map Number

Switzerland - Map XIII

WALES - MAP XIV
Index of Places to Stay by Map Number

Wales - Map XIV

AUSTRIA - Map I - Page 379

BENELUX - BELGIUM - Map II - Page 381

BENELUX - HOLLAND - Map II - Page 381

BENELUX - LUXEMBOURG - Map II - Page 381

ENGLAND - Map III - Page 383

FRANCE - Map IV - Page 385

GERMANY - Map V - Page 387

ITALY (continued)

PORTUGAL - Map VIII - Page 393

SCANDINAVIA - FINLAND - Map IX - Page 395

SCANDINAVIA - NORWAY - Map IX - Page 395

SCANDINAVIA - SWEDEN - Map IX - Page 395

SCANDINAVIA - DENMARK - MAP X - Page 397

SCOTLAND - Map XI - Page 399

SPAIN - Map XII - Page 401

SWITZERLAND - Map XIII - Page 403

WALES - Map XIV - Page 405

KAREN BROWN travelled to France when she was 19 and wrote *French Country Inns & Chateau Hotels* – the first book of what has grown to be an extremely successful series on European country inns. With 11 guides now on the market, Karen's staff has expanded, but she is still involved in the planning, research and editing of each book in her Country Inn series and returns frequently to Europe to update them. Karen, her husband, Rick, and their daughter Alexandra, live in the San Francisco Bay area.

CLARE BROWN has been a travel consultant since 1969, specializing in planning countryside itineraries to Europle featuring charming small hotels. Now her expertise is available to a much larger audience – the readers of her daughter Karen's Country Inn guides. Clare lives in the San Francisco Bay area with her husband, Bill.

JUNE BROWN has an extensive background in travel, having worked as a travel consultant before joining her friend Karen in the research and writing of her Country Inn series. June, who was born in Sheffield, now lives in the San Francisco Bay area with her husband, Tony, and their son, Simon.

CYNTHIA and RALPH KITE admit to a long-term love affair with Europe, where they have lived and travelled extensively. Ralph spent many years as professor of Hispanic literature at a major American university and Cynthia (Karen's cousin), who holds degrees in Spanish and French, is a production director for a national magazine.

KIRSTEN PRICE, a friend of Karen's since their school days, has lived and travelled extensively in Europe, including 8 months in England when she did the sketches for the original edition of Karen's *English, Welsh & Scottish Country Inns*. When not travelling, Kirsten, an avid skier, lives in Keystone, Colorado.

BARBARA TAPP is the talented artist responsible for most of the interior sketches and cover paintings for Karen's Country Inn guides, icluding *European Country Inns*. Barbara, born in Australia, now lives in the San Francisco Bay area with her husband, Richard, and their 3 children.